A Spartan Journey

Michigan State's 1967 Miracle on the Mat

Dale Anderson

A Spartan Journey
Michigan State's 1967 Miracle on the Mat

All rights reserved
Copyright 2016 by Dale Anderson

No part of this book may be reproduced or transmitted in any form or by any means without permission of the author.

For information contact:
    Dale Anderson
    7609 E Monticello Way
    Crystal Lake, IL 60014
    daa2000@aol.com

Printed in the United States of America

ISBN: 978-1-5323-0991-5

First edition

Edited by: Mike Chapman, Suzanne Fell, Renee Weingard
Cover design: Mike Chapman, Suzanne Fell
Page Layout: Suzanne Fell

Dedication

I dedicate this book to Doug Blubaugh.

Named Outstanding Wrestler in the World after the 1960 Rome Olympics, you were a great coach—and an even better friend.

May you rest in peace. In many ways you deserved better than you got here on earth, especially after you left the Michigan State wrestling program you loved so much.

Here is how I heard of Doug's passing: I was presenting a lecture on constitutional law when I looked at my cell phone during a break and noticed that my college wrestling coach, Grady Peninger, had called. A sense of dread flooded over me. During a break, I called him back. He told me, "Doug is dead. He had a motorcycle accident. You are the first person I called."

I must admit that, instead of sorrow, I found some relief in Grady's words. I told him, "Doug is in a better place." And I believed that from the bottom of my heart. We miss him, but I doubt he misses us.

As I write this, every member of that '67 national championship team is still alive and kicking. Only Doug, the most important cog in that miracle machine has passed on to a better place.

As you will read, the Spartans would <u>never</u> have won the NCAA Championship in 1967 were it not for Doug Blubaugh, so my main regret about his passing is that he is not alive to read about how much he meant to our sport, our team, and to me.

I will always consider myself very fortunate to have had Doug Blubaugh as a coach and, more importantly, a friend.

DA

Photo courtesy of Mike Chapman.

Acknowledgments and Explanations

I want to acknowledge the many people who helped me bring this book to conclusion (I apologize if I forgot someone): Dave Campbell, Dale Carr, Larry Anderson, Dan Gable, Don Behm, Bob LaBrant, Mike Narey, Jeff Mikles, and Rachel Mayes for their help in developing the drafts.

Special thanks go to my wife, Sandy, who provided so many helpful ideas on changes that needed to be addressed in the book.

I also want to thank my editors: Mike Chapman, Suzanne Fell, and Renee Weingard. Suzanne also completed the final formatting and getting everything print ready. I appreciate you all.

As a special note, I asked everyone on the 1967 team whom I could reach to make comments and corrections about everything I wrote. Many did make comments and corrections. I also tried to contact others whom I discussed in the book in order to be sure my recollections were correct. I particularly thank those who got back to me with their critiques.

I have written many law books, but this is my first try at "non-fiction." I put non-fiction in quotation marks as, who remembers what is truth—and what is fiction—after 50 years? I have done my best to corroborate every "fact" in this book, but sometimes our memories grow weak. Any mistake or omission in the book is mine even though I may be quoting someone else. I also want to apologize in advance for any mischaracterization.

> *In this book the reader will note many boxes with information. I included information in boxes when I thought there was an interesting point to be made, but that the point was somewhat tangential to the text. I hope the boxes are more enlightening and interesting than they are distracting.*

The perceptive reader will also note that I repeat some of the stories and information in the book in different contexts. I believed it was important to re-emphasize several important points and stories throughout the book.

Please consider, where appropriate, that all circumstances where gender is not an issue, that gender applies to both male and female, no matter how described in the text.

If you have any questions or comments about this book that you would like to convey to me, please do not hesitate to write to me at daa2000@aol.com. I welcome your feedback!

I will be donating the profits from the sale of this book to charities related to wrestling.

DA

Table of Contents

Dedication i
Acknowledgments and Explanations iii
Table of Contents v
Preface vi
Foreword viii
Introduction x
Chapter 1 Wrestling 1
Chapter 2 Spartans 9
Chapter 3 Michigan State Wrestling: A Brief History 19
Chapter 4 The Setting - 1967 29
Chapter 5 Me - Growing Up and Falling in Love with Wrestling 37
Chapter 6 Gable and Me 55
Chapter 7 Getting Recruited 1963-1964 79
Chapter 8 Iowa State - 1964 101
Chapter 9 Michigan State - 1965 107
Chapter 10 My Sophomore Year 1965-1966 123
Chapter 11 Our (Dysfunctional) Wrestling Family 149
Chapter 12 Coaches 179
Chapter 13 Our Magical Championship Year 1966-1967 201
Chapter 14 The 1967 NCAA Wrestling Tournament 217
Epilogue: Life's Lessons Learned from Wrestling 245

Preface

Magic Johnson, Michigan State University's greatest basketball player and leader of the 1979 NCAA championship team, told the members of the 2000 Michigan State NCAA championship basketball team that they would not fully appreciate what they had done for a long time, maybe 50 years.

As I relax in front of my fireplace, I begin to feel that way about our NCAA championship team of 1967—now some 50 years ago. That's one of the main reasons I wrote this book. This is a story I only later in life am beginning to fully appreciate. I hope readers will appreciate it too.

One motivating factor in my deciding to take on this project was my reading of "*The Dream Team of 1947*" by Arno P. Nieman. It is the wonderful story about the Cornell College wrestling team, located in Mount Vernon, Iowa. Energized and driven to success by a number of wrestlers from West Waterloo High School, Waterloo, Iowa, Cornell upset all the major wrestling powers to win the NCAA wrestling championship in 1947. Nieman's book sparked in me the idea that maybe our program at Michigan State, exactly two decades later, was equally as interesting and produced just as great a miracle triumph, only in far different ways and for far different reasons.

An important ingredient in this mix is that I love rags-to-riches stories and stories where someone has to overcome great odds to win. So I also love to watch movies like "*Rudy*" or "*Hoosiers*" that depict that theme. In some ways our team in '67 was like the Hoosiers. Who could imagine that a team that managed to score only one point in the Big Ten tournament in 1964 could win the national championship just a short three years later? Has any team, in any sport, that was last in their conference won an NCAA championship just three years later? I would bet that it has never happened, except at Michigan State. And how could we have done that when the majority of wrestlers on the team were "mere" walk-ons? That was easily as great a miracle as a small high school in Indiana beating a large and mighty one in the Indiana state championships. And how could I, technically a "walk-on" at Michigan State, win a national championship in 1967? You'll soon read why that was as unlikely as walk-on Rudy being carried off the Notre Dame football field after the game against Georgia Tech.

Maybe these stories of old need to be told, if for no other reason than they are not forever forgotten. For those of you who know nothing or little of the '67 Michigan State story, it probably should be told at least once by someone who was there. In some respects, I am as good a person as anyone to explain what happened to the best of my ability and recollection.

I tried to induce many great authors to write this story. But ultimately I decided I would write about our "Miracle on the Mat" 1967 team and tell the story as a travelogue of my (wrestling) life; not as an autobiography—but as a "Spartan Journey."

DA

Foreword

In 1964, Dale Anderson was a senior when I was a sophomore at West Waterloo High School. He was the captain of our wrestling team. I watched him closely in order to figure out what gave him an edge in his matches. One thing was that he seemed to work himself into a fever pitch before his matches, and I realized that that strategy might give me an edge too.

When I graduated two years later, I seriously considered attending Michigan State because Dale was there and because Doug Blubaugh, one of the greatest coaches of all time, was there too. Also, Coach Siddens, our high school coach, often spoke highly of Dale and Michigan State.

The main reason I did not go to Michigan State was because I wanted to stay close to home. I was an Iowan at heart; I needed my parents to be close, and, maybe more important, my parents needed me. Finally, Coach Siddens and my friends were all in Waterloo, and I needed them to be close to me, especially during my early difficult freshman year in college.

Right before I was to fly to MSU on a recruiting visit, I cancelled the trip as I had never flown before, and I had already decided to attend Iowa State. So I didn't think it was fair to use Michigan State's money to take a trip, knowing I was not going to attend school in East Lansing.

Two years later during the 1966-1967 academic year, I became aware that Michigan State could win the national championship, as the Spartans beat Iowa State in the Midlands that year when the Cyclones were ranked second in the country and then MSU beat Oklahoma University at Norman, Oklahoma, when OU was ranked #1 in the country.

I went to the NCAAs at Kent State in Ohio as a freshman in 1967 to watch the competition (as freshmen were ineligible for varsity competition back then). Again, I watched Dale closely to see what helped him have an edge…just like in high school. Again, I could see that he got his edge by imposing his will and intensity on his opponents by constant attack and motion.

After watching that tournament, I thanked God that someone finally stepped up and showed everybody that there are great wrestling teams out there besides the Okies!

Dale helped my thinking about how to wrestle and how to win.

I hope he will help everyone who reads this book to better understand wrestling in the '60s, how Michigan State won the NCAA wrestling championship in 1967, and how to be a better wrestler or coach—or person!

Dan Gable

Introduction

Looking back from the perspective of a half a century, it seems to me that 1967 was a magical year in the history of college wrestling.

The NCAA tournament debuted in 1928 in Ames, Iowa, and since that time two states, Oklahoma and Iowa, have held a firm grip on the official team title. Of course, Oklahoma State (originally known as Oklahoma A&M) was the kingpin, but its arch rival Oklahoma University had climbed into the winner's circle, too. And three Iowa colleges—Cornell, Iowa State Teachers, and Iowa State—had each claimed one team title by 1967. (The University of Iowa did not win its first championship until 1975).

1967 was very different. In 1967 the Spartans were unstoppable. They stormed to the Big Ten title and then ran over the field at the NCAA tournament held on the campus of Kent State University, Ohio.

Ironically, Michigan State enjoyed a powerful Oklahoma-Iowa connection that helped them to think like champions and boost them into the top spot. Their head coach was Grady Peninger, who earned All-American honors at Oklahoma State under Coach Art Griffith, and the assistant coach was Doug Blubaugh, one of the giant figures in the entire history of amateur wrestling.

Blubaugh had wrestled at Ponca City High School in Oklahoma under Peninger and then moved down the road to Stillwater to become an NCAA champion for Oklahoma State in 1957. After winning a gold medal at the 1960 Olympics and being named the outstanding wrestler in the entire world, Doug embarked on a long coaching career. Peninger brought his former high school star to East Lansing, and Blubaugh's presence in the MSU wrestling room became a key factor in the team's successes, both from an instructional standpoint and for inspiration.

The Iowa angle was represented by an indefatigable junior named Dale Anderson, who had wrestled at West High School in Waterloo, Iowa, under Bob Siddens, the same coach who guided Dan Gable's high school career a couple of years later. Anderson won two state titles for Siddens and provided considerable energy and drive in the Spartan room, winning three Big Ten and two NCAA championships.

Growing up in Waterloo, I followed Anderson's career and saw that he and Gable were cut from the same fabric—non-stop, incredibly intense competitors who pushed foes to the breaking point, both mentally and physically.

The lessons they learned in the West Waterloo practice room helped guide them all through college and far beyond. While Gable embarked upon the most storied coaching career in college annals, Anderson went on to become a successful trial lawyer, author, law professor, and senior investigative counsel to Congress in Washington D.C. He now writes books on constitutional law and lectures all over the country on matters related to constitutional law.

Michigan State's strength was in its never-say-die attitude, cultivated by Peninger and Blubaugh, embodied by Anderson, and adopted by the entire Spartan team. Anderson claimed his 1967 title with a dramatic come-from-behind win over Masaru Yatabe of Portland State.

Many football fans remember 1967 as the year of the first Super Bowl (won by Vince Lombardi's Green Bay Packers); boxing fans recall that 1967 was the year that marked Muhammad Ali's final fight before being stripped of his world heavyweight crown for refusing induction into the armed services; baseball fans know that Carl Yastrzemski (of the Boston Red Sox) won the Triple Crown, the last time a major leaguer would do that until 2012. But for me, a wrestling fan, it will always be the year that Michigan State broke into the ranks of wrestling's elite programs and changed the college wrestling world forever.

I have had the distinct pleasure of attending about 50 NCAA tournaments. On this, the 50th year anniversary of that remarkable event, I can say that 1967 event was one of the most exciting and significant of them all.

I read Dale Anderson's stirring account of that magical season with tremendous interest and highly recommend the book to anyone who has even a passing interest in the history of wrestling in America.

Mike Chapman, Newton, Iowa, author of 27 books

Chapter 1
Wrestling

ଔ

> *"It is not the critic who counts; not the man who points out how the strong man stumbled or where the doer of deeds could have done better. The credit belongs to the man who is actually in the arena, whose face is marred by dust and sweat and blood, who strives valiantly, who errs and comes up short again and again, because there is no effort without error and shortcoming, but who does actually strive to do the deeds, who knows the great enthusiasm, the great devotions, who spends himself for a worthy cause; who, at the best knows in the end, the triumph of high achievement, and who, at the worst, if he fails, at least he fails while daring greatly, so that his place shall never be with those cold and timid souls who knew neither victory nor defeat."*
>
> *-Theodore Roosevelt*

It was Saturday, March 25, 1967, the final evening of wrestling at the NCAA wrestling tournament. It was my junior year at Michigan State, and I was literally about to enter the arena of which President Roosevelt spoke above.

Shouldn't I have been thrilled? Instead, I was feeling an incredible burden for which no one could prepare me.

Feeling the weight of the world on my back, I was well aware that if I won tonight, not only would I win the national championship, Michigan State would win the NCAA championship as a team. We, the Spartans, would become the <u>first</u> Big Ten team in history to win a national wrestling championship as no Big Ten team had ever won the NCAAs in wrestling.

If I lose tonight, we are just another Big Ten team that could not withstand the pressure of the Big 8, particularly the Okies, again. The Okies had won the national championship almost every year for the past 40-50 years. They were virtually unbeatable. Everybody knew that, even me.

I had not been wrestling well as I had not slept. I had let the pressure get to me. Sleep deprivation was affecting my reactions, intensity, and desire. Also, I had been unable to eat—too nervous. So I had no fuel; I had no energy. I had been wrestling on adrenalin alone. The anxiety was killing me or at least driving me crazy. I was simply worn down and worn out.

Why had I allowed myself to become so constantly anxious? Why didn't I just relax and watch television with my teammates? That would just not have been me. Worse still, I was wrestling an opponent in the finals tonight who was much better than I was. And everybody knew it.

I wanted to hide. But there was no place to hide. I decided to walk to the coliseum to clear my head in the cold night air. I shivered a little as I was wearing no jacket, and I could see my breath as I began the trek to the "arena."

I tried to focus on how to win the biggest match of my life, but I found it impossible. I just kept thinking about being humiliated in front of the biggest crowd in NCAA wrestling history. I was alone, and I knew I would be alone when I shook hands in the middle of the mat in less than an hour.

If I had just gotten more rest—and re-energized. But it was too late for that now. I realized that I needed to hurry as I was a bit late. I knew I could make it in time if I walked a little faster and took a short cut.

I began to think, "Were my coaches asking where I am?" They were probably beginning to wonder why I'm late, as I am never late. Suddenly, I was lost. How did I get lost? Probably I was day dreaming again, got off course, and lost my way.

And this was a very bad part of town, really rough characters standing around everywhere. I would have asked them for directions, but I was afraid that questions might result in something much worse than being lost.

All of this chaos was causing me to lose what little focus I had—winning the NCAA championship, for me and my team. I needed to focus on finding my way to the coliseum. I changed directions, but no matter which way I went, I just got further and further from my destination.

After a short period, I was really lost. I had no chance of making it on time to wrestle. I was filled with dread as I was about to be the first wrestler in history to lose in the finals of the national tournament by virtue of just not showing up.

What will people say—that I was afraid? They would be right. How did this happen to me? How can I explain it to my coach and my friends and my family—the entire wrestling world?

Then...I woke up.

Long after my last wrestling match I had that dream, or one close to it. Anyway, don't tell Freud; I have no desire to have it interpreted.

I'm seventy years old, and I still have dreams about wrestling. Sure, they are only very occasional and not nearly as dramatic as this one, so probably not worth worrying about. Many of my wrestling dreams involve being late and/or getting lost. Some of them involve making weight. I'm never just a pound over. Usually, I'm about thirty pounds over! (Maybe my dreams are telling me it's time to go on a diet!)

I think that most of my dreams, including the wrestling dreams I have had, were positive, very good dreams. If you never had a dream about wrestling or making weight, you probably were never a (real) wrestler. If you were a (real) wrestler, you've had those dreams. I would bet on it.

I haven't wrestled competitively in fifty years. So I haven't had to make weight or wrestle for fifty years. So why do I still on occasion dream about it? I think the answer is that once wrestling is in your blood and your brain you'll never get it out. And competing and making weight were always integral parts of wrestling.

Also, all wrestlers have to identify with the Roosevelt quote, even if they have never heard it before. What could be more identified with wrestling than "the man in the arena"—alone, winning or losing, but not among those afraid to compete?

Wrestling has to be a little like being in a fox hole in WWII, a time you never can forget, no matter how hard you try. Talk to veterans who have fought in war. If they say they have forgotten or never dreamt about those days, they are lying—or they never fought in the war. Every day in the wrestling room was like being in that fox hole. Raise your head up and get it knocked off. I got mine knocked off a lot.

But I still wouldn't trade those (wrestling) days for anything in the world. And I'll never forget the moment I became "addicted" to wrestling—in a good way. Even though I went through a lot of tough times during my wrestling career, it was all well worth it. I'd bet that most wrestlers feel the same, whether they wrestled third team in high school or won an Olympic championship.

Wrestling builds character and teaches you how to get back on your feet when you're down. Wrestling also makes you tough; but to be a wrestler in the first place, you have to be tough. The first time you ever step on that mat, you know you are in a different world than you ever were in before, a very tough world. But once you've done it, as Roosevelt said, "Your place shall never be with those cold and timid souls who knew neither victory nor defeat."

What is the Hardest, Toughest, and Oldest Sport?

Who doesn't know that the sport of wrestling is synonymous with toughness? I have seen a number of studies and surveys that try to test out what is the "toughest" or the "hardest" sport. All of them that I have seen conclude that wrestling is the toughest and the hardest.

So what does "tough" or "hard" mean when applied to sports? I'll defer to a sports science expert, like Kevin Neeld, for the answer. He used the criteria of strength, speed, quickness, cardio, and overall durability to determine the toughest sport. Based on those criteria, Neeld concluded that wrestling was number one, followed by football, rugby, hockey, and lacrosse.

Another "study" by Ian Warner discussing *The Five Hardest Sports to Train and Compete In* tried to evaluate "what sport takes the greatest toll on an athlete "mentally, physically, and emotionally?" You guessed it. Warner concluded that it is wrestling.

Although this is sort of a subjective inquiry, wrestlers agree, and probably most of the world agrees, wrestling is the toughest and the hardest sport.

Wrestling is also our oldest sport, going back at least 5,000 years. According to wrestling historian Mike Chapman in his book *From Gotch to Gable*, "Wrestling was an honored sport in ancient Greece and Rome. A form of wrestling was incorporated into the Olympic games around 708 BC." Wrestling is now a huge sport with kids participating in tournaments even in pre-school. At the post-collegiate level athletes are sponsored and train year round to wrestle in the Olympics.

Why are Great Wrestlers Great? Why is Anyone Great?

A subject of constant debate over the years among wrestlers and fans is what is the most important attribute of the greatest wrestlers? Young wrestlers ask themselves, "What can I do to be the greatest wrestler in the world?"

Is it hard work? Is it quickness, intensity, strength, intelligence, flexibility of mind and body? All of the above? None of the above? Is there anything else one can think of? Are there other traits more important than these? It goes without saying that great wrestlers have to be in great shape and have great technique, technique that perfectly fits the wrestler's particular wrestling style.

This started me thinking about what factors cause a person to be successful in anything. Malcolm Gladwell wrote an interesting bestselling book, titled *Outliers*, about people who distinguish themselves and why. According to Gladwell, although there are many factors that determine success, the one that stuck in my mind was the number of hours necessary to achieve success. He claims 10,000 hours are necessary to be successful. Obviously, all great wrestlers devote 10,000 hours to wrestling. So there must be more to greatness than the number of hours spent trying to perfect one's art.

One thing is for sure. Nobody's perfect—in life or sports.

The two greatest wrestlers of my era were Jojiro Uetake and Dan Gable. I doubt there would be great debate about that assertion, at least among my generation. Uetake was never beaten and was a three-time NCAA champion (Oklahoma State University) and a two-time Olympic champion. And most people reading this book already know that Gable (at the time) was an unbeatable Olympic champion in 1972.

I wrestled both of them in 1967, the year the Spartans won our national championship. I worked out with Uetake during the summer of 1967 in preparation to go to Japan with Athletes in Action as he was helping us to learn the international style of wrestling. And I wrestled Gable in the Midlands tournament over the Christmas break in 1967, during the 1967-1968 season.

Uetake was as sound a wrestler as anyone could possibly be. He had about reached his peak as a wrestler. He won the Olympic championship in 1964 and would win four years later in 1968.

What was his greatest strength? I think his coach, Myron Roderick, once said it was his balance, his feel, his touch—some things hard to define or explain. Gene Davis, Uetake's teammate, said it was his competitive spirit. I would probably say it was his quickness. But I don't think people give him enough credit for his strength. He was very strong. I remember tying up with him and thinking that his arms felt like iron bands (or was that just my imagination?). To look at him, one wouldn't think he was that strong.

In 1967 when I worked out with Uetake, he was at his very best. In 1967, when I wrestled Gable, he was nowhere near the wrestler he would be five years later when he would win the Olympics and not one opponent would score a point on him. As for me, when I wrestled both, I was a bit over the hill. I had accomplished all my goals in wrestling and was eager to move on to something different.

I asked Dan himself what made him tick. What was it that inspired him to such heights? I will explain his answers later in the book.

I really didn't get to know Uetake well enough to figure out what made him tick. And I also don't know who would have won had Dan and Jojiro wrestled at their peak(s) at the same weight. But I will say, there could not be two wrestlers more diverse in styles and thought processes that define wrestling greatness.

> *The most important thing a young wrestler can do is to figure out his/her own strengths and weaknesses and create a style around that. That's what I did. My style was very aggressive-frenetic characterized by constant motion. I had more endurance than almost anyone and felt I could almost always wear anyone down, so they were vulnerable to easily conquer in the middle or the end of the match.*
>
> *If you are a young wrestler, ask yourself, "What is my strength and how can I make sure I develop my wrestling style around it?" If you don't know, maybe it would be well to talk to your coach(es) as this issue is, and will be, crucial to your success as a wrestler.*

Because I could usually push my opponents to exhaustion, it normally didn't matter to me what style my opponent had as I was going to be so aggressive and intense that eventually they would get tired and quit. I also never gave any thought to whether my opponent was tall or short. Many, maybe most, quit before they even started. That little bit of (even psychological) tiredness gave me that little edge I needed—even against the best wrestlers.

Any experienced wrestler would agree that styles are important and that certain styles match up best with certain other styles and vice versa. What wrestlers will always disagree about is what makes a truly great wrestler.

Long after 1967, a number of us ex-wrestlers were sitting around a table somewhere philosophizing and debating the question of the importance of various wrestling styles, attributes, and characteristics, when a friend of ours, Jim Duschen, former East High School and Iowa State All-American and Hall of Fame wrestler walked up.

Since we had already made up our own minds as to the answer, we asked Duschen, "Jim, what is the most important characteristic or attribute a wrestler can have to be a winner?" He immediately responded, "Respect for the coach." Although it seemed at the time to be a non sequitur, I think, in retrospect, his answer was spot on. I will discuss later the coaches that had an influence in my life. In my opinion, in wrestling everything starts with the coach. I was blessed to have had the all-time greatest.

Chapter 2

Spartans

ଛ

> *"Either with it or upon it"*
>
> *That was allegedly the quote every Spartan heard when marching off to battle centuries before the birth of Christ. The quote is about the Spartan shield uttered by Spartan mothers and wives to their sons and husbands as they marched off to battle.*

I love that quote. To me, the quote means that you leave it <u>all</u> on the mat every time you wrestle. If you have to be carried off the mat (as I have), that's fine too.

I also love this Michigan State Spartan quote from Lou Anna K. Simon, MSU President, "Spartans Will—It's not just what we do, but why and how we do it, that distinguishes us as Spartans. As Spartans, we have the heart, the talent, and the tenacity to make an extraordinary impact."

Spartan Discipline

I looked up the word Spartan. It means "a person of great courage and self-discipline; exhibiting courage in the face of pain." In the context of that definition, I think I'm a Spartan in name only as I am neither disciplined nor courageous in any sense of the words. And I am not just being modest. My family and friends all know this and would vouch for the fact that I am neither disciplined nor courageous.

Probably my best quality was, and is, "mental toughness." Spartans were mentally tough, and I am mentally tough. Wrestling makes you mentally tough, but you have to be mentally tough in the first place to even participate in wrestling.

Many great football players who have also wrestled have quickly admitted that wrestling requires much more mental toughness than football. That's why the University of Iowa football coach, Kirk Ferentz, has commented many times that he loves to have former wrestlers on his football team as they provide the physical and mental toughness necessary to compete at high levels. And their toughness rubs off on their teammates. Michigan State also has a lot of ex-wrestlers on the football team, and look what they have done!

As an example of my mental toughness, long after my wrestling career was over, I ran a couple marathons (just like the Spartans!). I had not trained much, as I knew all I had to do was put one foot in front of the other for 26 miles. It's not like making ten free throws in a row. It's simply a matter of making up your mind—a reflection of mental toughness—not skill. I sincerely believe that almost every wrestler could easily run a marathon if they put their mind to it as, in my opinion, it is much easier than wrestling.

Another characteristic of mine for some reason, for good or bad, I was obsessed. Lots of wrestlers say they were or are obsessed when it comes to wrestling. I know levels of obsession are subjective, but I think I was more obsessed than any other wrestler, ever, especially my senior year in high school. I really had no obsession to win a state championship or a national championship. I was just obsessed with wrestling. I would think about it <u>a lot</u>. I would imagine wrestling my opponents when I was day dreaming, which I did a lot, unfortunately, even in class. (Rudy and I could have been blood brothers on this one.)

From almost the first moment I stepped onto a wrestling mat, I was obsessed. When you are obsessed, you don't miss practice, you don't drink, you don't take drugs. You learn to "just do it" right, you always make weight, you can't wait to tie up with an opponent in a match, etc., etc., etc. Who needs Spartan discipline when you're obsessed (and mentally tough)?

Don't get me wrong. I always admired people who were disciplined. A good example would be my best friend in college, Dave Campbell. He always went to class. He always studied hard for exams. He went on to become a hospital administrator of some repute at our country's best hospitals. That is certainly a position that requires a lot of discipline. And I admire him for his discipline. But that was not me.

I have often said and thought that wrestling is way too tough a sport for those who are not obsessed with participating in it. It is not a sport that you can do on discipline alone. No way.

A few years after I graduated from Michigan State, I was asked to give a pep talk to the Michigan State wrestling team in the wrestling room. I always hated doing those as I always seem to say the wrong things. I told the Spartan wrestlers there that I personally wasn't much into the character trait of "discipline" per se. I said I didn't think one had to be disciplined to be a national champion (as I certainly wasn't). I told them it was more important, at least for me, to be obsessed.

I don't think the coaches liked my speech much.

Pat Milkovich, four-time NCAA finalist and assistant coach at the time, was downright upset at me for telling wrestlers that discipline was not a critical trait for wrestlers. I responded that I didn't tell them that. I just told them that I wasn't disciplined back when I wrestled. I was obsessed. The more obsessed I was, the better wrestler I became.

Mental Toughness

I think I got my mental toughness mainly from my mother but also my dad. They were both extremely tough-minded—maybe it was the Great Depression of the 1930s or maybe it was our Viking heritage.

There weren't a lot of hugs and "I-love-you's" in the Anderson household. (In fact, I don't remember any.) But I can tell you that my father worked very long hours, virtually every day, to bring home the bacon so we could eat. My mother, bless her soul, was the toughest and smartest woman, mentally, that I have ever seen or known or imagined. I could write a book about her mental toughness. Their toughness somehow became mine, either by nurture or nature or both.

Did they love me? I think they showed me rather than told me. That seemed to be more the approach that parents took in the 50's. My parents never babied me or mollycoddled me, so that was a big factor in my mental toughness.

In third through sixth grade I would get up early and go down to my dad's creamery in Roland, Iowa, and help to make cottage cheese. I have fond memories of those days as the entire family had responsibilities to which they attended. We did everything together when it came to work. I spent most of my time singing and stamping the date on cottage cheese cartons. I was the fastest cottage cheese carton stamper in history. I should have applied to Guinness book of records. I always had very fast hands and excellent hand-eye coordination.

When we moved to Waterloo, Iowa, in sixth grade, I had a morning paper route for a couple of years. I was glad when that came to an end—probably because of my discipline challenges. I had little interest in getting up that early every day to deliver papers, and I rarely tried to enlist new customers as making more money has never been a big motivator for me.

I believe my father recognized early that "discipline" was never going to be one of my strong suits. He used to give me the discipline lecture frequently during my childhood, but it always went over my head. He would often say something like, "We need to exercise some discipline around here"—meaning, of course, that **I** had to exercise some discipline. He always put the emphasis on the wrong syllable—de **SYP'** lin. He finally gave up and accepted me for who I was—undisciplined, but very mentally tough (and stubborn)!

After I started wrestling, I would at times lose all control and eat a half gallon of ice cream or a whole loaf of bread. Dad would try to understand that I had starved myself for a week and was now recovering. He would try to explain that if I just ate normally, but minimally, I would not have to starve myself. I'm sure it all made sense to him, but not to me. I simply never developed the discipline to eat moderately.

A lot of wrestlers in my era cut 15-20 pounds every week for eight years during wrestling season. That was me, and I certainly do not consider that effort being disciplined or even mentally tough. That is just what one did to wrestle. If you say you are going to make weight, you make weight. No "the-dog-ate-my-homework" lame excuses. I always made weight. I felt strongly that if I did not make weight, I would be letting my teammates down. More importantly, I would be letting myself down. And I felt that wrestlers on our team who didn't make weight did let our team down.

I can remember many times not being able to eat for days before the meet and not being able to drink at all the day before the meet, even though I had to work out hard. My fingers would get so dry, I would put a bowl of water near the bed just to stick my fingers in during the night, all night. (Probably lotion would have worked better, but I never thought of that.)

So, if cutting (making) weight does not require real discipline or mental toughness, what is extreme mental toughness when applied to wrestling? I would say wrestling all season with a broken bone in my arm, wrestling all season with torn cartilage in a knee, wrestling with mononucleosis, or wrestling with and in pain almost every day of most wrestling seasons.

Most normal people would say that if I wrestled with all of the above, I was just stupid. And they are probably right. But wouldn't one also have to agree that it imitates to a degree the mental toughness of the Spartans over 2,000 years ago?

> *At this point let me express my admiration for those veterans who have been in battle or people who have been in automobile accidents and experienced incredible pain and injuries and can still smile and fight through it all. My mental toughness does not even remotely compare with theirs.*

Frankly, from my way of thinking, there are only a few ways for wrestlers to deal with bad injuries and pain.

1. You can quit, or you can stop wrestling until you are healed by some means such as surgery.

2. You can adjust your wrestling to mitigate the pain and problem. Gable discusses this approach in his book, *A Wrestling Life, The Inspiring Stories of Dan Gable.* Shortly before the Olympics in 1972, Dan hurt his knee badly, such that the doctors said he would have to have it operated on. Dan decided instead to have his old high school coach, Bob Siddens, devise a dog bone tape job for the knee. After that, he began to learn how to wrestle defensively, as he could no longer wrestle aggressively with a bum knee. No one scored on Dan at the Olympics in Munich in 1972. What an incredible transformation! What would the legend of Dan Gable be had he decided to take his doctors' advice and wait for the 1976 Olympics?

Dan Gable wrestling in the '72 Olympics

3. The third way is just to forget about the pain. That's what I did for most of my high school and college career. I would just apply mind over body. However, in my senior year in college I began to avoid situations where I could potentially get hurt, particularly situations where I could hyper-extend elbows or knees. Also, I decided to try methods 1 and 2 on particularly vexing injuries.

The Spartans of Old

So...what about the original Spartans, the Spartans of old, and why do I identify so much with them? I think it's because they were tough and because they introduced wrestling to their Olympic games hundreds of years before the birth of Christ.

Almost everyone knows that wrestling became part of the "games" in ancient Greece—and that Greeks were wrestling around 700 B.C. The Spartans were excellent wrestlers and were a great fighting force in Sparta, Greece, some 500 years before Christ was born.

Anyone who watched the movie "*300*" saw that a few hundred Spartans fought hundreds of thousands of Persians at Thermopylae to a draw for about a week. The Spartans were tough, mentally and physically. And their courage was immeasurable.

I loved the fact that the Spartans went toward the battle at Thermopylae. They didn't run away from it. They didn't fear the battle and they didn't fear dying. That's the way I liked to think of myself—always going forward toward the problem—not running from it. Eagerly, get to the middle of the mat, and claim it as my own.

The Michigan State <u>Spartans</u> - Athletic Greatness in the '60s and 50 Years Later

I cannot imagine a more suitable moniker for me or our Michigan State teams of the 60s. And I loved it if others thought of me as a Spartan—as I will always think of myself as a Spartan.

About a century ago Michigan State's nickname was the "Aggies." I am so glad they changed that name. What could be worse than being an "Aggie"—a spider? a duck? a wolverine? Heaven forbid!

Presently, during this period 2014, 2015, and 2016 as I write this book, the Spartans have arguably the best football-basketball combination athletic program in the country. Both Spartan football and basketball had rough endings to their seasons during the 2015-2016 academic year. But no one can underestimate the respect garnered by both teams winning their Big Ten championships and being ranked at the top of the AP and Coaches Polls during portions of the season.

Campus Insiders selected the top 16 teams based on only the football basketball combination. They dubbed it "Hoops and Helmets." Michigan State was #1; Oklahoma was #2. Although there was no time period on the selection, it would seem that over the past few years, the #1 rating would be accurate.

The football team has ended the last three seasons in the top six in the country, finishing third in 2014, fifth in 2015, and sixth in 2016. And now, finally, Michigan State has a top ten recruiting class in both football and basketball.

> *I am a proud loyal fan of Dantonio and the football program at Michigan State. In that context there is one statistic of last year's program that I can't resist writing about. Everyone knows that traditionally, Ohio State and Michigan get the 5-star athletes and the Spartans develop the 3-star athletes into 5-star players.*
>
> *For example, in the National Football League draft, Ohio State had three players picked in the top 10 and five in the top 20! Michigan State had one—and he was not even a 3-star recruit. He was a walk-on!*
>
> *Now here comes the stat I love. Michigan State with a boatload of 3-star kids go to Columbus and beat Ohio State's 5-star athletes on their own home field. And the kicker? We did it with second and third string quarterbacks and a last second field goal by a kicker who grew up in Ohio—but was rejected by the Buckeyes!*
>
> *Now tell me that's not a program to bleed green for.*

This year, the basketball team was ranked first in the country and the football team won the Big Ten championship and was selected to play in the four-team playoff for the national championship. Also, relatively recently, the MSU basketball team was named the "National Team of the Decade" (2000-2010) by *Sports Illustrated*, and in 2015 the Spartans made it to the Final Four (again).

Although in the mid '60s there was no Directors Cup to award to the best college sports program in the country, Michigan State had arguably the best all-around athletic program in the country. The football team went undefeated during the 1966-1967 academic year—the same year we won the NCAA wrestling championship. And many Spartan teams won NCAA championships during that period, including the soccer and hockey championship teams. The Spartans also had individual national champions in other sports like gymnastics, track, and swimming.

The catalyst for these great teams and individuals came from the top; the president

John Hannah, President of MSU in the '60s

of the school, John Hannah, was a giant and a legend among university administrators across the country. He could usually be seen at our wrestling meets and other sport activities. He even wrote me a couple letters and mentioned me in one of his speeches during a banquet I attended. He also took the time to write me a letter of recommendation to law school, which I'm sure was instrumental in my admission to numerous top ten law schools.

Possibly even more important, Biggie Munn, athletic director who coached NCAA football championship teams at MSU, was "all in" in his support of our wrestling program. Biggie once said that the greatest sporting event and most exciting meet he ever attended was when our wrestling team beat the University of Michigan in 1968, my senior year. In that meet our heavyweight Jeff Smith pinned Dave Porter, a two-time NCAA champion, to win the meet in front of what was the biggest crowd ever to attend a Michigan State meet. I'll write more about that later.

From a personal perspective, Biggie sent me notes encouraging me during my time at Michigan State. He sent some of them to me even when I was a freshman! Think of that! How many athletic directors in the country send minor sport athletes notes of encouragement? Name one. And have any of them sent one to a "nobody" freshman wrestler, telling him to keep his chin up, that times will get better? That was the character of Biggie Munn. And that is why MSU had the greatest sports program in the country.

Biggie Munn, Athletic Director in the '60s

Great programs start with great coaches, but those coaches must be supported by great administrators.

A lot of Michigan State alumni are very proud right now of our sports programs and for good reason. We are all dusting off our Spartan caps and t-shirts to wear proudly the Spartan symbols once again. I am hoping this book will encourage former Michigan State wrestlers to be proud of what the wrestling program accomplished, even if the accomplishments I am writing about occurred a half century ago.

There was no Spartan era like the mid '60s. And there will never be one like it again. Even Spartan football stars of today say that the present teams may not be as good as the teams in the '60s, but deserve to be in the same conversation. I would agree—maybe not as good, but in the same conversation.

Chapter 3
Michigan State Wrestling: A Brief History

ଔ

> *"Go Green! Go White!"*
>
> Michigan State University fans bleed green (and white).

Spartans have a fan base that has grown exponentially because of the recent fantastic fortunes of the football and basketball teams. Spartan fans love their Spartans. Every Spartan fan knows that Michigan State is always number one—no matter what the pollsters or statistics say.

Whenever I am wearing my Spartan cap, a day doesn't go by when someone doesn't greet me with "Go Green!" To which I am supposed to immediately reply, "Go White!"

How good was Michigan State football prior to the Dantonio era? How good was basketball prior to the Izzo era? Who cares? That was then, and now is now! And this is another golden era of Spartan sports.

What about Michigan State wrestling? Probably most wrestling fans would prefer to remember the good old days when Michigan State won seven Big Ten titles in a row, a record at Michigan State that still stands and may never be broken. No Spartan athletic program or team has won as many as seven straight Big Ten titles. And it all started with us in 1966. I am proud of that fact and will state it again and again in this book.

But…let's get real. Most sports fans in general, including wrestling fans, have very short memories, and 50 years was a long time ago. Very few remember the heyday of Michigan State wrestling, and so….a good reason for this book.

If you asked wrestling fans what university has the best wrestling program, probably most fans right after March of 2016 would say Penn State. They would be both right and wrong. They would be right if they are talking only about the 2016 national champions.

But what about 2015? Penn State did not win that year, but Penn State was and is the national powerhouse program these days. No one would doubt that. What about before Penn State during the "Gable" era? For decades in a row, during the '70s, the '80s, and the '90s, Iowa won the NCAAs almost every year.

However, if you consider which school has the greatest program <u>ever</u> over the past century since the beginning of college wrestling, based solely on the "numbers" (NCAA championships, top 10 appearances and all-Americans), it isn't even close. Oklahoma State University wins by a landslide in all four salient categories with:

- 138 (individual) national champions,
- 440 All-Americans,
- 31 NCAA championship teams, and
- 78 top ten teams.

And what's more depressing (especially for Iowans) is that nobody is ever going to catch them—at least in the lifetime of anybody reading this book.

Iowans can grouse that many of those championships were won in the '20s and '30s when very few programs participated in the NCAAs and that sometimes the weight brackets back then contained only a few wrestlers, mostly Okies. But in fairness, the first NCAA championship was held at Iowa State in 1928, and guess who won that tournament? Also, the NCAAs were held all over the country after that, and the Okies seemed to win them all. OSU, in fact, won the first 10 out of 11 NCAA championships.

Maybe the complaint by Iowans is somewhat justified anyway, but there is no getting around the statistic. I remember so well in the 60's, there was something awe-inspiring and jaw dropping about the "Okies" in their black and orange uniforms. There was an aura about that team—the most unbeatable team in any sport in NCAA history. As an Iowan, I "hated" them. But, at the same time, I had to respect them. And I must admit, when they all came out on the mat, they took my breath away, all demigods of wrestling who would have been worshipped back in Greek times.

But that was then, and now is now. And for now here is the big picture, the top 10 college wrestling programs historically. No matter when you read this book, the placement of these teams is probably not going to change much or at all (except that Michigan State might soon drop out of the top 10 in favor of Ohio State).

	NCAA Individual Championships	All Americans	NCAA Champ Teams	Top 10 NCAA Finishes
Oklahoma St	138	440	31	78
Iowa	81	307	23	60
Iowa State	68	287	7	56
Oklahoma	66	269	7	62
Penn State	29	189	5	47
Minnesota	22	172	3	36
Michigan State	**25**	**136**	**1**	**25**
Northern Iowa	21	119	1	19
Lehigh	27	139	0	40
Michigan	22	176	0	41

These are the objective criteria of historian Jay Hammond, the official historian for the National Wrestling Hall of Fame. What other criteria would one use? It is apparent that Oklahoma State stands alone at the top and Iowa stands alone in second place. Again, I doubt seriously that these two are ever going to change as first and second—at least in our lifetimes.

Iowa has one record that won't be broken. Dan Gable, the Iowa coach, has coached more NCAA championship teams than any other coach, according to wrestling historian Jay Hammond. And ironically, although Oklahoma State won almost all the NCAA Championships during the first 40 years, Iowa won almost all of them for 20 years or so during the '70s, '80s and '90s.

Iowa State and Oklahoma are even statistically, as both have won seven NCAA championships. I gave a slight nod to ISU as the Cyclones have more individual national champions and more All-Americans than Oklahoma (and I'm an Iowan).

Penn State really stands alone at number 5. It will probably take a decade for them to catch Iowa State or Oklahoma, but it is also very unlikely that any program below the Nittany Lions is going to ever catch them. The most important reason is that Penn State has won the championship the last three out of four years. There is no reason that Penn State, under the leadership of Cael Sanderson, will not continue to win championships.

So the top five programs are probably not going to change for a while, if ever. The sixth best wrestling program is Minnesota, mainly because it has won three NCAA team championships and is at least equal to any other program below it on the other criteria.

The next four are really grouped together. I have weighted winning a national team championship higher than the other criteria, when all other criteria are basically equal. MSU and UNI rank higher than Lehigh and the University of Michigan. All else being close, I believe being a national champion as a team has to trump the other criteria. (Neither Lehigh nor Michigan has ever won an NCAA championship.)

But who cares who won the championship in 1967 or any other year, particularly if you are an Ohio State or Penn State fan? That makes sense if you only care about recent years' champions.

Where does the 2015 NCAA champion, Ohio State, rank? I, and anyone objective, would probably place it at eleventh—in front of Illinois (12th), Oregon State (13th), Wisconsin (14th), and Nebraska (15th). Depending on when you read this book, Ohio State has had about 20 NCAA champions, about 90 All Americans, far less than any in the top 10; 1 NCAA team championship; better than two in the top ten and about 20 top 10 finishes, better than only one in the top 10.

One important statistic is that although the Big 6 (the Big 8, now the Big 12) virtually owned the NCAA tournament for the first 40 years, the Big 10 has virtually owned it for the last 40 years.

Speaking of Michigan State, in the '60s and early '70s, it was the fourth or fifth best program overall historically. But sadly, in the past 40 years or so, the Spartans have slipped in all criteria.

But this book is not about the history of Spartan wrestling; the context for the 1967 team was one where all of us on the team in 1967 could look back with pride on what the program had accomplished. And we wanted to continue that proud program tradition.

The program just before and just after our NCAA championship was called by many a (mini) dynasty at least within the context of Big Ten competition. "Under Peninger and Blubaugh, the Spartans became the terror of the Big Ten, rolling to seven consecutive titles," wrote Mike Chapman, the sport's most prolific author, in his book, *The Encyclopedia of American Wrestling*.

So let's review the history of the Michigan State University wrestling program.

The 1920s–1950s

The Michigan State wrestling program had a most inauspicious beginning in 1922. The team wrestled four meets. In the first meet, State lost to Indiana 39-5 and then to Iowa State 50-0. The roaring '20s were not kind to our program.

> *According to Mike Chapman, there was one previous coach in the history of wrestling with the intensity of Gable, and that was Edward Gallagher. Gallagher built Oklahoma State (then called Oklahoma A & M) into a fighting force in the 20's and 30's that no team could begin to contend with for years. Gallagher has the highest winning percentage (95.2%) of any coach in college wrestling history. It was during this period that OSU built up an insurmountable lead in national championships.*

The '30s saw an undefeated Okie travel north to East Lansing to coach the Spartans. His name was Fendley Collins, and he was to lead the Spartans to respectability through the '50s.

Official NCAA wrestling championships did not begin until 1934. Just two years later, in 1936 Michigan State notched its first individual NCAA champion, Walter Jacobs. It was clear to all that the program was on the right track and improving year by year.

In 1940 Gallagher, at OSU, died. During this period Collins began to recruit in Oklahoma and actually threw a scare into the Okies in 1941 and 1943 by taking second place in those national tournaments. Unfortunately, the tournament was canceled in '42 because of World War II. There is a relative consensus among historians that prior to 1967, the '42 team was MSU's best team. In fact, when we traveled to Oklahoma in 1967, the newspapers even announced that ours was the best team since the 1942 Spartans, 25 years earlier.

Fendley Collins, MSU Wrestling Coach

After the war, Collins began heavily recruiting in Michigan while continuing to recruit in Oklahoma. As a result, the late 1940s and 1950s produced a number of individual national champions and a couple more near national team championships.

The 1960s

The early '60s were good to Michigan State, with MSU winning its first Big Ten championship in 1961 while still under the tutelage of Collins. But the program was about to get a lot better when Grady Peninger and Doug Blubaugh took over a couple years later. Grady and Doug initially inherited six Okies from Collins, but soon realized that they had great high school wrestling right in their back yard. Soon, great Michigan wrestlers like Jack Zindel and Mike Bradley came to State instead of the University of Michigan.

Simultaneously, Grady began to seriously cherry pick the best wrestlers in the country including Don Behm from Illinois and Dale Carr from Virginia. Later in the '60s, after the Spartans won a national championship, the Spartans were able to induce the Milkoviches from Ohio to enroll and brought in eventual three-time national champion Greg Johnson from the Lansing area.

> *The Spartans lost the recruiting battle against Michigan when it came to one of the greatest wrestlers ever in the state of Michigan—Dave Porter, a wrestler out of Lansing. Porter, a two-time NCAA champion, ended up with the best record in U of M history and created some great stories in the MSU - U of M wrestling rivalry. Porter wanted to be on a team where the team could win the NCAAs. In that context he made a big mistake, as he would have been on a national championship team in both wrestling and football had he stayed in East Lansing. An irony which was not lost on him to his bitter disappointment, as U of M never won a national championship in either football or wrestling during his enrollment there—and Michigan State did!*

The Spartan program hit its apogee in the late 1960s when it won four Big Ten championships in a row (1966-1969) and one NCAA championship.

The 1970s

The '70s started the way the '60s ended—three Big Ten championships in a row and finishing second at the NCAA tournament twice and third once. As mentioned, anchoring the team were Greg Johnson at 115 pounds, four-time NCAA finalist; two-time NCAA champion Pat Milkovich at 126; and Tom Milkovich, four time big Ten champion and NCAA champion at 142.

In 1972 the bottom fell out of the program when Doug Blubaugh left to take the head coaching job at Indiana. That was a fatal mistake for both Doug and Grady, but it was also a huge mistake for Michigan State. Michigan State wrestling has never recovered. Grady tried to talk Doug out of taking the head coaching job, probably promising Doug the head coaching job at Michigan State when Grady retired, but Doug just couldn't wait.

Doug Blubaugh, MSU Assistant Wrestling Coach

1980s–2016

Unfortunately, the Michigan State wrestling program presently finds itself in the cellar, not just in the Big Ten but in the entire country. The program has definitely fallen on hard times.

Spartan fans are optimistic that the program will right itself with the introduction of new coaching leadership. One fact that gives alumni hope is that back in 1964, Michigan State was last in the Big Ten and three years later, we were #1 in the country!

Michigan State NCAA Individual Champions

Michigan State is still in the top ten in total number of individual national champions and will remain so for a long time. They are listed in chronological order below:

Walter Jacobs
(1935-1937)

William Maxwell
(1941-1943)

Burl Jennings
(1941-1943)

Merle Jennings
(1941-1943)

Gale Mikles
(1946-1947)

Richard Dickenson
(1946-1949)

Gene Gibbons
(1948-1951)

Bob Hoke
(1950-1954)

Jim Sinadinos
(1952-1956)

Ken Maidlow
(1954-1958)

Norman Young
(1957-1961)

Richard Cook
(1962-1966)

Dale Anderson
(1965-1968)

George Radman
(1965-1968)

Greg Johnson
(1969-1972)

Tom Milkovich
(1970-1974)

Pat Milkovich
(1972-1976)

Kelvin Jackson
(1993-1995)

Franklin Gomez
(2005-2010)

Chapter 4
The Setting - 1967

ଓ

> *"It was a time of sex, drugs, and rock and roll versus the silent majority (a group that apparently didn't care for illicit sex, non-prescribed drugs, and rock and roll). Nobody knows who won. I really didn't have time for either one. I was too busy wrestling and trying to get through school. What did I miss?"*
>
> *Dale Anderson*

Jairus (Jay) Hammond, official historian for the Wrestling Hall of Fame, wrote in his book titled *The History of Collegiate Wrestling* that college wrestling is divided into three eras—the Prewar Era, the Postwar Era, and the Modern Era.

He notes that the Modern Era of college wrestling began when Michigan State won the NCAA Championship in 1967, taking the prize away from the Oklahoma schools. We were a watershed moment in the history of college wrestling.

The Modern Era was more or less consummated when Gable and Iowa subsequently took the championship away from the Okies year after year after year. Our win let Iowa and Gable know that there was no reason for Oklahoma to ever dominate wrestling again. And it hasn't.

Ron Good in *Amateur Wrestling News* claimed that this period was the best wrestling ever. Mike Chapman, who has attended nearly 50 NCAA tournaments and has written 17 books on wrestling, agrees with Good, "The college wrestling of the 1960s was as good as I've seen."

That was 50 years ago, long before today's collegiate wrestlers were even born. So what were times like in 1967? What were most Americans doing and thinking about in the 60s?

Many people living in the '60s remember those days as characterized by the liberal media as sex, drugs, and rock and roll or maybe race riots or maybe Vietnam or maybe all of the above. At the same time, Richard Nixon tapped into a larger segment of society which he named the "Silent Majority" in the '60s. This group, which did not express their opinions openly, did not engage in illicit sex, did not consume drugs, and did not listen (much) to rock and roll. They didn't join the protests against the war, and they didn't get involved in the race riots.

Sex, Drugs, and Rock 'n Roll

I didn't know much about the sex part, and I knew even less about drugs. But it was impossible if you were a college student, to avoid the barrage of great rock and roll during our 1966-1967 wrestling season. On Valentine's Day, February 14, 1967, Aretha Franklin introduced her version of the greatest rock and roll song of all time *"Respect,"* which our team implicitly took on as our theme song right through to the national tournament in March. Aretha sang, "All I want is a little respect…" That's all we wanted. During that period I saw kids look at our 1967 team the way I once looked at Oklahoma State wrestlers—with respect—and sometimes a little awe. It was an amazing feeling to be ranked number 1 in the country.

As far as great rock and roll songs went, it was impossible to ignore them as we were only a stone's throw from Motown, the heart and soul of the greatest music of the '60s. Our team's "soul man" was Mike Bradley from the Detroit area, three-time Big Ten Champion and NCAA runner-up at 177 pounds in 1967. He always made sure he had his big portable player with him so that we could hear all the latest and greatest Motown hits every day in every locker room when we traveled. It brightened our spirits and clearly fired us up. A lot of great songs were released right during this period that had a lot of soul and fire like James Brown's, "I Feel Good!" Who wouldn't feel good and fired up after hearing that song! Mike made sure we heard all those great songs loud and clear—and nobody complained!

Dale Carr, our 145 pounder, recently reminisced about Mike and these songs, "I do remember warming up to the music of Motown, thanks to Bradley." Carr further commented that "actually Motown is still the only music Bradley listens to…"

Vietnam

This was also a time of turmoil that makes the political disorder of our present time look tame. There was a war in Vietnam, and the United States was neck deep in it. The Waterloo draft board was particularly patriotic in making sure all of its citizens were either exempt, deferred, or in the army.

It seemed that no one was exempt, except those in school or those who could convince the military doctor that they were sick, injured, or homosexual. Some guys tried all three to escape the rice paddies. I remember the sick feeling that washed over me each time I got a notice from my draft board warning me that I must assure the board that I was enrolled in college each term and carrying at least 15 credit hours, or I would be immediately subject to the draft.

The war created a huge schism in society with almost everyone having a strong opinion, usually based on whose ox was being gored. Some kids even gave up their United States citizenship and fled to Canada. Hundreds of thousands joined marches for peace all over the country. These marches dwarfed any protests we've seen in the 21st Century. And these protests would continue year after year until the war ended well into the '70s. But in the '60s it seemed the war would never end. Many times during 1967 my friends and family would send me notices of the death of another one of my classmates. Even worse, college campuses were sometimes literally on fire as buildings were torched and even blown up.

Race Relations

Another enormous issue of the day was race relations. Many believe this is a tense time between races. Today is a picnic compared to 50 years ago. Every bi-racial city was a powder keg for violence and rioting.

> *During this period, my best friend Don Buzzard, who lived on the East side of town where almost all Waterloo African Americans lived, was one of the greatest athletes in Waterloo high school history. One night, we decided to go into a bar patronized only by blacks on the northeast side of town, just for "fun." Neither of us drank (and we were too young to drink anyway), but it just seemed like something fun—and dangerous—to do. Waterloo had one of the nastiest race riots in the country in 1967.*
>
> *This bar was in the worst part of town. There was probably no worse place for a white person to be in any city in America. When we entered the bar, everything seemed to stop—including time. The world stood still. There was not one white person in the bar. What did we expect?*
>
> *I was sure we were about to die. Suddenly, we spotted a good friend of Don's and mine, Willie Hoosman, a state champion wrestler at East High and later a wrestler for Iowa State. Willie welcomed us into the bar, and only then did the mood change dramatically, and all was well. I'll never forget that moment when time (and my heart) stood still.*

A century after the Emancipation Proclamation, the President and Congress decided to create a Civil Rights Act that had teeth and thereby broke the back of segregation in the United States.

Michigan State was one of the first northern universities to "steal" great African American athletes from the south as most southern schools would still not recruit them. Some schools even had informal rules that no black athlete could play for them. Football players like Bubba Smith (of "*Academy*" fame), George Webster, and Gene Washington, recruited in the south, became All-American stars and made Michigan State the number 1 football team in the country.

Mike Bradley (177 pounder) from Michigan and Jeff Richardson (heavyweight) from Pennsylvania were the only African-Americans on the wrestling team at the time. They were anchors of our team, simply great guys with big hearts whom we could count on for a win when it mattered most—to close out the meets.

Two of my happiest sports moments at MSU came from Mike. The first one was in 1966 at the Big Ten Tournament and the first of seven that Michigan State won. If Brad (Mike) won the Big Ten Championship at 177 we would win the team title. The scores were very close as going into the final round, Michigan, Michigan State, or Minnesota had a chance to win the tournament. Mike beat Bob Ramstead from Minnesota to give us the championship. That was one of my most exciting moments wrestling at Michigan State. More about that later.

My second moment of happiness related to Mike was reuniting with him when I returned to Michigan State for the 1967-1968 academic year in the fall. Michigan State football had just come off of an undefeated regular season and was about to embark on another undefeated season. Mike saw me watching the team football practice. He ignored the practice and ran all the way across the field and gave me the biggest hug I can ever remember. I felt then that he was a true friend. He may have long forgotten it, but I never will. Mike was (and is) a great guy and friend.

Jeff Richardson, our heavyweight and All American wrestler, played pro football for the New York Jets when they won the Super Bowl with Joe Namath quarterbacking after college.

The 60s—those were great days! And 1967 was the greatest of the great—at least at Michigan State!

The Six Day War

While the Vietnam War continued on interminably and the best of our young men were being killed in a far-off land that nobody seemed to really care about, Israel was making fast work of its Arab neighbors by achieving a decisive victory in one of the shortest wars in history. This war ultimately was probably more important than the one in Vietnam.

Syria, north of Israel, really started the war by continuing to bombard Israeli settlements just across the border. They then began to mobilize for battle. Egypt mobilized its forces in the south. Soon Jordan, Iraq, Kuwait, and Algeria sent forces to make quick work of the Israelis.

The Israelis, however, struck preemptively, bombing the planes and tanks on the ground. The Egyptian air force was obliterated without a moment's notice. Soon the other invading countries and all ground forces were destroyed by the Israeli air, tank, and troop attacks.

The Arabs capitulated after just a few days. As a result, Israel doubled their land mass and established themselves as a country to be reckoned with. This area is a sore spot even today as it continues to be an area of dispute for Jews and Muslims.

The United States Supreme Court

As an attorney, I remember some incredibly important decisions during this period. The controversial case of *Miranda v Arizona* had been decided (5-4) just prior to the academic year and was the source of great debate not only among law students but even among undergraduates at Michigan State.

Also in the '60s, unimaginable as it might seem, it was illegal in many states for people of different races to mix and marry. *Loving v Virginia*, decided by the United States Supreme Court in 1967, changed all that. Miscegenation soon became a notion of the past. Most people now don't even know what the word means.

Soon the *Terry v Ohio* case would give peace officers the power to "stop and frisk" when the officers had "reasonable suspicion" that a crime was occurring and that the suspect was armed and dangerous.

The Blizzard of '67 and Terrible Winter Weather

An event seldom remembered was that in January 1967, what is arguably the worst snowstorm in history (yes, all of history) was recorded. I checked out Google "blizzards" or snowstorms, and an article by Ed Grabianowski listed the ten worst blizzards in world history. I think #8 was a terrible blizzard over in Siberia somewhere. #1 was the Midwest blizzard of '67 where over 70 people died just in the Chicago area! Many other Midwesterners lost their lives. The 50+ mph winds created drifts up to 15-16 feet! Some Michigan State students were hurt badly jumping out of second story windows at their dorms.

The Lansing Journal on January 27, 1967, wrote in one of its largest headlines ever, "State of Emergency Declared In Lansing's Worst Blizzard."

THE STATE JOURNAL

State of Emergency Declared In Lansing's Worst Blizzard

Snowdrifts Shut Factories, Stores

To make matters worse, the temperature in January dropped to 23 below zero! Mother Nature was not kind that winter in East Lansing, Michigan. I'm just glad that by 1967 I had had two years to acclimate myself. Iowa weather was bad, but nothing like this! Many of us during this period considered transferring to Arizona State. ☺

Other Sports Besides Wrestling In '67

As far as other sports in 1967, the Green Bay Packers won their first Super Bowl. And suddenly, the Lombardian terms "blocking and tackling" became synonymous with "learning fundamentals" in the nomenclature of every area from education to business (and even wrestling).

In basketball, people were still talking about Wilt Chamberlain scoring 100 points in one game. At the college level, under Coach John Wooden, UCLA was beginning its streak of national championships from 1967 to 1973, a streak that no basketball program was ever going to come close to matching. (Gable later won nine NCAA team championships in a row coaching the University of Iowa.)

Everybody knows about the Triple Crown in horse racing, but what about baseball? In baseball, who could forget Boston's Carl Yastremski's winning the Triple Crown and then Boston losing to St Louis in the World Series? No baseball player would win the Triple Crown again until 2012, almost 50 years later. And tennis—who would have guessed that no men's champion would ever win the men's Grand Slam (all four tournaments in one year) after Rod Laver in the '60s?

Remaining Questions

Three huge questions remain to be answered and will be answered later in this book:

- How did I end up at Michigan State?
- How did the other members of the team end up at Michigan State?
- How in the world did we win that national championship in 1967?

Chapter 5
Me - Growing Up and Falling in Love with Wrestling

ଓ

"I remember the exact moment I knew I was addicted to wrestling"

Dale Anderson

Fort Dodge, Humboldt, Clear Lake, Spencer, and Marshalltown

I was born in a Fort Dodge, Iowa, hospital exactly nine months after Japan surrendered in War II. Since my parents didn't drink, I guess they found other ways to celebrate what they believed was the greatest moment in American history.

My early years were spent on a farm in Humboldt, Iowa. We had neither running water nor electricity, and we had an outhouse. My father was born in the same house in Humboldt.

He was apparently best friends with Frank Gotch's son. Frank Gotch was the most famous wrestler of the early 20th Century. His world championship match in 1911 against Hackenschmidt, known as the Russian Lion for his great strength, was so big that the crowd of 30,000 virtually filled Comiskey Park in Chicago.

Those were the days when wrestling was one of the most popular sports in the country, and Gotch was the biggest wrestling name in the world, as he was the world champion. Mike Chapman has done extensive research on Gotch's career and asserts that Gotch is the primary reason for Iowa's love affair with the sport.

I am the youngest and on the bottom left side.

Chapman has written several books on the subject including, *Gotch: An American Hero* and *From Gotch to Gable: A History of Iowa Wrestling.*

> *I wish now I had asked my dad some questions about growing up in the same town as Frank Gotch and being best friends with Gotch's son.*
>
> *One of the best things I ever did was to videotape my mother when she explained her childhood and life.*
>
> *I would like to suggest that you do an autobiographical videotape of your parents while they discuss their lives growing up. You will never regret it. And it will be a wonderful legacy to hand down through the generations.*

I grew up while my father moved from town to town in Iowa. In kindergarten, we lived in Clear Lake. In first grade, we moved to Spencer. In second grade we moved to Marshalltown. I mainly played cowboys and Indians in Marshalltown and, of course, listened to the Lone Ranger on the radio.

> *Many of us old timers remember that some of the greatest singers of our time, including Buddy Holly, Richie Valens, and the Big Bopper, died in a plane crash right after leaving Clear Lake, Iowa, in 1959. That was the day the music died according to Don McLean, who sang about it in the song American Pie, which became the #1 song for four straight weeks.*

I remember only one athletic event that I participated in Marshalltown. We were playing football in our back yard. I was by far the youngest, probably at least five years younger than anybody else participating. We were called in for supper to eat, so we had one more last play. We either won or lost depending on this play, a touchdown or nothing.

I ran out for a pass. Nobody guarded me at all. There was no reason to. My brother threw the pass to me. If I caught it, we win, as I was already in the end zone. I remember distinctly the point of ball hitting me in the chest and bouncing harmlessly to the ground. It was a most disgraceful start to my athletic career. I'm sure my brother said something similar to what Rudy's brother said to him just before heading back home to eat supper in the movie *Rudy*. That's probably why I remember it so well. I felt terrible and never forgot it. Always catch the ball with your hands—not with your chest. (Even the pros fail to do that sometimes.) My chest still hurts where the point of that football hit me—or is that just my imagination?

Roland

We moved to Roland in third grade. By this time my sister, who was eleven years my elder, had married and moved out. So there were just my two brothers and me—Myrl in the eighth grade, Larry in the tenth grade, and me in the third grade.

Roland changed everything for me. I don't remember being happy before Roland; I don't think I was. But in Roland I became accepted by my classmates, which happened very soon after we arrived.

Roland was an athletic little town with about 700 residents. It was like the town in "*Hoosiers*" in many ways as Roland beat some very big schools in the state basketball tournaments during this period in the '50s when there was only one state tournament for all high schools, large and small. I thought that Roland was a much kinder town than the one in the

Hoosiers. It certainly was kind to me, providing me with great feelings of nostalgia as I write this book.

When we arrived, one of the greatest basketball players in Iowa history was playing for Iowa State University in Ames, Iowa, just a few miles down the road from Roland. His name was Gary Thompson. Though just 5'8" tall, he became a first team All-American for the Cyclones and beat out Wilt Chamberlain as conference player of the year. Sports Illustrated named him as the fourteenth best athlete in Iowa history. As an alumnus of Roland High School, he was, of course, a hero for all of us kids. Gary Thompson had a profound influence on every kid (and adult) in Roland in the 1950s. He was a class athlete that everyone looked up to. One of the greatest lines I heard about him was that he was the guy every father would love to have their daughter marry.

Gary Thompson, Roland and Iowa State basketball star

The first time I saw a basketball game in Roland, I was hooked. I was every bit as addicted to basketball during our life in Roland as I would later be addicted to wrestling. My oldest brother, Larry, was on the varsity team, which made watching the team even more exciting. He played on one of Roland's greatest teams.

I was a better spectator than I was a player, especially at first. For example, I was not even close to being the first person chosen whenever we played pickup games in any sport. I was just plain behind my classmates as they had been playing sports for several years, and I was just learning in the fourth grade.

In the fifth grade, one of my friends told me that he picked me relatively early when choosing sides for his basketball team because I could "argue good." I never asked him what that meant or what it had to do with basketball, but I'll never forget his saying that to me. Maybe that's why I became a lawyer.

I played basketball every day for hours and hours, even in snow and zero temperatures. Sometimes I played with my brother and his friends as not many kids my age lived in town. Most of the kids my age lived on farms and would play basketball in their barns when it got cold. I loved to do that. During school and recess, we always chose up sides quickly and played until, reluctantly, we were forced to respond to our teacher's order that we return to class.

Our family lived just a couple of blocks from the school, so I would walk to school at night and shoot baskets on my own. When it got dark, I could turn on the lights and shoot as long as I liked. Later, I bought a skeleton key and used it to sneak into the school and shoot on the same court where Gary Thompson and our state championship team played. Every shot was for the state championship, so every shot was important, at least in my imagination. Roland would be down one point and my shot would make the difference if we were going to win—or lose. I cherish that time of my life.

> *So here is my point. There is no more important thought process during practice than to think and practice like a "winner." Here is how I did it. If I was to make five free throws in a row (to win the state championship) before I went home, I would never leave only making four. Never. Later when I wrestled, if I were to set out to run an hour, I would never just run an hour. I would always run an hour and more. All the time, I would tell myself that the little bit extra would be the difference between winning or losing my next match, between feeling strong in the overtime and being pooped. Also, I would often wrestle my future opponent in my mind as I ran. That would really crank up my adrenalin and make the run so much easier. Finally, I distinctly remember thinking that I was going to make my opponent pay for every drop of sweat that fell from my face.*
>
> *So when you practice, think what would win your next match or game.*

By the time I hit sixth grade, I had improved a lot and could usually make four out of five free throws. We played really competitive games in the gym against each other and other schools. In one game I had to make both free throws at the end of the game for our team to win. I did—great memories. I sometimes fantasize that in a parallel universe, if we had stayed in Roland, we would have won a state championship in basketball. I know we would have.

Aside from basketball, I loved all sports from football to table tennis. And I loved all kinds of games from chess to cards. Since there were very few kids my age in the town of Roland, as most lived on farms, we had to be creative and modify how the games were played during non-school days or the summer.

As a relatively extreme illustration, sometimes we played baseball with a basketball. Obviously, when a batter hits a basketball, the ball is not going to go very far, so you can play the game with only a few players on each side. One time when we were playing this game, I hit the basketball as hard as I could. Because the ball was resilient, the bat bounced back and hit me in the forehead, knocking me cuckoo. I was out like a light. My forehead swelled up like a golf ball. Nobody knew what to do. I was just lying there unconscious. When I finally regained consciousness, I went back to playing the game, too stupid or hard-headed to realize that I probably had just suffered a concussion. (Besides, back then, I'm not sure anyone knew what a concussion was.)

My parents never even commented on the huge bump in the middle of my forehead. Even if they had noticed it and asked about it, they would have just told me not to play baseball with a basketball anymore. (And they might have added that that was a dumb thing to do.) There is not one chance in a hundred that my parents would have suggested taking me to a doctor. Probably the closest doctor would have been in Ames, about 20 miles away. Going that far over a bump on the head was a non-starter in our family. I don't remember any of us ever going to a doctor until my junior year in high school when I fractured and separated my shoulder playing football.

Anyway, I still have a relatively obvious bump there in the middle of my forehead as a reminder of (one of many instances of) my poor judgment.

Much more intense than my experiences with kids my own age were the ones with my brother, five years my senior. I loved playing games with his friends. He expected me to play all sports with him and his contemporaries—and up to his level. If he threw me the football, I was expected to catch it, every time. If I threw the ball to him, the pass was supposed to be over the shoulder. If he threw me the basketball and no one was guarding me, I was expected to shoot—and make the basket. There were no excuses, no Mulligans, no do-overs. Playing with older kids made me really tough and competitive with kids my own age. For example, nobody ever wore pads or helmets while playing football, and the game was always tackle. No one would ever mention playing a sissy game of two-hand touch or flag.

If we played ping pong, I was expected to play at my brother's level (but not better). One time I beat my brother in table tennis. I told him that I wanted to quit. We had played enough. But for him there was no quitting until he won. We were playing in the basement. Later, while he was retrieving the ball, I made a dash for the stairs to get out of there before he could stop me. Suddenly I felt a paddle hit me right between the shoulder blades. There was no quitting in the Anderson household. You played until you dropped or lost.

> *Big brothers have incredible influence over their younger siblings. Too many older brothers refuse to mentor their siblings. I think that is a mistake—for both. No matter how many fights we were in growing up, I learned so much just being around my older brothers and appreciate what they did for my development, particularly in sports.*

Waterloo

During my sixth grade year, our father bought a dairy in Waterloo, so again we had to move. My oldest brother had graduated. But my other brother was in the middle of his junior year, a tough time to move from a high school of about 75 to a high school of around 2,000 kids, most of whom were pretty cliquey. My brother loved Roland and soon hated Waterloo in general and West High School in particular.

I hated the move, and I had a very difficult time fitting in. In Roland, I sincerely felt that everyone in my class was my friend. When we moved to Waterloo, I had to start over making friends. That was not easy for me as I was not that gregarious.

Initially, one big problem in Waterloo was that the grade school I had to attend had no grass or basketball courts. It looked and felt like an inner city school, surrounded by a substance like macadam or blacktop. The only "sport" anyone played was four square. Four square was a sissy game where 4 people stood in one of four squares more or less in a circle. The object of the game was to sort of bounce a ball into someone else's square and make the person miss it.

There was really nothing to do at my new school except be embarrassed in class because I was at least a year behind Waterloo kids academically.

The other thing I did was fight. I got into lots of fights, and I got into lots of trouble—some of it even "legal" trouble. I didn't like fighting and would do almost anything to get out of a fight, including trying to talk my way out of it or walking away. Maybe sixth grade is a time that all kids fight. I really didn't want to hurt anybody, and I didn't want to get hurt, so it was not a fun period for me.

I would come home with bruises or black eyes. My parents wouldn't say anything. Maybe they didn't know what to say or maybe they thought fighting was a natural part of growing up. Bullying was rampant.

Often if the bullying went too far, as beyond words, I would fight. The only thing that switched a trigger for me as I was pushed into more and more fights was being touched, usually pushed or slugged. When that happened, I often became sort of like Ralphie in *Christmas Story* when the bully pushed Ralphie too far. Sometimes I went into such a zone I didn't even remember what happened afterward. One time I beat a bully's head against a driveway. I think I was sort of in a different world for that brief period of time.

It was not something over which I had a lot of control of at the time, so I was somewhat relieved when I could channel that energy almost exclusively into wrestling. By that time, basically high school, the bullying stopped anyway, as bullies do not like to fight wrestlers, for obvious reasons.

One big side benefit of wrestling is that you never again have to worry about being bullied. One extreme example occurred when a few of us went to Chicago while we were still in our teens. I was the only wrestler in the group. Suddenly, in a relatively isolated moment, we were accosted by a group of young black toughs. They asked for (wanted) our money. I immediately asked them for money. They didn't know how to respond. We walked away. I was not nervous during that period at all. Wrestling did

> *that for me. I'm sure all of the "kids" in our group would vouch for what I say about this "encounter."*
>
> *Wrestlers never need to be bullied again.*

Even though I might have technically lost fights, I never quit. Once the fight began, I would never quit. The other guy always was the one who quit. And I usually let him quit even if he technically won the fight. One thing I always prided myself in was that I never quit.

To make matters worse, I was a follower, and I started following the wrong crowd as most of the "good" kids already had their own friends. There were exceptions, of course, and they have my undying appreciation.

After only a few months in elementary school, I graduated to West Junior High School where there were approximately 400-500 students in the seventh grade. There was no seventh grade football team. In fact, I don't think there were any sports teams specifically for seventh graders at all. This made no sense as all we seventh graders did after school was get into trouble and fight. This made my life even more miserable as I was definitely hanging around with the wrong kids still during the fall of my seventh grade year.

Seventh graders were, however, allowed to try out for the eighth grade basketball team. Even though I was by far the shortest kid on the team and I had not played basketball at all in about a year, I could compete with most kids my age. Frankly, the best five basketball players in my sixth/seventh grade class in Roland could play evenly with the best five players in seventh grade at West Junior, even though West Junior was more than ten times bigger. So fortunately for me, I made the eighth grade team in the seventh grade and got off the streets.

In eighth grade, I tried out for the West Junior High football team. I was a fifth string quarterback until the coach, Bill Lane, saw something in me (that no one else saw) and, thank God, gave me a shot at playing first string. From that moment on I played first string quarterback pretty much through junior high and high school. I am forever indebted to him for giving me that chance. I had limited speed and arm strength, so I was an average quarterback. My best football skill was my quickness. I noticed recently, looking in my scrapbook from a statistic compiled by someone about the football team, that I had an average of seven yards per carry my senior year. Not bad.

During this period, I was also proud to be named to an all-city baseball team at second base.

> *One of the ironies here is that one year later Dan Gable made the all-city team at second base too. Not many people would think of Gable as an "all around" athlete because he was so focused on wrestling; but he was really good in many sports, including swimming, before he decided to focus completely on wrestling. Dan loved baseball, and I think he wanted to be another Mickey Mantle when he was in grade school and junior high. With his focus, maybe he would have been.*

Now in eighth grade, I began to feel that I finally fit in and was finally loving school, sports, and my social life. At this time, I still did not know what wrestling was—except for the fake professional stuff we watched on television.

But Larry, my oldest brother, who was attending the State College of Iowa, later University of Northern Iowa, in nearby Cedar Falls came home one day and showed me some wrestling moves. I liked it but was in no way hooked. That was just my introduction, on the floor of our home. I remember it as if it were yesterday.

In our physical education class at West Junior High everyone had to try all sports. When we tried wrestling, Jim Harmon, who happened to be Coach Siddens' first national champion, winning the NCAA title for Iowa State Teachers College in 1953, also happened to be student teaching and encouraged me to try wrestling as I think he saw something in me that I didn't know about. I do remember that I won my matches in my physical education class relatively easily.

I had always liked to wrestle, just goofing around. And my brother would beat me up a lot, so I think I was pretty tough considering I had no idea what wrestling was or any of the moves or technique. Mr. Blue, the physical education teacher at West Junior High, was also greatly encouraging. Both Harman and Blue knew that I was presently playing first team on the eighth grade basketball team, but that didn't stop them from pushing me toward wrestling.

In a basketball scrimmage game soon after that, I was engaged in a violent scrum (like a pig pile) over the ball on the gym floor, and I ended up fighting aggressively, maybe violently, for the ball with an opposing player. He was lying on his back, and I was on top, and we both had a hold of the ball. I eventually yanked the ball away from him and scored.

My coach suggested that I might be a little too rough (and ungentlemanly) for the game of basketball and that my aggressive disposition might be better directed to wrestling. I had to agree. I don't remember touching a basketball after that.

My dad told me to stick out the year with the basketball team—never quit. But it was too late for that. I began wrestling and made the junior high team for the last meet of the year. I got beat.

West High School

Our junior high school was seventh through ninth grade with high school being tenth through twelfth grade. The high school probably had an enrollment approaching 2,000 students.

Prior to wrestling season every year, Coach Robert Siddens would open the wrestling room at the high school to anyone, including junior high kids. So some of us ninth graders shuttled a couple of miles up to West High after class to see what it was like to wrestle at the high school level.

I will never forget the moment when I knew I became addicted (in a good way) to wrestling. I think it must be the way a crack addict feels when he gets hooked. I had just finished a workout at West High, and I went down to my father's dairy afterward. As I stood there in the dairy, I realized I was hooked. I really loved wrestling. I will never forget that feeling or that moment in time.

That year, only two of us were chosen from junior high to wrestle on West High's team, as those two weights (95 and 112) were particularly weak for West. West had a state champion, Paul Miller, at 103, and I couldn't beat him even though I was a 112 pounder. The first meet, I tried out and won and was to wrestle varsity. I was to compete against a state champion from Cresco, Don Henry, at 112 pounds. I couldn't wait to wrestle him. I actually thought—no, <u>I knew</u>—I could beat him. I was obviously delusional. At the last minute Coach Siddens mercifully inserted an older senior, Dick Bear (whom I had beaten relatively easily at tryouts) in my place. Henry pinned Bear in the first period. I was inconsolable as I was sure I would have beaten Henry.

The rest of the year I wrestled a few matches—and did not do well as, frankly, I was just not very good, especially compared to high school competition. I won only one varsity match that year. But at least that qualified me for a letter.

I just didn't understand how to "play the game" mainly because I was so inexperienced and very aggressive-dumb. "Aggressive-dumb" is an expression that characterizes a wrestler who goes after his opponent without any thought of protecting himself from getting taken down.

> *Some would say that I wrestled that way even eight years later when I was a senior in college. I disagree. For the most part, I think I wrestled aggressive-smart in college. At least by then, I knew all the dangers and consequences of aggressive wrestling and was pretty good at responding to any opponents' counters. The best person to drill with on my aggressiveness was Don Behm, as he would take advantage of every mistake I made. Better to get taken down in practice than in a meet or tournament.*

My sophomore year at West I started out where I left off the year before. I played quarterback on the sophomore football team, and we went undefeated. Coach Siddens was our backfield football coach, which made our season even better and a lot more fun for me.

However, I still had little idea what I was doing on the wrestling mat. For some reason that was intuitive; I was way overly aggressive on my feet which just left me open for my opponents' counters. In a meet against Osage I wrestled a senior. I think his name was Gary Pollard (but I could be wrong). He beat me something like 14-2. (Whatever the score was, it was very bad for me.)

When I went to school the following Monday, the assistant football and track coach, Dick Dotson, rushed up to me feigning concern. He said that he read the score in the paper and thought maybe I had lost my arms or legs or something, obviously wondering how anybody could get beat that badly if he had two normally operating arms and legs. I was not amused.

In fact, my feelings were hurt as I really liked that coach, and I was already feeling a lot of pain from getting slaughtered. It was obvious at that point that I wasn't any good on my feet, in the riding position or in the down position. I just was no good.

I'm sure Dotson was so tough on me thinking it would help me do better on the mat. Maybe it did. But I've never thought it was a good idea to use humiliation as a way to motivate. Many coaches back in the '60s thought it was. I always disliked coaches who humiliated their athletes.

> *I really appreciated the fact that our wrestling coach, Siddens, never used humiliation to motivate. The worst he ever said about me in front of the team was after a meet against Cedar Rapids Jefferson my junior year. Our team got slaughtered, and I got beat. While talking to everyone in the wrestling room, Coach said that he thought there was one wrestler on the team who would never get beat again in high school. I knew he was talking about me. I was captain of the team as a junior, and I got beat. I was mortified. At that moment I made up my mind never to lose again. As a small consolation, the wrestler who beat me, Alan Sieverson, won the state championship that year, and I won the state championship at the weight below him. I had actually gone up a weight to wrestle him in the dual meet, so in the final analysis I didn't feel too bad losing that match. But when Coach Siddens mentioned me by implication, I was embarrassed and, more importantly, motivated to never let it happen again.*

During my sophomore year, Dick Dotson wasn't the only one making sarcastic unkind comments to me about my wrestling abilities. West Waterloo High School at the time did not tolerate losers. (Unfortunately, they do now.)

About mid-season, the captain of the wrestling team (he was also captain of the football team) and the athlete voted "most valuable" in our high school, was psychologically preparing me for the big meet of the year against East Waterloo, our cross town rivals. In the Waterloo Courier prior to that big meet, the newspaper always put the pictures of all the wrestlers on the front page of the sports section. Our wrestling captain told me that maybe my opponent might be afraid of me if he (was dyslexic and) read my record backwards. He thought that was a clever comment. I thought it was cruel, but relatively typical of the comments directed at me.

Kids can be cruel and brutal. This was a particularly tough comment that I never forgot especially since I really looked up to that guy. I had to pull myself up by my bootstraps and perform. It was a "Just Do It" Nike moment in my life.

My name and picture were in the paper—and my record. I was the only wrestler on either team with a losing record. It was extremely embarrassing. I was to wrestle Obie Saddler from East High, who would go on to take second at the state tournament at 112 pounds that year.

Let me reiterate. For anyone reading this who doesn't know wrestling, it is obvious to even the dumbest wrestler that the more aggressive one is, the more one leaves himself open for "counters" and getting scored on. Some wrestlers, in fact, practice nothing but counters. (So try watching two counter wrestlers. It's like watching paint dry. Is it any wonder some people think wrestling is boring?)

Anyway, I was the opposite. My instincts told me to be aggressive, and my aggressiveness was killing me. As I said, I was just plain "aggressive-dumb." But I could not change who I was and the way I wrestled. It was clear to everyone, including me, that my super aggressive style was the main reason that I was getting beat and getting beat badly. Coach Siddens knew it too, but he was not going to tell me to stop being aggressive, as that was just not me—or him.

Maybe if I had been smart(er), I would have slowed down and not tried to shoot takedowns every five seconds or so. But that was not my style. And I never would have achieved the heights of wrestling I did if I would have slowed down and tried to slow down my opponent.

I really wanted to make my style work at the high school level, even though I didn't have anybody who did what I did so that I could model myself after them. Nobody else was that dumb. And nobody was really encouraging me as I don't think anyone had seen that before.

However, on that night of the East-West meet in front of a packed house, I somehow beat Obie Saddler! That was my turnaround match in high school. And maybe it was because the captain of the wrestling team made fun of me, got me mad, and forced me to prove myself.

From that moment on, I wrestled one way—straight ahead and super-aggressive. And I won most of the rest of my matches my sophomore and junior years and all my matches my senior year—all because my style was way too intense for most of my opponents to deal with.

The only person during my period of defeat who didn't question the stupidity of my aggressive nature was Coach Siddens. He always stood by me and never moved someone else in at my weight who might have done better. He knew, I think, that once I became "aggressive- smart," I would become a champion.

By my junior year, I began to feel that most of my opponents were afraid of me because they knew that I was coming after them every second of the match. I'm sure that was a scary feeling (as anyone who wrestled Dan Gable knows). If an opponent happened to take me down, I would be back out and after them within seconds. There was no place to hide.

Frankly, my best skill became my ability to escape or reverse from bottom. My philosophy and intuition in wrestling has always been that the only way a wrestler can take chances on his feet is if he knows he can escape or reverse any opponent right away. This fact eliminated any fear of being taken down and therefore made me even more aggressive on my feet. So I worked the hardest on escapes and reversals. I prided myself at almost never being ridden for more than a few seconds.

> *If I had ever been a high school head coach, I would have created as the foundation of every wrestler's skill the ability to always be able to escape or reverse in about 10 seconds. I believe that a bottom wrestler should virtually always move first and continue moving until he has escaped or reversed. No excuses.*
>
> *So if you are young, learn moves on bottom that will get you out on anyone you wrestle. And always move first and keep moving until you get out.*

I believe that getting off the bottom position is totally attitude. Coach Siddens used to say that. How badly do you want it? If you want it bad enough, you will work on moves that work every time, whatever your style is. My style was constant motion on the bottom until I got out. It might be the second or third move, but I learned to always get out, even if it was the eighth move.

Further, it is extremely exhausting to be ridden for long periods of time and demoralizing for the wrestler and his team. So my advice for young wrestlers would be to learn to get out from underneath—and get out fast. That will help every aspect of your wrestling the most, by far.

I draw support for my philosophy on this from no lesser legend than Bill Koll, Iowa State Teachers College, a man like Uetake who never lost a college match. According to Jay Hammond, Koll's "top lesson was that getting ridden was a cardinal sin…"

I absolutely agree with Koll. Even if the wrestler wins, he should not be congratulated if he got ridden out, in any period. In the long run, inability to escape or reverse will kill you, especially in the big matches. Too many kids who wrestle a lot of international styles can't get out from the bottom when it comes to folk style, and it really costs them when they compete in state and national tournaments.

At the college level, I saw a match where Tom Brands, three-time national champion and University of Iowa head coach, got taken down over and over by a University of Michigan wrestler, Joey Gilbert. Over and over Brands would then escape. At one point Gilbert took Brands down, and it looked like he was pinned. Brands didn't seem to mind that the Michigan wrestler was much slicker than he. After many take downs and many escapes, Brands could feel that the Michigan wrestler was spent. Suddenly Brands began to take the Michigan wrestler down over and over. The final score was something like 23-14 with Brands winning. Ultimately, the match really wasn't that close. You can watch this match for yourself on YouTube.

Later, I saw Mark Ironside, University of Iowa, accomplish a similar result when he wore down Cary Kolat from Penn State.

Contrast that with another great wrestler who won the national tournaments every year from when he was 6 or 7 years old until he was

16 or 17. And he pinned almost all of his opponents. His father asked me for advice. I told him that in the long run, his son was not going to win the NCAAs if he didn't learn how to get out on the bottom. The kid's problem was that because he pinned almost everybody in the first period, he never thought the bottom position was important. He never even got to NCAA finals, let alone win them. Lots of people may have their reason why he never won an NCAA championship. I say the biggest reason was that he never learned how to escape or reverse (and he loved counter-wrestling).

In 1963, my junior year, I won the state championship at 120 pounds. I was the only West High wrestler to win a state championship that year, and the team finished fifth.

> *One thing that really helped me to win my junior year was keeping a journal all during wrestling season. I still have that journal. I think I could write a book just based on my memories and notes from that. I think Gable kept journals too during the wrestling seasons. I'm not sure what he would say about the practice of writing in a journal every day, but I think for me, the journal was crucial for my success my junior year. I think for most wrestlers, it is a very good idea. Start it today; you won't regret it. Maybe just start by writing down your goals for the year or the month. Then keep track in your journal of how you are doing to accomplish those goals. It only takes a few minutes every night to keep up.*

The next year, my senior year, Gable came on the team as a sophomore.

Chapter 6
Gable and Me

❧

> *"After wrestling, everything in life is easy."*
> *Dan Gable*

What wrestling fan or wrestler doesn't know and admire Dan Gable? This chapter is more about me and my relationship to Dan and his family than about Dan. Most people have read about Dan and know about him.

You don't have to be a wrestling fan in Iowa to share the respect for Gable. When Sports Illustrated wrote an article on the greatest athletes in the history of Iowa sports, Dan finished first.

Wrestling people often ask me about Dan as we wrestled on the same high school team in 1964, and we both won a state championship in 1964 and a national championship in 1968. I am often asked what made Gable so great. Frankly, nobody knows. I don't think he does, really.

My guess? I think Gable's best quality by far is and was his ability to "will" himself to greatness and a unique ability to borrow from others approaches that worked for his particular special skill set. His will created in him his hard work ethic. He constantly thought about wrestling, leaving absolutely nothing to chance (I think he still does that). But he also had one of the best sixth senses at "borrowing" the best from other wrestlers and adapting the characteristic to his particular style. When he became a coach, Dan borrowed the best from other coaches and, again, adapted whatever the characteristic was to his approach to coaching.

> "I'm a big believer in starting with high standards and raising them. We make progress only when we push ourselves to the highest level. If we don't progress, we backslide into bad habits, laziness and poor attitude."
> -Dan Gable

When I asked Dan to tell me what he thought made him great, he said it was from the beginning a "body type and brain—mentally." He also said he loved to practice, "The extra practices became just normal for me.... I loved to practice." He also thought it was his level of success with every victory making him want to take on "higher and higher goals."

Finally, he mentions the timing of losses, "The losses were so far apart that they were almost good for me." He got pinned in junior high, but he never lost in high school. He was undefeated as a freshman and as a sophomore in college and won the NCAA championship as a sophomore in 1968. Then he got beat up when he tried out for the Olympics in 1968, getting pinned by a former West High wrestler, Tom Huff, and beaten badly by Bobby Douglas. Somewhere during that period, even Rick Sanders gave him a double arm bar/chicken wing lesson. So Dan knew then he had a long way to go to wrestle internationally.

He obviously grew after his match with Larry Owings in 1970; and by 1972, there are rumors that nobody could beat him. He said from the start that he was a "lifer in the sport from the beginning." I know Dan has always thought that he outworked his opponents. He probably did that too.

One thing about Dan that I like to think I shared was that he had such a big tank, great endurance, in that he never seemed to get tired. That's an incredible advantage in any match. Because he never got tired he pushed opponents to their breaking point the same way I did. Beyond that, who knows? I think a lot of wrestlers would like to hear about some magic potion or idea that the wrestler could steal and be great like Gable.

Beyond his ability to will himself to be great and his amazing energy, Dan has said that he would constantly try to think what his next opponent was doing to prepare. That used to give him incentive to push harder to outwork and outthink him.

I had a similar way of thinking. When I would run, I would always squeeze grips. As I ran, I would think about how my next opponent was going to pay for every drop of sweat that poured off of me. Usually, I would actually imagine myself in the match wrestling as I ran. That sure made the time go faster and make the run easier during the adrenalin rush.

Dan went on to coach at the University of Iowa where he might well have established himself as a better coach than a competitor. In surveys and polls, he usually is ranked in the top ten coaches of all time—not wrestling coaches—coaches of any sport. In a recent survey he was ranked just above Coach Krzyzewski (Coach K), a coaching legend at Duke, and just below legendary coaches like Knute Rockne, Connie Mack, and George Halas.

How did he reach these heights in both wrestling and coaching? When I knew Dan he was just a sophomore in high school who wrestled in a group right beside mine in the West High wrestling room. He wrestled in a weight class five weights lighter than mine. Who in that wrestling room would have dreamed that he would become a wrestling legend?

Me Wrestling Dan

As an aside, Dan also has an incredible memory when it comes to the sport of wrestling. Plus, Dan apparently kept an exhaustive journal from which he could reference almost any information related to wrestling, however trivial.

Relatively recently, Dan and I were at a wrestling tournament in Waterloo. We were asked to participate in a panel discussion. Coach

Siddens and other wrestling greats, like Chuck Yagla, NCAA champion and most outstanding wrestler, were on the panel.

I was asked by someone in the audience if Dan and I ever worked out. My response was no. When we were in high school, I was a 127 pounder as a senior and Dan was a 95-pound sophomore. I just had no recollection of ever working out with Dan as I outweighed him by about 30 pounds in high school.

Dan interjected. His memory was a lot better. He was sitting next to me, and he corrected me. He said that we had worked out. He then smiled knowingly, giving me the impression that he had bested me in the workout. (Got to love that competitive spirit!)

Dan is a great guy, in my opinion, and he does not lie. So I took his word for it. Later he told me that he thought we had worked out in his basement when our weights were similar later in college. I don't remember that, but my memory is terrible.

Frankly, I have had a lot of people over the years tell me they beat me in practice. I never have any recollection of it. It doesn't surprise me. I was not a very good "practice" wrestler. So it wouldn't surprise me at all that I was bested, especially by Dan, a guy who wrestled the same during practice as he did in his matches.

I do want to mention a couple of things about context and my working out with Gable.

John Irving, a famous author who has written many classic books, including *The World According to Garp* and *Cider House Rules,* who won an academy award for best adapted movie, and who has been inducted into the National Wrestling Hall of Fame, once wrote, "When Dan Gable lays his hands on you, *you* are in touch with grace." (This was the last sentence in an article about Gable in the April 1973 issue of *Esquire* magazine.)

By that measure and assuming that what Irving said is true, I am probably the only person in the world who worked out with Gable—and doesn't remember it—but Gable does!

One other thing that Gable once said which I found particularly flattering was during a meeting with Mike Chapman, Gable, and me. Chapman asked Gable if he was ever afraid when he went out to wrestle anyone. Gable said he was afraid of me when we wrestled at the Midlands. I took that as very high praise. If I thought of myself as a wrestler when I die, I would probably put that on my tombstone.

Most wrestling fans know that we (Dan and I) wrestled in the finals of the Midlands Tournament at 137 pounds. I was a senior; Dan was a sophomore. I was a returning national champion, undefeated throughout my junior and senior years. Dan had never lost in high school or college. I will describe the match later—at least the little I remember of it or was told about it. (I have heard that somebody videotaped the match, but I have never seen the video.)

Dan and Me in High School

But let me start at the beginning in my relationship to Dan. Dan was a sophomore at West High when I was a senior. I was a returning state champion. I frankly did not know Dan at all. He had his friends in his class, and I had my friends in my class. I don't remember ever talking to Dan during the season except to encourage him before his matches—as he did for me.

I "went with" a girl I really liked during my junior and senior years, so I spent most of my spare time with her. She bore my bad moods with humor and grace. And, at least ostensibly, she willingly shared me with wrestling. Even at the time, I felt sorry for what I put her through during my obsession with wrestling.

I didn't fraternize with guys on the wrestling team too much or anybody else for that matter. I think I was sort of a "lone wolf" when it came to small talk or seeking out friends. It really wasn't me. But I was voted president of the student body and varsity club at West High. Since no one ran for office at West High, we were more or less shanghaied into it. I guess most students thought relatively well of me, at least within a social sense.

Dan was kind of shy as I remember him and didn't have a girlfriend to my knowledge. I believe he had friends in his class who wrestled. I did not know who Dan was in any personal way until he started wrestling and winning and winning and winning as a sophomore.

When we started wrestling season, Coach Siddens apparently told Dan that if he could make the 95-pound weight class, Dan could wrestle varsity and not have to try out. I'm pretty sure 95 was a hard cut for Dan as he probably weighed at least 115 or 120 pounds off season.

All weight classes worked out in certain spaces on the mat in the wrestling room. Dan worked out with kids his weight (95-112) in an area next to those of my weight (120-133). I think I would have been a bit surprised if he could beat the seniors who wrestled 103 or 112 on our team. The 112 pounder, Billy Cannon, for example, was state runner-up the year before. Dan said he thought he had an edge on the 103 pounder, Kenny Kohlmeyer, so I will take him at his word. Anyway, my point is that Dan had some very good workout partners as a sophomore, guys whom I think could possibly beat him or at least go even with him at that time.

In meets his sophomore year, I was very excited to see him constantly win. Sometimes his matches were very close, but he always came through. So we began to depend on his win; he never let the team down. He always made weight—and he always won. So in every meet, we knew we were going to start off a win.

I know he has said that he worked really hard as a sophomore. But most of us were working hard, I think. It was almost impossible to make it through a Siddens' practice if you weren't in great shape.

Every morning I would run around the gym while the basketball team shot free throws before school started. Then I would usually skip library period and run for an hour mid-day. Dan and I were probably the only ones on the team who were self-motivated (obsessed) enough to work out on our own many times a day.

I remember vividly always carrying a "gripper" that I would squeeze during spare times in the wrestling room, during running and even during classes. I would climb the rope in the gym many times a day without using my legs. I got so that I could scamper up the rope very quickly. I then tied a rope to a tree branch in my back yard so that I could practice climbing the rope off season. I attributed the very strong grip I developed to climbing the rope and squeezing my gripper. I always thought that a strong grip was one of the most important factors in winning <u>as a strong grip ensured control of an opponent.</u>

Back in the '60s, we simply did not know anything about weight training. So no one I knew lifted weights or anything like that. At least I never saw anyone lifting weights. Many coaches insisted that lifting weight would make you "muscle bound" (whatever that meant). We mainly did isometric or isotonic exercises by pulling on ropes, push-ups, chin-ups, etc.

Dan Gable wrestling in high school

Preparing for matches

I believe strongly that I was the most obsessed person on the team my senior year. I'm sure Dan would argue that he was. Maybe we both were, especially in our respective senior years. I think Coach Siddens would agree with that.

During my senior year I began to build up energy against my opponents during the week that made me "crazy" to attack them when the referee first blew the whistle. This was a much more aggressive frenetic pace than I had ever set for myself my sophomore or junior years.

Within the psychological realm, I frankly couldn't explain or understand the frenzy I worked myself into. And I'm sure that my opponents thought I was nuts. Maybe I was. What I would do before my matches was to go into a sort of trance. I would almost hyperventilate, as my breathing would get way out of control. Most of the time I wasn't trying to do it. After a while, it became very natural.

Back in the mid-'60s I don't know if anybody else did this. I frankly don't know if anybody does it now—maybe it's not recommended by your local physician....

I did hear that Bill Koll, three-time NCAA champion, worked himself into a fever pitch before matches back in the '40s. In the book *From Gotch to Gable: A History of Iowa Wrestling* written by Mike Chapman in 1981, there is a similar story to mine about Koll. Koll's teammates told stories of how Koll would work himself into a fever pitch before he ever stepped onto the mat. It must have worked as he never lost a match in college and was twice voted outstanding wrestler in the NCAA Tournament. Koll characterized his style as "controlled anger."

Everybody is different when they warm up. I would say that Koll, Gable, and I represented the outer edge of frenzy. (I know some readers will wince when they read my name in the same sentence as Koll and Gable. You can relax. I'm not saying I was as good as they. I'm simply saying we had similar pre-match and match intensity.)

Someone like Tom Huff, University of Iowa, maybe the best wrestler to ever come out of West High, would represent the other end of the continuum. Tom would stretch out and reflect almost complete relaxation before his match. Maybe he didn't want to waste even an ounce of energy until he was on the mat. But when I watched him warm up, I would think he was getting ready to go to bed he was so relaxed.

> *And then there was Ray Brinzer, University of Iowa. Dan and I were talking to Ray right before one of his matches. I think Dan wanted to get Ray prepared for his match. But Ray was much more concerned about a misspelling of someone's name on the scoreboard than he was about his future opponent. When Brinzer insisted that he was going to go tell the scorekeeper about the misspelling, Dan and I just looked at each other in disbelief. Ray got beat. It didn't seem to bother him. Right after his match, he wanted to talk to me about the Roman Empire and its comparison to Greece in world history.*
>
> *It takes all kinds!*
>
> *But I think everyone would agree that Ray definitely was an outlier when it came to preparing for a match.*

Another thing I began doing was to try to view (look at) my opponent as I paced back and forth, revving up my body before matches. That really got my adrenalin going. I don't remember a match my senior year when I didn't have a very good sweat going before I ever took the mat. I almost always shot within a second or two of the referee blowing the whistle. I'm not sure many wrestlers did that back then either. I rarely see it even now.

Finally, before a match I would never think of what I would do when the referee blew the whistle—I never had an idea of what moves I would use. I simply let my nervous system/instincts take over. All I thought about was being super-aggressive and going directly at my opponent—over and over and over—until he quit or I pinned him or both.

If my opponent took me down five times in the first period, that made the score 10-5 as I could always quickly escape. And I could be pretty sure my opponent was scared and exhausted by then even though he was way ahead. The rest of the match was mine, as I always felt it was easy to make up five points if my opponent was tired and psychologically beaten. I even was down five points in the national finals my senior year, 1968, and was confident I could make up the difference. I did.

When I started to feverishly pursue my opponent, I could almost always feel him quit. Everybody has a place where they quit—some sooner, some later. But everybody quits; everybody has a breaking point. Most of the time, the biggest factor is psychological. If my opponent almost immediately knows that I am going to come after him every second, he is probably going to try to conserve his energy, and he will probably quit sooner than an opponent who says, "Let's wrestle!"

I would guess that many of my opponents in high school and college were stronger than I and/or had better technique and/or were quicker. But I never found any opponent who was nearly as aggressive as I was. Win or lose, 99% of the time, I was coming after you if you were my opponent. And most of my opponents knew that. It was an incredible psychological advantage.

I don't think I remembered what I did in the vast majority of my matches I wrestled after my junior year in high school as I went into some kind of a zone, and I didn't come out of the "zone" until the match was over.

> *The Urban Dictionary defines "the zone" as being completely unaware of what's going on around you as you are so extremely into what's going on right in front of your face.*
>
> *Basketball players like Michael Jordan and Steph Curry have been described as being in the zone when without forethought, they seemed to make baskets from anywhere on the floor. Most of the time great athletes create a zone by being relaxed, yet highly focused.*
>
> *I have been told that some wrestlers, like the Brands, can go into a zone for days or weeks. That might be a zone where they are very focused, but it wasn't a zone like mine. Again, think of Ralphie beating up the bully. Then think of Ralphie being in that crazed sense for several days. No way could anyone do that without being committed to an asylum.*

My "zone" was way further out there. It was a little bit more like Ralphie when he beat up the bully in the Christmas Story. Once I was on the mat, I almost never heard anyone. I got myself into such a fever pitch that all I was doing was totally relying on my nervous system or instincts and training to react, but everything was straight ahead. Any move I was going to do was already built into my nervous system, so there was no need to think about what I was going to do. I just let my body take over. Absolutely no thinking, so it was virtually impossible to be nervous. How can you be nervous if you're not thinking?

I think professionals in sports psychology would characterize this state as relying completely on muscle memory, instincts, or mental state mindset. I like to think of it as one's nerves reacting rather than just muscles, but I don't want to get too academic about this state of being. I just believe strongly that wrestlers wrestle better if they are in the zone than if they are not. What that zone is may be different for different wrestlers.

If I found it difficult to get into the zone, I would begin to hyperventilate with quick breaths breathing out by my mouth, without breathing in, and always focusing on my opponent and how I was going to attack him.

The reason I say this is that I think Gable took on some of those very aggressive traits to suit his style of wrestling. I don't know if he completely cut out the world when he wrestled, but I suspect he was into very heavy focus and concentration.

Dan's Comment to Me Right Before My Final Match in High School

I only remember one thing that Dan ever said to me in high school. It was after he had won his state championship match as a sophomore at 95 pounds. I was very excited for him, but the only way I was going to win my own state championship was to begin to prepare and get into my zone. So after congratulating him, I needed to begin to focus as my match was within the hour.

I started to hyperventilate and go into a frenzy. Dan came up to me to encourage me and said instead, "You're crazy!" Those were his exact words. Why that brought me out of my zone, is why I will always remember it. I almost never "heard" anyone talk to me before a match, and I don't think I ever heard anyone when I was out on the mat. I was just too focused. So I have no idea why I remember those words as if they were spoken yesterday.

Recently, I asked Dan if he remembered saying that, and he said he didn't. But there really was no reason for either of us to remember his saying that over 50 years later.

Dale Anderson wrestling in the Iowa State Wrestling Tournament

Something Coach Siddens said to me every time he shook my hand before I went out on the mat to wrestle my senior year that I will never forget was, "Wrestle like the champion you are,"—every time. He never varied. That brought me briefly out of my zone, but I really liked his comforting and motivating words. I was a champion. All I had to do was to wrestle like one. I don't remember Coach Siddens ever coaching from the corner of the mat during a meet. I think he knew that either the wrestler knew what to do based on his instincts and his practice sessions, or he didn't. And there was nothing a coach could add during the match. I don't think I ever heard one word any coach or spectator ever said while I was wrestling.

About being "crazy" before my last match my senior year in high school; Dan was right. I was crazy—crazier than ever. I went into a zone and pinned my opponent, Rich Mihal, from Cedar Rapids Jefferson in the first period. In many respects, I probably should never have even beaten him. Rich had earlier in the year beaten the wrestler a weight above me during our dual meet with Jefferson. The next year Mihal went up two weights and won the state championship. He later won the Big Ten Tournament at a much higher weight and took second at the NCAAs. He might have been a better wrestler than I—but not that night in 1964.

Coach Siddens later told me that he frankly worried about Dan and me when we went into our frenzied pre-match pacing as he thought we might wear ourselves out before we ever stepped on the mat. Sometimes I must admit that I wrestled in big matches on adrenalin alone, but that was not because of my pacing. That was especially true of my championship match in 1967. But Dan and I were in such good shape that it was almost unimaginable that we couldn't go hard an entire match no matter how much we fretted and "frenzied" on the sidelines.

The Buzzards

Along with Dan, there was a small group of elite wrestlers in Waterloo at the time. My best friend my junior and senior years was Don Buzzard, an East High School student. He was the best athlete in Waterloo in 1964. I recall that he was all-state in football, wrestling, and baseball. Besides our athletic wrestling compatibility, we did not drink or smoke, which also made us somewhat unique among Waterloo athletes or maybe Waterloo high school students in general. Although there was a rivalry of extreme proportions between East and West High, I always rooted for Buzz—except when he wrestled us. It did not matter as he always won.

Dan has often mentioned publicly that Bob Buzzard, Don's older brother, was a big influence on him. Bob, who wrestled at Iowa State and was ranked first in the country at 137 pounds, was at least four or five years older than Dan; so it should come as no surprise that Bob could beat Dan up pretty good at the time. However, Dan did not like the idea of being beaten up by anyone, even in practice and even if Bob was much bigger. So Dan took his beatings from Bob very personally—and very hard.

Don's and Bob's father, Don Senior, was sort of the "godfather" of wrestling fans in Waterloo. He owned a grocery store in town where wrestling fans would gather and tell stories about wrestling. Don Senior was big and really rough around the edges, but he was always good and encouraging to me. Everyone called him "Old Man Buzzard"—but I didn't. I respected him and always called him Mr. Buzzard. I think he felt that I was good for his son, Don Junior—or Don and I were good for each other. We <u>were</u> good for each other.

Dan with his parents after a day of fishing

Mr. Buzzard was probably the first person in the country to buy a wrestling mat for his kids back in the early '60s. He bought it from Harold Nichols, head coach at Iowa State University, at cost. In the summers we would come home from our construction jobs and then head over to the Buzzards to work out on their mat, which we would place out on the grass next to their home. Those were really fun times. I have wonderful memories of working out there. Gable remembers going over to the Buzzard's home to watch us wrestle, but he said he doesn't ever remember participating. He said he thought of us as committed wrestlers.

I thought of it as fun. Dan's father, Mack, ultimately bought that mat and put it in Gable's basement. Dan still has it.

I don't remember Dan ever hanging out at Buzz's supermarket, but Mack Gable, Dan's father, was a regular there. He would sometimes be a little tipsy. He loved to hang out and hear wrestling stories. And he was always asking advice especially from Don Senior and sometimes even me. I'm sure Dan got his inquisitive nature from Mack, who was always asking questions about wrestling and everything else. He was always extremely deferential to everyone there at the store, never wanting to argue or debate. I thought of him as a really nice guy. I think Mack was always looking for an edge for Dan. (That got to be a trait of Dan's too, looking for an edge and always finding one.)

Mack was also a welcomed regular in the West High wrestling room when we would practice. I really liked the fact that wrestling meant so much to Mack that he would come in almost every day just to watch Dan and the rest of us work out. No other parent did that, although many parents would come and go during practice. I'm pretty sure it meant a lot to Dan. I was even more impressed by Mack because the wrestling room was virtually always very hot and uncomfortable for the average spectator in the room.

Diane

That brings me to an important story about Dan and his sister, Diane. At the end of the 1964 school year, an event occurred that forever changed the lives of many of us within the Waterloo wrestling community. This story has been told many times, but I will tell it from my perspective.

Diane Gable was brutally murdered. The Gables lived in a middle class peaceful neighborhood. I doubt there had ever been a murder or even a robbery or burglary there previously.

Diane was very cute, personable, and a couple years older than I was. Diane loved wrestlers and loved to be around them. And she loved Dan and was his biggest fan.

Tom Kyle was the murderer and virtually everyone in West High knew him and of him. He was the adopted son of the president of a bank in town. He was a bad seed. To put it bluntly, Kyle was loony, very dangerous and unpredictable. Virtually everybody knew that long before 1964. His parents seemed to have no control over him at all.

Possibly his worst character trait was that he was a bully, probably the biggest bully at West, although West harbored more than its share. Most kids probably did their best to stay clear of Tom Kyle.

For example, he had a ring he often wore on his finger with sharp prongs sticking out that would gouge deep in someone's face when he slugged them, possibly scarring them for life. He loved to let everyone know about his ring to intimidate and bully them.

Kyle was also big, so he presented an imposing kind of scary matchup if he decided to bully you. But again, he was just a bully, whom if one stood up to or fought, would back down.

Tom Kyle after his arrest

Earlier in my life, he might have bullied me. But not after I learned how to wrestle (and fight). I even got in fights with him. One time I knocked him over a table in the lunch room.

I didn't have any difficulty handling him as he did not know wrestling, so it was easy to control and subdue him. After a while, Kyle knew to stay clear of wrestlers and others who knew how to wrestle and fight, preferring to pick on the weak and helpless.

As I mentioned above, Diane loved wrestlers and loved to party. Apparently while the Gables were out of town fishing at the Mississippi River, Kyle, uninvited, came to a party at the Gables' home or broke into their home after the party and committed the terrible crime. I'm not sure of the details. I don't think anybody is. I don't think they matter. We do know Kyle lived close to the Gables' home.

When I found out about the murder, I was for some reason most empathetic toward Mack. He seemed very fragile. After the murder, he would go to Buzz's Grocery to seek sympathy. He was a wreck—drinking more and crying more. He would go to the store to unload. His psychological and physical pain was palpable, and it hurt anyone around him. Since I spent a lot of time at Buzz's market, I would listen to him and try to comfort him, but there was no comfort for him.

Meanwhile, he was getting terrible phone calls from weirdos saying terrible things to him about Diane. He would tell us word for word what they would say before he could hang up. Back in the '60s, of course, there was no caller ID. When the phone rang, you didn't know who was calling. So you always answered the phone. Unfortunately for Mack, some really sick people had gotten his phone number and were constantly calling him to drive him even closer to the mental institution or worse. All of that just caused Mack more and more psychological pain. He tried to salve it with drink, but as everyone knows, that was a mistake in judgment. The drinking simply made him more depressed and maudlin. It was a tortuous vicious circular downward trip for him. I was really concerned that he might commit suicide. He just saw no reason to live.

This period during the end of my senior year should have been a time of celebration. But how could I celebrate? The year started with President John Kennedy getting murdered. The year ended with Diane getting murdered. Mack asked me if I would be a pallbearer for Diane. Even though I was not close friends with Diane, I told him that of course I would and that I would do anything else I could do to help. All he had to do was ask. I just didn't know what to do to help. I felt so helpless. I guess most everybody did.

I always liked Mack, and I think he liked me. I hope so. I didn't know Dan's mother, Katie, at all, but apparently she was going through the same process, trying to drown her sorrows. Dan, now an only child, was the only sane (and sober) person in the house. He had to take on the role of the adult, trying to pull his family together but all in the midst of alcoholism and trauma.

I am at great pains to remember and recite this, but I don't recall ever trying to comfort Dan during this period. I don't think I even talked to him. I assumed his friends were there to get him through this. And our wrestling coach, Bob Siddens, was the guidance counselor at West High, so I know that he did all he could to help Dan. But I should have been there for him too. My only real connection with Dan was that we were two state champions on the West High wrestling team of 1964. I was the (supposed) leader of the team, and I should have been there for him. I regret that I wasn't.

I give Dan himself a lot of credit, actually all the credit, about this. He was only a sophomore in high school, and he was now trying to "take care of" his mother and father and still remain sane himself. I could never have done that. I think somehow he "willed" his way out of this terrible situation. How he did it, I can never imagine. But whatever he did, I really give him a lot of credit.

I don't want to "talk out of school" here. Most of the painful facts have already been written about many times. I am simply discussing them from my perspective, remembering some of it as if it were yesterday.

> *If there is a lesson here, I think it is that when you know someone is really hurting, you need to let them know you are with them and for them. Maybe they need to talk—or maybe you can just listen or do something with them to take their mind off their problem(s) even if only so briefly. One day you will regret doing nothing. I know I do.*
>
> *Another lesson is that drinking does not help you solve a problem. It usually makes the problem worse.*

At the funeral there were all kinds of media, including a lot of crude sensationalists. There were also crazies there, some of whom were saying very cruel things.

Two things I remember most about all of this afterward: One was that Mack wrote me the nicest thank you letter for acting as pallbearer. He said Diane would have been proud to have had me carry her to her resting place. I was amazed that in his pain he could even think to write a thank you note to me. I appreciated it and have always thought kindly of his class at that moment of great pain.

The second was that I had very bad dreams about the murder afterward. Sometimes I'm not sure they were dreams.

Wrestling Dan

When I came back to Waterloo for Christmas break my senior year in college four years later, I was told that Dan was wrestling 137 and that we would probably meet in the Midlands tournament at some point. I was happy about that and thought it would be a great match. I always looked forward to wrestling really good opponents.

I had some great workouts at West High over the Christmas break—some, I think, were too good. I developed a severe electrolyte disorder, probably from sweating too much without replacing electrolytes. Sometimes during the break we would lose 8, 9, even 10 pounds at a practice. I don't think I had ever lost that much weight before.

Back then most of us had no idea what electrolytes were, and most of us had no idea what we should or shouldn't eat or drink. I never had had a problem with this before. It was clear that I did not properly replace those electrolytes lost.

During the Midlands tournament, I felt unusually weak. In the semis, I was getting badly mauled by Bob Campbell from Indiana, a wrestler I had pinned in the Big Ten finals the year before. I mean really beaten up; I simply had no energy. I felt totally fatigued and drained. I felt in many ways like my mononucleosis had returned to haunt me. Even though I was getting beaten badly by Campbell, I was trying my best. As we began the third period, Campbell sat out and pulled a hamstring. He had to forfeit.

Some people on our team wisely diagnosed at least one of the problems and said I had to drink some certain liquids to replace the electrolytes. I think I drank something like Gatorade. Actually, after I did that, I felt much better, but I was still a little anxious about wrestling someone like Dan whom I knew would push me to the limit. Psychologically, I was still a little shaky, but I was so glad to have replaced the electrolytes.

Later, I tried to figure out what caused my exhaustion when I was in such good shape? Ultimately, I have to attribute it to an electrolyte deficiency. So for the first and only time in my life, I decided to wrestle smart instead of frenetically, as I normally would have. That means I wisely tried to conserve my energy as best I could. This would be the one match I would wrestle smart—not in the zone—if only Dan would let me.

Dan later said that the only match where he was afraid before he went out to wrestle was against me. That made some sense too given when I was a senior, Dan was a sophomore in high school, and I was four weights heavier than he.

If you were a wrestler, think back to your sophomore year in high school and try to remember someone four weights heavier and two years older than you. Could you imagine beating him? Or think the opposite. You are four weights heavier. Can you imagine losing to a wrestler two years younger and four weights lower?

One of Grady Peninger's favorite expressions about this kind of match (between Dan and me) was, "One's scared and the other's glad of it." So he was scared, and I was very glad of it. This was the only match I ever wrestled where I wanted to slow the match down, wrestle smart, and win in the final seconds.

Fear of an opponent is a terrible feeling. I think most opponents were afraid to wrestle Dan. At least for a moment in time, I knew how they felt. I certainly didn't know that Dan felt the same way.

So neither of us did that much during the match until the very end. Dan was ahead in the third period 2-1, so there was no reason for him to be aggressive. In a couple minutes, he could walk away a Midlands champion, having again beaten a national champion in the finals. The previous year, as a freshman, he had beaten Oklahoma State NCAA champion Masaaki Hatta 8-3.

> *Gable became famous as a pinning phenom. But an area Dan never was given much credit for, in my opinion, was his skill on bottom. For example, twice during our match in the Midlands finals, I had Dan in cradles, but it was like trying to cradle a worm or a snake. I never had experienced that from anyone as once I got my hands locked the next thing that always happened was that the referee slapped the mat. I heard that Dan's teammates at Iowa State affectionately called him "weasel" for his ability to always weasel out on bottom. Had I known that, I*

> *doubt I would have tried to cradle him and would probably have just tried to ride him as long as I could.*

At the very end of the match with about 15-30 seconds left, I picked up the pace and (allegedly) took Dan down with time running out. Instead, the ref gave me one point for Dan's fleeing the mat just as the regulation match ended. I don't remember it well at all, but I think when I got in on him with a single, he turned and dove off the mat, both of us going off. Many people watching thought I should have been given the takedown. Some have even told Dan that.

Had I gotten the takedown call, I would have won the match in regulation 3-2. However, I have always felt that if you have to win because of a referee's call, then you have to be ready to accept the ref's call when you lose.

Anyway, since I only got one point for Dan's fleeing the mat, we tied in regulation. That was probably the worst thing that could have happened, as in 1967 the overtime portion of the match was three minutes (one, one, one)—way too long for me in my (psychological) condition.

Before going into the overtime, Mack told Dan that I was getting tired. He was right. And again, I couldn't figure out why. I had trained so hard. I should have been stronger than Dan for the overtime, as I had what I thought were fantastic recovery skills, and Dan knew that. Of course, I knew that Dan had great recovery skills too.

Based on Mack's advice, Dan decided to be the aggressor in the overtime. He shot, and I tripped him back and put him on his back with a counter. Dan got off his back, and I was given two points. (If the match were held now, that would have been the end of the match.)

I do remember vaguely having him in a cradle at that time, but he quickly squirmed out of it. I had Dan in an inside cradle during the regulation and outside cradle (from the other side) during the overtime. Those are about the only things I remember about the match and probably the only things I could have told anybody about the match even right after it was over.

The match went on another two and half minutes. I think the match was as good as over as Dan had a lot more stamina then than I did. And Dan won in overtime 6-2.

> *Dale Carr, who resides in California, said recently that he was talking to a former Illinois coach who watched the match and thought it was the best match he had ever seen. I frankly thought that neither Dan nor I wrestled our best, but that we would both wrestle our best in the NCAA finals later that year.*

Getting beat at the Midlands definitely re-motivated me to win another championship in '68 and to do it by beating Gable. So I started training very hard every day with one goal—to beat Gable. I doubt very much that I would have won the national tournament my senior year if I had won the Midlands as Dan was my main motivation for winning the NCAAs in '68. Every moment after the Midlands, I prepared for the NCAAs that year, thinking only of beating Gable with total focus.

Shortly before the NCAA tournament in 1968, Coach Siddens, our old high school wrestling coach called to tell me Dan was going down to 130 pounds. I immediately told Coach I was going down to 130 too, as my only motivation for wrestling at that point was a rematch with Dan. My saying that was pure delusion. There was absolutely no way I could have ever gotten down to 130 again.

I would bet that it was a hard cut for Dan too. I'm sure he made the cut for our old coach whom we loved so much. Bob wanted to see us both on the victory stand. I know without a doubt that Dan was not running from a rematch with me. No way.

After we both won our championship matches at the 1968 tournament, Dan and I sat together briefly. He said he was glad he didn't have to wrestle me again. I think I was too. It was better in the long run that we both took home a championship, even though we both knew it would have been a great match.

Because I did not wrestle competitively at all after college, I lost track of Dan. We did, however, cross paths again in the 1980s when Title 9 morphed into a quota and was destroying hundreds of college wrestling programs across the country. Both Dan and I tried to help wrestling programs all around the country. Dan worked hard to strengthen programs from the inside. I tried to figure out ways to destroy the quota. But we were caught in a political movement much bigger than we were and could do little to help programs that were unwilling or unable to help themselves.

I have great respect for Dan and all he has done for wrestling. No one has worked more unselfishly for the sport of wrestling than Dan Gable. Everybody knows that.

In a recent e-mail to me, he said, "You realize that wrestling was on and off the mat for me. Pretty much full time for me my whole life! You were able to do notable work in the law area. Besides Family is the other part that guides us all—and includes our Faith and Directions." That pretty much sums up Dan—the three "f's"– frankness, family, and faith. I respect that.

> *Dan went undefeated in high school and college, except the last match of his college career. Most people know that he attributes that loss for his great victories later, especially winning the 1972 Olympics.*
>
> *Not many people know that a number of the wrestlers during my era, around my weight who lost their last match in college or failed to win the NCAAs, went on to wrestle in the Olympics with great success. Besides Gable, during my era and around my weight, there were, for examples, Rick Sanders, Don Behm, Gene Davis, the Hazelwinkels, Bob Buzzard, Bobby Douglas, and Tom Huff who tried out for the Olympics in 1968 and/or 1972.*
>
> *I would suggest that most wrestlers in my era who won the NCAAs did not even try out for the Olympics. I just had no desire to. My goal was to win the NCAA and go to law school. I accomplished everything I wanted or dreamed of in 1967.*
>
> *I'm not sure if I would have been motivated to continue wrestling if I had lost my last match at the NCAA tournament in 1968. Maybe...*

Finally, Dan is a guy who is impossible not to like.

If they took a poll to determine who is the most popular Iowan, I think Dan would still win hands down over all the football coaches, all the politicians, everyone in the state of Iowa. That is how much Iowans still love Dan, a coach who has been out of the system for about 20 years now. Maybe someone already took that poll.

Anyway, with his state of popularity, during one recent short period, some people in the state of Iowa wanted Dan to run for Governor. A number of us told him that the moment you run for Governor, your popularity would go from 99% to 49%, depending upon what party you choose to run in. I'm glad he decided not to run. Even had he won, it would have been a step down for him in my mind and in the minds of most Iowans.

Maybe someday he'll retire and relax, and we can talk about the good old days.

Chapter 7
Getting Recruited
1963-1964

ം

> *"Do not hire a man who does your work for money, but him who does it for the love of it."*
>
> **Henry David Thoreau**, <u>Life Without Principle</u>

In high school I definitely wrestled for the love of the sport.

Almost all of my scrapbooks and wrestling memorabilia were lost in my many moves from place to place since the '60s and '70s. I feel somewhat bad about losing so many mementos from the 1960s. But I must admit that "things" really haven't meant that much to me. I think I am a minimalist—the fewer possessions, the better.

I do still have a few scrapbooks from my high school days that my mother and girlfriend put together, and while looking through these in anticipation of writing this book, I came across a few recruiting letters, one of which was from Myron Roderick, the Oklahoma State coach. He said he wanted me at OSU and said I "could be a three-time national champion." The letter was dated the day that Diane Gable was murdered, so either I or my mother just stuck it away in my scrapbook and forgot about it—until 50 years later.

Had I gotten the letter my sophomore or junior year, I probably would have slept with it under my pillow as Roderick, even then, was thought by many to be one of the greatest coaches of all time—until Gable hit the record books.

My experience of being recruited during my junior and senior years was probably like a lot of athletes. I reacted to it worse than most.

I had no idea what it was to be recruited or how to respond to recruiting overtures by a college coach. The coach has such a big advantage because he basically knows what the recruit wants to hear. I'm sure what every recruit wants to hear is how great he is. The recruit is young, impressionable, and has no idea what the coach is doing. Some coaches will make promises and then forget them, etc., when the recruit comes to the school in good faith on what the coach promised.

Don Behm, who wrestled 130 for Michigan State, the weight below me, said about recruiting, "I was a very naïve kid. I had no idea even what the Big Ten was or who was in it. I was REALLY uninformed...." Behm was a state champion at New Trier High School, north of Chicago, one of the most progressive, upscale high schools in the country—and yet there seemed to be no way back then for a high school athlete, even in the most modern school system, to figure out what was going on in the recruiting process. Behm was also heavily recruited by Roderick.

Dale Carr, who wrestled at the weight above me, 145, said that when he was recruited by Oklahoma from famous Granby High School in Norfolk, Virginia, he was being recruited as a 130 pounder. He said that was one of the main reasons he didn't go to Oklahoma University. At least Tommy Evans, the coach at Oklahoma, was scrupulously honest. That's what I heard.

So Behm was recruited by one Oklahoma school and Carr was recruited by the other. That is not faint praise for those two. I'm pretty sure the experiences of Behm and Carr were relatively typical of most great high school athletes in that time period who were being recruited by major universities. I'm not at all sure what athletes nowadays are told about the recruiting process. All of the rules, I've heard, have changed and become so very strict and technical.

My junior year was my first experience with the recruiting process. Apparently, Coach Siddens had told my parents during my junior year that I was likely to get a college athletic scholarship, but they did not tell me that right away. Coach Siddens was naturally reluctant to push me toward any particular school as he wasn't sure what I really wanted to do. I didn't know either at the time.

Grady and Doug Visit

The first coach to recruit me was Grady Peninger during his first year as head coach at Michigan State. He actually came to our house in 1963, my junior year. My parents loved him. Very early in the conversation, Grady told me and my parents that he was offering me a "full ride" at Michigan State—room, board, tuition, books, and fees—all paid! And it was still my junior year in high school. Wow! I kept thinking, how can this be happening to me? Did I hear that right?

Grady Peninger, MSU Wrestling Coach

Second, he told lots of down-home stories and made a lot of corny quips, mainly for the benefit of my parents. One of the quips I remember was when he looked at me and said something like, "You know, Dale, that a national championship in wrestling and ten cents will buy you a cup of coffee when you graduate. What's important is getting that college education."

My mother especially ate that kind of talk up because it made Grady appear to put priorities in the right place. My mother, like almost all mothers, didn't care that much about my winning or losing in sports. She just prayed that I wouldn't get hurt! Getting a good education was her second concern. Her third, final, and most important concern was my falling under the influence of those commie professors she had been told about in church. (Despite my mother's prayers, I did become a commie.)

Then Doug Blubaugh, 1957 NCAA Champion and 1960 Olympic champion at 160.5 pounds (and voted by FILA the best wrestler in the world) came to visit. I didn't have a clue who he was.

Doug was even better than Grady at telling down-home stories. Doug was so straight forward that my parents got committed to Michigan State before Doug even left the house. His honesty as he talked was unmistakable. Doug couldn't tell a lie if he wanted to. Since my dad lived on a farm for most of his life—and all Doug knew or cared about was farming (and wrestling)—Doug's moving into my parents' heart was like a marriage made in heaven, at least for my parents. And they couldn't have cared less if he was the greatest wrestler in the world.

Doug Blubaugh, MSU Assistant Wrestling Coach

As far as my parents were concerned, I was going to Michigan State. The discussion was over. There was no need for anyone else to come calling as they were not welcome—Dale Anderson and Michigan State were already married up. No need to get the shotgun for this wedding.

For one thing, my parents told me straight out that they didn't have any money to send me to college. So I was on my own (and therefore I had better go to Michigan State where my education would be free!). That was good enough for me—almost.

After that, especially my senior year, when coaches came to our house to recruit me, my parents would leave and go for a walk, as my folks were going to be faithful to Grady and Doug—no talking to other coaches behind Grady's and Doug's back!

But like most kids my age, I was going through my rebellious stage, wanting to break free of my parents and their telling me what to do. So their love for Grady and Doug kind of rubbed me the wrong way sometimes. Had they disliked Doug and Grady, I probably would have gravitated toward them. As a result of my rebellious turn, I had some very interesting recruiting experiences and adventures on my own.

Here is one of the more interesting and amusing:

Northwestern (and Other Brainiac Schools)

West High was one of the top academic schools in the country in 1964. Bob Bowlsby, West High graduate, former athletic director at Iowa and Stanford, and now Big 12 Commissioner, told me that during our tenure at West High we were in the top 1 percent academically in the country. That surprised me, as I had never thought about our status in the country academically. However, during this period (1963), we were given the Bellamy Award as the "best" high school in the state of Iowa (whatever that meant). So I shouldn't have been too surprised that we were pretty good. I guess it was all sort of subjective.

But I will say I found West High very difficult academically, at least for me. In many of my math and science classes, I had little idea of what was going on, but everybody else in the class seemed to reflect self-assurance that the subject matter was all quite easy. So I should have suspected that the curriculum was pretty difficult compared to most schools. But I guess I just thought I wasn't very smart. I think I was the token jock in all of my accelerated classes.

Also, I know that when I moved to Waterloo as a sixth grader, I felt I was already a year behind my classmates at Whittier Elementary School. I always thought I was just dumb as I had little idea what was going on academically. My senior year I decided to take a typing class. I did pretty well in that. I would have done better but the girl who sat in front of me turned around just as the timed test began and pulled the paper out of my typewriter. So I lost a lot of time putting the paper back in. I probably got a gentleman's "C" in the class too.

As a result of West High's general academic status, we had recruiters from some top-rated universities visit West High to recruit students who were at the top of the class academically. One such institution of higher learning that came to recruit was Northwestern University, located in Evanston, Illinois.

When the recruiter came to West High, a number of us gathered in a conference room to listen to his spiel. I noticed that everyone in the room was far superior to me academically, at least in grade point.

One of the first things the recruiter said was that if I was not in the top 10 percent of the class, there was absolutely <u>no reason</u> for me to be there in the room. He said, unless my GPA was in the top 10 percent of the class, I had <u>no chance</u> of acceptance at Northwestern. He then added that I was wasting his time and mine to be in the room. He didn't pick me out by name or look directly at me, but after this third reminder, I was sure he had heard I was going to be there and wanted me to know for sure that I was not welcome.

I froze. I felt everyone was looking at me (or was it just my imagination?). What was I doing there? Why did I think I belonged in a group with all the top students in my class? I was an interloper (and I didn't even know what that word meant)! Northwestern was a school where rich people sent their smart kids. I was definitely out of my element.

Suddenly I felt like Rudy did trying to get on the bus to go visit Notre Dame. I was a fool to think I could ever get into a school like Northwestern, filled full of brainiacs who would just look down on me—a dumb jock. Besides my embarrassment, it seemed an eternity after the speaker made the comment that he continued with his presentation. Deep in the recesses of my brain I was wondering if he was waiting for me to leave.

> *I was in "accelerated" classes at West, but for some reason, I rarely finished a homework assignment. And I didn't do that well on exams because I didn't study for them. So I received average grades. I was often called into the guidance counselors' offices and there told that I could do better. But I never did. The counselors would ask me why I thought I wasn't doing better. When I said I didn't know, they would dismiss me.*
>
> *Who knows why I never could keep up? For one thing, I never learned how to study in high school. There was no class in how to study. Maybe there should have been. For another, I spent so much time and energy participating in sports that I just didn't have the time or energy for school work. Finally, I didn't care a lot about doing well academically like a lot of the kids my age. Sometimes, and for some unknown reason, I found myself embarrassed when I was doing well in a class, as I was a jock. And, as legend had it at West, jocks don't care about school—only sports.*

> *The only class I did well in was algebra, I think in eighth grade. I was put in a class of students one year ahead of me. Our teacher stumbled on the bright idea that as soon as we got into class and sat down, we had to pass our homework forward, back, or to the side. Then that person would grade our work based on the answers the teacher gave. I never minded if the teacher graded my incomplete paper, but I was not going to hand my homework to a fellow student undone. I loved algebra, I think mainly because I always finished the assignments and therefore understood it.*
>
> *These days a teacher would probably be fired for requiring students to pass their homework to a fellow student. It would probably be a violation of privacy rights for which the student could sue the school.*

Anyway, I sat through the lecture from the recruiter and then immediately forgot about Northwestern, believing it was way out of my league. A couple weeks later, I got a call from the Northwestern coach, Ken Kraft. He talked to me a bit about Northwestern. And then he said he had a full scholarship waiting for me there at Northwestern!

To say I was shocked would be a gross understatement. I told him that a Northwestern recruiter told me that I had no business even thinking about applying for admission to Northwestern, or even being in the room where attendance at Northwestern was being discussed.

Anybody reading this could only infer that I was about the most naïve kid in America, a real hayseed from Iowa. And they would be right.

I responded incredulously to Coach Kraft's explanation. "You are telling me that, not only can I get <u>into</u> Northwestern, <u>but that my entire four years will be paid for</u>!" Talk about cognitive dissonance!

(Do you remember "It's a Wonderful Life" when Jimmy Stewart/George Bailey is talking to Lionel Barrymore/Potter and Potter is offering Bailey a job? Bailey looks around the room and asks something

Ken Kraft, Northwestern Wrestling Coach

like, "Are you talking to me?" Maybe that was DeNiro. Sorry. Anyway, that's how I felt.)

I was so naïve about recruiting. I didn't know what to think when he said he was talking to me and that this was a real offer. I really thought he must be kidding. Coach Kraft must have talked to Coach Siddens to get my academic record or how would he have known that I could get in even under the lowered standards?

Coach Kraft assured me that he was on the level and asked me to wait by the phone. About ten minutes later, the recruiter who had visited West High called. He said that when he told everybody in the room at West that I shouldn't even be in the room if I wasn't in the top 10 percent of my class, he wasn't talking to or about <u>me</u>. He was talking about "normal" high school students!

I told him and later Coach Kraft that I still thought he was talking about me (and in fact, he <u>was</u> talking about me). I decided that I was not interested in attending a school where (I thought) I would end up at the bottom of my class.

Northwestern may, or may not, have been a good school for me. I will never know. But now it doesn't matter, as I am glad I ended up a Spartan at Michigan State.

> *I will say that over the years there are few college coaches (or coaches at all) I have more respect for than Ken Kraft. His 50 years devoted to wrestling at Northwestern are impressive. And he is truly a gentleman. Of all the college coaches I have ever known, he reminds me the most of my high school coach, Mr. Siddens, a man of great class. I can give no coach a greater compliment. Anyone reading this who knows Ken Kraft and Bob Siddens knows exactly what I mean.*

Later, when even the Ivy League type schools recruited me, it was easy for me to decline as I just didn't think I fit very well in a brainiac environment.

Iowa

Had Gable been the coach at Iowa, I would have gone there in a second—and probably paid my own way. I've never seen him coach, but

I can tell by the results he produced. He is without a close second (in my mind and the minds of many) the greatest college coach of all time. The reason is simple. He took all the great motivational tools he "borrowed" from Coach Siddens and applied them at the college level. He has always been a genius at borrowing the best from others (probably including Nichols and Blubaugh) and then applying what he has learned to his own style and personality. In my way of thinking, he is more than anything the extension of Coach Siddens at the college level, the only type of coach I could have trained under without a hitch.

Unfortunately, he was not the coach at Iowa. How could he be when he was still a sophomore in high school? And there were no college coaches like Siddens for whom I could win a national championship.

Anyway, I was being recruited by a great coach at Iowa who was also way over the hill and who should have passed the baton years ago. My rationale for not going to Iowa (not even considering Iowa) was simple and probably very unfair. If Tom Huff, without question in my mind <u>at the time</u> the greatest wrestler to ever come out of West High (and a guy who later pinned Dan Gable in the 1968 Olympic trials), can't win a national championship at Iowa, how was I going to? It was a rhetorical question that nobody could answer for me. But I could easily answer it for myself. The Iowa coach was a great guy, but no longer a great coach. I think what put the final nail in that coffin for me was that nobody at Iowa seemed to care at all about wrestling. You could just about hear a pin drop during their meets as their crowd attendance was terrible.

I desperately wanted to stay in Iowa as I was an Iowan, but where could I go?

Oklahoma State

One of my most fun adventures my senior year (and my junior year) in high school was driving to the NCAA and Big 8 wrestling tournaments. The Big 8 Conference had (and has) Oklahoma State and the University of Oklahoma which had between them won almost all of the national championships since wrestling began in the early '20s.

Mr. Buzzard, Don Senior, drove Don Jr. and me. And we had a fantastic time! Attending those events was just like actually wrestling in the NCAAs for me. I could "feel" every move and loved watching the matches, all of the matches. It was a fantastic opportunity for me. To be frank, I enjoyed watching the NCAAs in high school as much or more than I did wrestling in them.

And always at these tournaments we could work out with other high school kids in the wrestling room. I loved that part too.

That year (1964) Oklahoma State, as usual, won both the Big 8 and the NCAA tournaments, with Oklahoma and Iowa State far behind. Oklahoma State was very strong that year, far, far better than any other team in the country. They were simply unbeatable.

> *One of the things that impressed me most when I attended national tournaments my junior and senior years in high school was the plaque the national champions got. They were beautiful. I really wanted one of those more than anything!*
>
> *(from left) Bill Harlow (191), Jo Uetake (130), Gene Davis (137) in 1966*
>
> *After my junior year in college, 1967, when I got the plaque, the football team players at Michigan State who won the NCAA championship that year apparently complained that they didn't get a big plaque like the wrestlers got. So the NCAA gave out a much smaller plastic encased medal to all subsequent wrestling champions. I was given one of those in 1968, but I lost it.*

> *My 1967 plaque hangs conspicuously on the wall of my den right next to where I am typing this book. I am very proud of that plaque. I guess I find it interesting that a plaque would motivate me since I really didn't care much about "things."*
>
> *What really motivates you to be good at wrestling or something, anything else?*

For some reason, Myron Roderick, the Oklahoma State Coach, decided to recruit me. Roderick was one of Oklahoma State's greatest wrestlers, a three-time NCAA Champion. He was a great athlete and could hold his own in virtually any sport. He also was one of their greatest coaches. He had a silver tongue. As they used to say, he could sell ice to an Eskimo.

Myron Roderick, Oklahoma State University Wrestling Coach

I think that Coach Siddens was probably providing a very positive reference for me to all college coaches as he was the head referee at many of the big college tournaments. He must have been my "PR" man during that time as Roderick for some reason decided that he wanted me at OSU.

After the Big 8 Tournament, Roderick called me into his office and asked me if I was interested in attending OSU. I told him I was not. He asked me why. I told him that I "didn't want to **be** an Okie. I told him that I wanted to **beat** Okies." I thought it was a clever turn of a phrase at the time (for a high school kid), especially since it came right off the top of my head. But now I think it was unnecessarily confrontational and downright disrespectful, given that Roderick was being more than civil with me. Apparently, though, that quote has gotten a lot of mileage as I've heard it quoted back to me by a lot of people.

Roderick asked me why I said that, and I told him that I hated the Oklahoma State style of wrestling—take 'em down, let 'em up, take 'em down, let 'em up, etc. I told him that I also hated the way Okies rode the edge of the mat. In other words, if someone shot a takedown on an Okie, the two would go out of bounds. But if the Okie shot, the takedown would occur in the middle of the mat. For some reason, that seemed like cheating, <u>and I told him so.</u> I told him that I like teams that wrestle in the middle of the mat—like I wanted to!

> *During my wrestling career I rarely talked to my opponent. One of the times I would talk was if he would stand on the edge of the mat. In those circumstances, I would tell him to stay in the middle of the mat and "wrestle." Another time I would address my opponent would be if he would fake an injury in order to take a breather.*
>
> *I didn't mean to act arrogant or cocky, but it was very difficult to wrestle someone who wrestles on the edge of the mat or who fakes injuries.*
>
> *Another time I would talk when I wrestled would be when I would have an opponent pinned and the referee would not slap the mat. I would tell the ref that "He's pinned." Often the ref would respond, "You do the wrestling. I'll do the reffing."*

I should have just been frank and told him that I was in awe of Okies, but that I hated them because of their dominance over Iowa. Had I said that, I probably wouldn't have gone through what he put me through later. But I just left Roderick with my disgust about their technique. Roderick got a bit angry at me, so we ended that recruiting conversation.

Later, Roderick told Coach Siddens what I had said. Coach Siddens told me about their conversation. He said that Roderick did not consider my response disrespectful, just confrontational. Siddens said that Roderick apparently liked how feisty I was.

Again, I think the reason I felt comfortable speaking my mind to Roderick was that I had already decided I was going to Michigan State, and Grady had already offered me a full ride there. So I didn't feel at all like I had to say the "right" things to him in order for him to give me a scholarship.

After the Big 8 tournaments I attended, I made up my mind that no Okie was ever going to beat me. I was a proud Iowan and was not about to ever lose to an Okie. That didn't mean I didn't respect Oklahoma State. I had to. They had won almost every national championship since college wrestling was invented in the early 1920s, almost a half century earlier.

But that didn't mean I needed to like it. And it didn't mean I had to take a "back seat" to OSU wrestlers.

> One thing Coach Siddens said constantly to us that I will never forget was to never take a "back seat" to anybody. I really liked that expression and used it as one of my many mantras through life. There is nothing wrong with losing or getting beat. There is something wrong about taking a back seat (a little inadvertent rhyme there).
>
> This could be taken a lot of different ways by a lot of different people. To me, it meant don't be passive. Be the aggressor—win or lose.

Roderick continued to try to recruit me many more times, even visiting me in Waterloo a few times. During one visit he told me that his national champion at 130 pounds was a very small 130 pounder. Roderick said he would move him down to 123 to make room for me. That very small 130 pounder was Yojiro Uetake! Cut him to 123? Yeah, sure!

For those who skipped the earlier chapters and/or who have been living on Mars rather than the United States and therefore know nothing about wrestling, Uetake, a two time Olympic Champion, might well have been the greatest wrestler in the history of our sport, certainly every wrestling pundit would agree at the level of Gable or Sanderson or Smith as he was never beaten in the NCAA competition. I wish I would have thought to ask Roderick if he had mentioned to Uetake that he was thinking of cutting him to 123. Unfortunately, that question never occurred to me. Even now, I'd love to know the answer.

Roderick said that I would have a great 137 pounder to work out with in Gene Davis, future national champion and later bronze medal winner in the Olympics. I became acquainted with Gene. Gene said that Roderick wanted him to cut to 130 also, again, to push Uetake down to 123. In my opinion, Davis was a really big 137 pounder! I thought he was kind of a big 145 pounder really. In fact, for a while Davis was ranked first in the country at 145.

> One thing I regret that I didn't do during Roderick's visits was to play table tennis with him. I heard later that he was a hustler/ringer in the game and that nobody could beat him.

> *I was a state champion in the sport and had played in exhibitions with a world champion. I'm not saying I could have beaten him. But it would have been a fun time that I missed out on as I just didn't know about his ping pong prowess (a little alliteration there).*
>
> *Since he was a "talker," he might have talked me into going to OSU while playing ping pong.*

Frankly, I had no intention of wrestling 130, and there was no way he was going to move Uetake down to 123 to make room for me anyway—not going to happen. Probably in his mind, he was thinking of moving me down to 123. Although I was somewhat flattered that he would even say that he would cut Uetake to 123, I knew it was BS. I was a very naïve kid and loved to be flattered, but even I knew Uetake was not going down to 123 to make room for me. However, anyone who knew Roderick knows how engaging he was and how he could get kids to come to OSU and get kids to produce for him.

> *I trained with Uetake in the summer of 1967 before I went to Japan with the first Athletes in Action wrestling team ever. One thing I do know and want to reiterate is that Uetake was and is one of the nicest guys I have ever known in the wrestling world—or any other world. And one other thing about Uetake—he was so nice that you never really knew for sure if he was really trying. While I'm at it, I want to mention that Davis was an equally nice guy and later became Director of Wrestling for Athletes in Action.*

If Roderick didn't need anybody at 130, why was he even recruiting me? Had Coach Siddens told him that I was going to be a national champion somewhere? Uetake was a couple years older than I, so maybe he was thinking of having me take his place upon graduation, so at least he could get a couple years out of me. Was that what he was thinking? Did he want to keep me from wrestling for ISU? I'll never know.

Finally, in fairness to Roderick, I recently corresponded with NCAA champion Gene Davis about Roderick. Gene said that he really liked Roderick during the four years he spent at OSU. So I have to think that had I gone to OSU, Myron would have treated me fairly, and I would have liked him.

Cutting Weight and Cutting Scholarships at Oklahoma State

There were two nasty bits of conduct that I was told coaches did in the '60s, and I had heard Roderick was one of the worst.

The first was to cut wrestlers down to a weight where they could hardly walk, let alone wrestle. The common wisdom of the age was that if you're really good at one weight, you will be better at the weight right below that as you will now be "bigger" than everybody else at that weight. That was a stupid philosophy that almost killed me my sophomore year in college.

The second was to cut wrestlers' scholarships if the coach was disappointed in a wrestler's performance. I told Roderick and every other coach that I would not attend any school where the coach could take away my scholarship at will. So no matter what Roderick said, I held out and continued to show no interest.

> *As I will discuss in more detail later, a lot of this recruiting went to my head—too many coaches telling me how great I was. And I believe I became a different person than I really was. I feel ashamed of my arrogant attitude now and wish that I had been more respectful of all coaches and everybody during this period. I think when you begin to be recruited by a lot of coaches, it can really change you as a person if you are not ready for it and are not properly grounded. It certainly changed me—and for the worse. At least for a short period, I was not me. I have tried to apologize to everyone whom I may have not given appropriate respect during this period. But I still have a lot of people yet to go.*

I was now in my senior year being recruited by a lot of schools, and I was becoming very confused about where I would find the best "fit" for me.

Since I didn't know the difference between Harvard and Iowa State, I really had no way of gauging how I would fit into the academic or athletic atmosphere of any school; but I was pretty sure that the Harvards of this world were not a good fit for me as I would have a zero chance of winning a national championship there.

Ever since my junior year in high school, I felt my loyalty was to Michigan State, since Grady and Doug had offered me a full scholarship when nobody else had talked to or even tried to recruit me until my senior year when I started really beating my opponents badly. But I wanted to stay in Iowa, as I was and always will be an Iowan at heart.

> *I'm not sure how most coaches handle circumstances where an athlete enrolls at a school and then gets hurt such that he can no longer compete. At Michigan State a two-time state champion, Charles Beatty, broke his neck wrestling during a practice in the Michigan State wrestling room. I gave Grady a lot of credit for the fact that he kept Beatty on scholarship during the duration of his university education. That was one scholarship Grady couldn't use to build the program, and every scholarship is crucial for that purpose. But I also think that a lot of wrestlers gave more to the program, knowing that Grady made that sacrifice. Another factor in Grady's favor was that he never made much of the sacrifice. Grady told my parents that if I was ever injured and could not wrestle, I would not lose my scholarship. And it was just more or less taken for granted that an injury that ended a career did not impact one's scholarship at Michigan State.*

Also, no one really discussed with me the difference in costs or quality of the different schools. Since all the schools were offering me full scholarships, did it make any difference that some schools (like Northwestern) were very expensive to attend and some (like SCI/UNI) were inexpensive, especially if I just lived at home? And was one school better than another academically for me? I had no idea.

State College of Iowa - Northern Iowa University

State College of Iowa (SCI) was in Cedar Falls, kind of a suburb of Waterloo. The school had some great wrestling teams as Iowa State Teachers College, one of which even won the NCAA championship back in the late '40s. My high school coach went there, and I really enjoyed going up to Cedar Falls to watch their meets. The gym was tiny by present standards, but I liked it because it seemed to always be full of spectators who made a lot of noise and loved wrestling.

Bill Koll was the coach at SCI. He was a legend at SCI, as he was the first three-time national champion who was never defeated, and he was the first wrestler ever to twice win the outstanding wrestler award.

Coach Koll would welcome us to come to his practices and even work out. I watched his techniques as he would explain moves. No one believes me when I tell them that he would explain moves to the wrestlers while smoking a cigar. Actually the cigar was usually not lit. But I found that habit rather bizarre. I can't get out of my mind one of the wrestlers hanging on to Koll's leg as Koll is kicking loose while holding a cigar and laughing. I kept thinking, "What's wrong with this picture?"

One of his wrestlers, Bill Dotson, became a national champion by beating a West High legend named Tom Huff, from Iowa, in the finals. Bill, referred to by his friends as "Beets," may well have been even more peculiar than Koll. One night after practice, Dotson began to bang his face against the door of his locker. I was standing nearby and saw this, so I am not repeating it secondhand. No one could figure out why he would do anything so seemingly insane. It wasn't like he was softly pounding his face. He was pounding it really, really hard. When he was done, his face was a mess. Another wrestler pointed out that there was a nail or a screw protruding from the door right where he was smashing his face. Had his face hit the protrusion, he would have been badly injured, maybe blinded if it would have hit his eye. It was a miracle that he wasn't badly injured anyway. This was the type of thing Dotson would do. This guy was a really nasty, tough animal—and weird! I wasn't sure I wanted Beets to be my college wrestling role model, but I loved his toughness.

So Beets and Koll were my (bizarre) introduction to college wrestling, college wrestling practices, college wrestling locker room, and college wrestlers.

Koll recruited me. Unfortunately, by this time, I had become a person I later realized that I didn't even recognize. For one thing, I told him right off that I wasn't going to any school that didn't offer me a full ride. So Koll began calling me "full-ride Anderson" to all of his coaching friends. That was probably not good for my reputation. I deserved the moniker.

This was not a time I am proud of. There were many periods of my life where my character waned. This was one of the worst. What the coaches were saying was going to my head.

As I was graduating in '64, I found out Koll was leaving for a coaching position at Penn State. His replacement was Patton. Patton was almost as nice and classy as Ken Kraft. What a great guy! Had he been the coach at Iowa, I might well have gone there.

But I just couldn't see myself going to State College of Iowa (SCI) in Cedar Falls for some reason, especially when my best friend Don Buzzard was going to Iowa State. And I still had the feeling that I really should be going to Michigan State. So SCI was a non-starter.

Iowa State

The most persistent recruiter at this point became Coach Harold Nichols (Nick) at Iowa State. Since a number of the wrestlers at Iowa State told me that Nick was like Roderick, in that they both cut scholarships and wrestlers to the bone, I was wary of him.

Concomitantly, Nick was also notoriously tight with money. I was told a story where a 130 pounder was in the car with Nick and some other wrestlers riding back from a tournament, and the wrestler told Nick that he was going to buy him a pair of pliers so he could "pinch those pennies" even harder.

Even though coaches could cut scholarships—and most of the best coaches apparently did do that, including those at ISU, OSU, and OU—I didn't like it; and I didn't think it was fair to athletes who were trying as hard as they could. As long as the athlete was trying, why should a coach be able to cut his scholarship? I think most coaches, like Roderick and Evans (the Oklahoma coaches), believed that the amount of scholarship was equivalent to the place you finished at the national tournament. They thought that wrestling was a job where a wrestler earned money based on results.

At that time, a coach renewed scholarships yearly. Some coaches reduced or cut the scholarship the next year if the wrestler did not perform up to expectations. It didn't seem right to me, especially if the wrestler was trying as hard as he could. Maybe coaches still do that. I don't know.

All of the talk about Nick and the ability of any coach to unilaterally cut scholarships made me uneasy about wrestling for him. Finally, Nick looked and acted a lot like my dad, whom I was presently rebelling against. And that, unfortunately, became a big negative to me during that time.

Harold Nichols, Iowa State University Wrestling Coach

Ultimately, Nick said he could allay my misgivings and give me comfort by typing up and signing a promise that he would not cut my scholarship. He even brought his own typewriter to my house!

I looked at the written promise he typed up, and I noted that it really didn't say what he said it would say. It only promised a scholarship for one year. It said only that he would not cut my scholarship the first year at Iowa State. I told him that I needed a promise that he would not cut my scholarship for <u>all four</u> years.

He then got really annoyed with me, sort of like Roderick did, and didactically informed me that the NCAA would not allow him to promise a scholarship for more than one year. I told him then that he had to promise in writing that he would <u>never</u> cut my scholarship in writing or we were done talking. He then typed that promise out.

I thought to myself that if I couldn't rely on a coach to not cut my scholarship just with a promise and a hand shake (like Coach Siddens), why would I want to wrestle for him for four years? For that reason alone to me, it made no sense at all to go to ISU.

I was really getting spooked and weird. I was talking and acting arrogantly and stupidly. I wanted a coach like Siddens. But there were no coaches like Siddens, at least that I could see. The closest to Siddens was Kraft, but he was at a school where I thought I could never win a national championship, and I might flunk out. I hated all the confusion and anxiety over the decision, so I decided I needed to just sign a contract and end the drama.

I signed a Big Ten contract, a letter of intent, to go to Michigan State mainly because Grady offered me a scholarship first—and my parents loved Grady and Doug. The contract was enforceable only among Big Ten schools. I knew that and so did Grady. But when I signed it, I fully intended to go to Michigan State. This is where Roderick came in again and began to encourage buyer's remorse about signing a contract with MSU.

Back to Roderick and Oklahoma State

Roderick heard that I had agreed to go to Michigan State, probably from Coach Siddens. So he visited me again and told me basically that agreeing to go to Michigan State was the biggest mistake of my life. He said that I had signed my own (wrestling) death warrant.

He said that if I were to go to a Big Ten school, I should have chosen the University of Michigan. In his silver tongued way, he persuaded me that I had chosen the wrong Big Ten school. He explained to me that Michigan State was last in the Big Ten, picking up only one point in the Big Ten tournament, and that Michigan was first in the Big Ten! Also, he explained that Michigan was much better academically than Michigan State.

Suddenly I thought, how could I make such a big mistake? Even though I already knew what he was telling me, I began to doubt my judgment (and that of my parents). For some reason, his logic got through to me and began to gain traction. Frankly, Roderick was a great recruiter. Anyone who knows him knows that. He knew exactly what to say and how to say it. I was young, foolish, and easily swayed by a fast-talking salesman.

Now I was really confused. I couldn't go to Michigan or any other Big Ten school that had recruited me as I had already signed a contract with MSU. My only logical escape was the Big 8. And so now, OSU was back in the hunt—and Roderick knew it.

It's Iowa State, by Default

It was about this time that I began again to be recruited by Iowa State, only not by Nichols. It was more subtle now. My best friend Don Buzzard was going to Iowa State. Like me, Don was a two-time state champion and virtually unscored upon his last two seasons in high school. The summer of 1964, he made the Olympic team as an alternate. We hung out together a lot during the summers of 1963 and 1964, going to dances, working out, and double dating.

We really wanted to go to college together. I know Grady wanted him at MSU and would have given him a scholarship.

Others in Waterloo began to push me toward Iowa State, even many adults with loyalties to Iowa State. I don't know if any of them had been prompted by Nick to recruit me, but the process was the same. They certainly didn't do anything wrong, but they did encourage me, even getting me a very good summer job right after my senior year.

I was loyal to Iowa; I was an Iowan (not a Spartan then), so I wanted to stay in Iowa and close to home and friends. I finally decided to take the road of least resistance. And so I went to Iowa State—a full ride and $15 a month, laundry money. That was the most any scholarship athlete at any school in any sport could be given at the time.

What more could any kid want?

> *At this juncture, I would like to write a word about bad judgment.*
>
> *One thing that I can be pretty sure of is that most kids in high school have bad or limited judgment during some period of their lives. For wrestlers, sometimes bad judgment results in getting in fights and maybe legal trouble. Sometimes it's worse. Kids drink and drive and kill or hurt someone. Or they get hooked on drugs or alcohol.*
>
> *You really don't want to go down that road. I did not do any of the above. My bad judgment was the result of not having any idea about the process of choosing the best school for me and then sticking to that decision—and becoming arrogant.*
>
> *I probably should have talked to Coach Siddens more about it or maybe prayed about it. But I always felt that I should make the decision on my own, so it never really occurred to me to get advice about this very important decision.*

> *I have made a lot of mistakes—I regret them all. But I particularly regret my bad judgment during the spring and summer of 1964, especially in not listening to good advice from people who cared about me, like my parents.*

Chapter 8
Iowa State - 1964

ଔ

> *"When Julius Caesar's army marched through the shallow Rubicon River in 49 BC, Caesar uttered the famous phrase 'alea iacta est'—'the die is cast.' It now means a point of no return."*
>
> **Crossing the Rubicon**

As soon as I decided I was not going to Michigan State, the die was cast. I was going to Iowa State.

The Fraternity

When I got to Iowa State, I immediately joined a fraternity—Tau Kappa Epsilon. There were no wrestlers in this fraternity. I was encouraged by friends to join, as the fraternity system was strong at Iowa State and the TEKE's were the best. I was told the TEKE's would be a home away from home and everyone in the fraternity would treat me like a brother.

It was a perfect fit in one way. All pledges had to sit at our desks for four hours in the evening, every weekday, every evening, and study. That was my first experience in learning how to study as I really never "studied" at night in high school. Maybe that's why I rarely finished a homework assignment. Frankly, I was surprised that I really enjoyed studying—and being forced to study. Pledges couldn't move, and we couldn't even whisper. All we could do was sit and do homework. This was an atmosphere made in heaven for me. It was the academic discipline I needed to succeed in college.

The fraternity had one other advantage over other college life. Parties were ready-made and virtually every Saturday.

The problem was that I really wasn't a party person at the time, and I still had a girlfriend back in Waterloo who was a senior in high school; so partying didn't work very well for me. Sometimes I did it anyway, but I never really enjoyed it. Since the fraternity was pandemonium on party weekends, there was really no use trying to study unless I would have had the discipline to go to the library (which I didn't).

The fraternity had one very nasty ritual, however, that was a deal breaker for me. My alleged friends who were active members tried to convince me that hazing me was good for me. The TEKE actives seemed to love hazing their pledges. I didn't know what hazing was; but after I was hazed, I knew I was not going to be a "frat rat" any more. I could not figure out how I was going to be a "brother" to people who abused me in what I considered to be the worst possible ways when I was a pledge. It wasn't the fact that I couldn't take being hazed. It was that friends don't abuse you like that. And I began disliking actives. So at that point I knew I had to get out of the fraternity. The problem then was that there was no place to go but to the dorm.

The Dorms

So I moved to the dorms. I soon realized that this was a very bad idea too. Dorms were chaotic compared to the fraternity. It seemed that I just couldn't get any homework done there. There was no peace.

Meanwhile, I was expected to work out, wrestling and training every day. I was finding myself actually disliking wrestling, and I was disliking school, and I was disliking everything else, including the coach.

This was a very depressing time in my life. In retrospect, I was acting like a spoiled brat. I had developed a very bad attitude waiting for the world to be good to me. Life didn't seem fair, and I didn't like it. I wanted to go back to high school.

Wrestling at ISU

Several times during the fall and winter terms my freshman year, I had to cut weight to wrestle, even though as a freshman I was ineligible.

Since there seemed to be little or no structure at all to the wrestling practices, it was very hard for me to lose weight or even get a good workout. It took a lot of self-discipline that I just didn't have. Since my obsession for wrestling was gone, or at least was now latent, I began to believe I was in big trouble as I couldn't imagine repeating this routine every day for four more years.

Frankly, I had no ability during this period to discipline myself to work out hard or make weight or to go to class or to study for class or to do anything that was remotely constructive. Somehow I got a B+ average fall term—I have no idea how or why. If I had to guess, I would say it was the great curriculum at West High that prepared me so well for college, and the fact that I was forced at the fraternity to (learn to) study.

I wrestled in one tournament as a freshman that Iowa State participated in, the Minnesota quadrangular. I won that tournament, beating a guy from Iowa, Bill Fuller, in the finals at 130 pounds. Making weight at 130 was torture. Fuller had finished third in the NCAAs the year before at 123, so I at least felt pretty good about that victory.

But I still had very bad feelings motivationally. I just didn't care about wrestling. I was mildly surprised that I really didn't care if I won or lost. I'm pretty sure Coach Nichols and others sensed it. Nick made me captain of the freshman team, perhaps to motivate me. It didn't. I did not look forward to going to practice (like I did in high school), and I did not look forward to competing.

Losing My Scholarship

Shortly after winning this tournament, I went to sign up for my winter term classes, but my scholarship was not registered. Since my scholarship was not registered, I could not register for classes for the winter term. I assumed the only person who could register a scholarship was Nick.

Exactly what I had feared most had occurred. This was the straw that broke the camel's back for me at Iowa State. Needless to say, this brought back memories of what I was told about Nick. I tried to reach him, but to no avail. He was incommunicado.

Most wrestlers back then said that if Nick could not be reached, he was probably out selling mats, as apparently he had a second job selling wrestling mats, which it was rumored brought in more money than his coaching job. Realizing my worst fears, I started calling coaches around the country to find out about transferring. That was a rash decision as the coaches that I contacted were apparently required by the NCAA to contact Nick and tell Nick that I was contacting them.

Since I knew nothing about transferring, I had no way of protecting myself in the process. I still don't know anything I could have done differently, except stay at Iowa State.

> *Dan (Gable) told me that when he went to Iowa State that he never had any problems at all with his scholarship being there every time he registered. So maybe I should blame this confusing situation on myself. I do know that Dan loved the practices where he could just grab someone and wrestle. That was not me, except in the off-season.*
>
> *Also, I believe Dan had written that he got very discouraged and homesick at Iowa State his freshman year and considered transferring or quitting. I could be wrong on that. Anyway, he stuck it out, and the rest is history. That decision was good for him, good for Iowa State, and good for Iowa.*

Maybe, had I been more mature, or had someone I could have talked to about this, I could have turned the situation around. I think I just always felt I had to make my own decisions without help. That was a big mistake.

So, as I was neither disciplined nor mature nor the type to seek advice, there was little chance that my future would have been good at Iowa State. Everything had fallen apart, and I couldn't put it back together. Neither could Nick.

When Nick began to get calls from coaches around the country telling him that I was calling them to transfer, Nick asked me to come into his office. I did. I told him about my scholarship not being registered, and Nick told me that it was all a big mistake and that he would fix it. I believed him (that it was a mistake).

He also said that no matter where I transferred to, I might be a big fish in a small pond, but I would never be a great wrestler on a great team, except at Iowa State. At that moment in time I had serious doubts that I wanted to be a great wrestler or be on a great team or that I wanted to wrestle at all. I frankly was miserable—about as unhappy as I had ever been since moving to Waterloo in the sixth grade, probably even worse. I just wanted to feel good again. I doubted I ever would.

Nick had numerous wrestlers and his assistant coach, Les Anderson, talk to me to try to dissuade me from transferring. By now, I'm not sure how Nick felt about me. He might have thought my best wrestling was behind me—and that I was burned out. He may have been right.

Transferring to Michigan State

By now, my mind was made up. I had crossed (back over) the Rubicon. My transfer was a fait accompli. I was gone.

I called Grady and told him that I wanted to go to Michigan State. I think I did feel that I had broken my word by not attending Michigan State in the first place, so I thought maybe this would make up for that.

> *As a result of my leaving Ames, I may have caused Iowa State to lose one, two, or three national championships. I have some regret about that, but I guess one could say that about anyone. Had Gable gone to Michigan State, he might have provided NCAA championships for the Spartans instead of the Cyclones.*
>
> *A few years later after I graduated, Nick and I did wrestling clinics together and got along fine. I assume that all was forgotten and forgiven between the two of us. It certainly was on my part.*
>
> *In retrospect, I realized that the fault was mine. High school coaches and college coaches are different. My high school coach was a surrogate father. He made me love wrestling.*

> *My college coach was my employer. He was giving me money to wrestle. When a college coach gives a "full ride" to an athlete, the coach deserves to see a great athlete give his all. The problem was that I had never been motivated by money. I had been motivated by an obsession to wrestle. And that obsession was now gone.*

So in late 1964, I was about to embark on a new adventure. Exercising even at the time what appeared to be bad judgment again, I jumped from the figurative frying pan into the fire.

Chapter 9
Michigan State - 1965

> *"Pride goes before the fall."*
>
> **Proverbs 16:18**

My parents drove me to East Lansing to begin winter quarter 1965, which started in January. It seemed like a very long ride. Fortunately at the time, Michigan State was on a system where winter term began later than at Iowa State; and therefore, even though I had enrolled at Iowa State for winter term 1964, I could still enroll at Michigan State winter term 1965.

It was also the coldest, most miserable month, weather-wise of the year. And in the winter, East Lansing can be dark and gray virtually every day—very depressing. I simply could not imagine a darker, drearier, colder, or more miserable place, except maybe Siberia. My only thought was, "What had I done to myself? What had I gotten myself into?"

I had just left Iowa State University where I was captain of the freshman team and on scholarship with a full ride—room, board, tuition, books, fees and $15 a month laundry money. And now I was broke and on my own in every way.

Registering For Classes

My first chore was to sign up for classes. I was a bit late for registration. Don Behm was apparently selected by Grady to shepherd me through this process, a maze even for an experienced student and impossibly confusing for me. Of the 40,000 plus students at Michigan State, I think I was the last one to register. The gymnasium where we signed up for classes was empty now with papers and other junk strewn around everywhere

There simply were no "academic" classes left for which I could sign up. I remember the following event distinctly as it is still seared into my memory over 50 years later. Behm was trying to be helpful, I think. Pointing to a page, he asked, "Do you want to sign up for this phys ed class?" My response, "Uh…No." "Do you want to sign up for this phys ed class?" "Uh…No." After about the tenth try, he asked, (in a slightly more exasperated way) "Do you want to go to school here?" I don't remember my answer to that question, but I know my mind was screaming, "No!!" Even 50 years later, I can still feel that bitter frightened emotion. What had I done? What am I going to do? Going back to Iowa State was out of the question.

Three things were painfully certain at that moment:

(1) I was without options.
(2) I felt alone.
(3) <u>I was totally alone</u>.

I had never been totally alone before. I had no family. I had no friends. I had no one. It was a frightening feeling. Was I just homesick or was I now in real trouble, way beyond that at Iowa State? Plus, I had a personality that would not let me reach out for help.

From Bad to Worse to Worst

When I think back on those days, I find myself empathizing with lonely people in the world who have no one and have nothing. That was me. I can easily understand why they turn to drink or drugs or worse. I was probably fortunate in that I didn't have enough money to even buy one beer.

I had to try to focus. How do I get out of this terrible fearful situation I was in? I could drop out of school again. But that option would have been even worse as even one semester behind in college meant the draft—and Vietnam.

I knew if I was going to go to school at MSU, I had to sign up for all physical education classes, then drop them all when better classes came open. That is, when other students dropped them. This meant that for the first week I had no idea what classes I was going to be taking. So before I even started attending classes at Michigan State, I was already a week or two behind the other students.

And the drop-add system at State was an incredibly complicated and difficult cumbersome process. It reminded me of the maze that mice go through in order to get a bit of cheese. You didn't do it by computer, you had to run all over campus going to the right building to drop a class and then going to another building, maybe across campus, to add a class. To make matters worse, Michigan State's campus is in the top ten in size (acreage). Walking from building to building on campus can take 30-40 minutes, depending on which way the wind is blowing and the temperature. The temperature was often below zero and, with the wind chill, 15-20 degrees below zero.

I knew I couldn't complain to anyone if my scholarship was not registered, as I had no scholarship. And contrary to what some believed, I received not one penny "under the table" from Grady or the athletic department.

I think I must have felt sort of like those guys over in Vietnam as it related to homesickness. Ironically, my first letter from home was from my draft board in Waterloo—not an encouraging moment when everything was seeming to go wrong, so wrong.

You would think that maybe I could find an enclave in the family of wrestlers. But our team wasn't like that to me. I even felt animosity there as I tried to fit in. At best, the feeling I got from the rest of the team was indifference. Maybe they thought I was a prima donna and that I deserved my fate. Maybe it was just my paranoia. I certainly wasn't a prima donna—not any more. In the final analysis, I think most wrestlers in the room were probably just trying to adjust and get by, the same way I was. But I just felt very alone, alienated. I was now a "nobody."

Jobs, Money, Studying, and Wrestling Practice

To be helpful, Grady got me three "jobs," so I could survive. Two of the jobs seemed relatively easy and benign—filling shotgun shells for Grady's shotgun shooting class and being involved in an experiment. In this experiment I was to be a guinea pig running on a treadmill with a face mask on. I liked the idea as I thought it might just help me get in better shape. I also worked at a car dealership moving cars.

During this period, I really had no money. The three jobs barely and ultimately provided only pocket change, maybe just enough to pay for my used books. My parents would not sign for any loans. Without their signature on a loan application, I remained broke. I couldn't even afford a cup of coffee and a donut.

So with no money, Rudy at Notre Dame, was wealthy compared to me. What Rudy and I had in common was St. John's Church.

Although I was not Catholic, I began to study at St. John's Catholic Church just off of campus and on the way to my room. St. John's actually became sort of a second home for me as it was set up to accommodate any college student. The basement was arranged so that students could sit at a table and study. The staff would have coffee and donuts available for students on the "honor" system. Students would take coffee and a donut and throw whatever money they could, or should, into the change bowl. I would usually take the coffee and donut(s), and then I would I would flick my finger around in the coin bowl. The coins would make a tinkling sound, and anybody nearby would (hopefully) think I was actually paying for my "treat"—but what for me was my meal. I was a pathetic fraud, but I was hungry (all the time). About all the nutrition I was getting was a donut.

What I liked best about St. John's was that everyone who studied there was quiet. It reminded me a bit of Tau Kappa Epsilon where everything was quiet and peaceful, at least during study hours.

I had no clothes to wear except a couple pairs of jeans. Every time I finished a wrestling practice, I would turn in my Spartan green wrestling t-shirt and get a fresh one from the supply cage. I would wear that all the next day to class, etc. Then I would work out in it the next day in practice and turn it in again after practice, the same for socks. That way, I rarely had to clean my clothes. I'm sure I was the butt of a few jokes in my classes when I wore the same clothes to class (when I went). (At least Michael Oher, the subject of the popular movie *Blindside* had his very own bumble bee rugby shirt! I didn't even have money for one of those. I was feeling a lot like the prodigal son, except I had no rich father to return home to.)

As I became more and more desperate in every way, my immune system began to break down. I was constantly flushed with fever and exhausted virtually all of the time, as I was not sleeping well either. My poor eating regimen and my inability to sleep was extremely enervating. And now I was feeling sick.

I had wrestled through sickness before and decided to tough it out. I tried to push myself harder, which simply made me sicker and sicker. It didn't help that I was walking around in brutally cold weather during a brutally cold winter.

Meanwhile, I was getting mauled, I mean really beaten up, in the wrestling room by everyone. I knew my wrestling partners were talking about me, and it wasn't good. Maybe I was just paranoid. I probably wasn't even good enough to be talked about. I always hated the hazing that went on in the wrestling room. It seemed so stupid. The best thing about being a nobody in the Michigan State wrestling room was that I wasn't even important enough to be hazed.

Even worse, the coaches were talking about me. I do know that. Finally, people outside the wrestling room began saying things to me that were downright cruel. I was reaching bottom. No, I had long since hit bottom. Maybe I deserved my fate.

I began to feel sort of like I have when I've driven through a blizzard during an ice storm. It was definitely time to pray, basically bargain with God—"God, if you will get me through this, I will do this and that and the other thing." (Probably one of them was to join the Peace Corps, which I never did). My prayers were pathetic, sort of like George Bailey's when he prayed in the movie *It's a Wonderful Life*. I was becoming sick in the head too. But I will say that prayer brought me peace—and at least then I didn't feel alone.

Going to Class

After a few weeks, I was able to settle in on classes I needed to take. I remember particularly an American Thought and Language (ATL) class that was mandatory for all Michigan State students. It was one of the few first-year classes that didn't register hundreds of students. There were probably 30 in the class. Most of the text and materials were liberal gobbledygook passed off as scholarly; but since I was now already a liberal, I didn't mind studying it at all.

What I minded was that the instructor appeared to be younger than I was. He was working on his master's degree and was trying desperately to stay one page ahead of the class. I quickly realized that my high school classes were much more rigorous than this class or any of my classes at Michigan State for that matter. Since this was the first class of the day, 8 a.m., I would typically pick up a school newspaper on the way and read it in class. This habit annoyed the grad student/teacher. So he got even. He gave me a D- (D minus) on my first paper I handed in. And he made a point of trying to embarrass me in front of the rest of the students in class by telling the class how bad my paper was. I don't think I was embarrassed, but I realized that this was one class where I had better not read the paper. I would save that for the second period of the day.

All of my other classes were frighteningly big—hundreds of students. A student could easily get lost in that large a group. So I tended to read the student paper or daydream. I soon learned that all large classes were graded based on the ability of the student to take multiple choice exams. I was already good at taking multiple choice exams, so that system was perfect for me.

But suddenly events would control whether I made it to class or not.

Sick and Injured

One practice while I was drilling with Behm, he executed a single leg drop and tore the cartilage in my knee. After that, when I would walk, I would feel like I was stepping off a curb as the inside portion of my knee would sort of pop out. I got used to pushing a part of my knee back in a lot, both during practice and while walking across campus. I refused to see a doctor about it. Frankly, I wouldn't even have known where to go to see a doctor, even though there was a hospital and clinic right on campus. If I would have known about the hospital, I wouldn't have known it was free for students. Nobody told me that. And it never occurred to me. I was really a country bumpkin when it came to health facilities and most other university freebies.

One night after practice, a janitor found me passed out on the floor of the locker room. I couldn't move, and I had no idea where I was or what had happened to me. When I awoke, I was delirious. I was transported to the hospital where a doctor told me that it was one of the worst cases of mononucleosis he had seen, as the disease had apparently infected my spleen and kidneys. I don't know much about mono, but apparently my spleen was in very grave danger of rupturing. Frankly, at the time I don't think I had ever heard of mono.

My understanding was that the only way that one dies from mono is if the spleen ruptures. Thank God it didn't. I remember my one feeling at the time was that of exhaustion, total exhaustion.

The doctor explained mono to me. I finally realized why I was so tired all the time. He said that I was done wrestling, at least for the season, maybe for good. I told him that wasn't possible. I had to wrestle to earn my scholarship! He also told me that I was done with school for the term. I told him, "No way" as that would mean the rice paddies of Vietnam for me.

Unfortunately, I was not going to be able to run on a treadmill anymore; so I could not earn a few bucks, and even filling shotgun shells was no longer an option. I had long ago been fired from my third job which involved moving cars for a car dealership, as I had wrecked one of the cars. So I had no job(s). And therefore I had no money.

With no ability to earn any money at all and being very sick and not on scholarship, I was now in really big trouble, even worse than before. I was reminded of that old verse in the Bible, "Pride goes before the fall," as I was the kid who told coaches that I would not even consider going to a college unless a coach offered me a no-cut full-ride scholarship. Now I had no chance of getting any kind of scholarship—ironies of ironies. Maybe a better verse for me would be, "You reap what you sow."

However I tell it or one thinks about it, this was all a most humiliating start to my college wrestling career.

Adding Insult to Injury—Grady Talks to Coach Siddens

In March of 1965 toward the end of my freshman year, Grady met with Bob Siddens, my high school coach, during the NCAA tournament in Laramie, Wyoming. When Coach Siddens asked Grady how I was doing,

Grady told him how terrible I was as a wrestler. Grady was not one to sugar coat a message.

But to add insult to injury, Grady said that I would <u>never</u> make the team at Michigan State. He said I couldn't beat anybody in the room. He informed Bob that he had a great wrestler at 130, Don Behm, who was a sophomore, and a great wrestler at 137, Dale Carr, who was a freshman.

Grady told Bob that Behm was a two-time state champion from Illinois who almost made the 1964 Olympic team (and at the 1965 NCAA tournament where the two were talking, Behm probably came the closest of anybody in America in the semifinals to beat Uetake).

Carr was a two-time state champion from Virginia and who as a freshman was ineligible to wrestle, so he was not at the national tournament. But had freshmen been eligible, Carr would be wrestling 137. Grady made Carr out to be even better than Behm.

So there was no place on the team for me to fit in. I was a very big 130 pounder and an average sized 137 pounder. Since I was a nobody on the team, I'm not sure if Grady even knew that I was probably wrestling with mono and that I was in the hospital recovering. I don't remember anybody visiting me there. I was, and still am, not one to tell anybody about my problems.

Keith Lowrance

Even worse for me, Grady said he had just recruited a wrestler allegedly better than either Behm or Carr, a virtually unbeatable kid at my weight named Keith Lowrance. Apparently, Keith was an undefeated two-time state champion from Granby who could wrestle either Behm's or Carr's weight. He had already beaten national champions while he was still in high school and was fifth at the 1964 Olympic trials as a junior in high school. Grady said that Lowrance had committed to Michigan State. Grady reiterated to Bob that I had no chance of beating Lowrance and that I had no chance of making the team, ever, at Michigan State.

Coach Siddens stuck up for me and told Grady, "You don't know Dale Anderson." Of course, I didn't hear about this conversation between Grady and Bob until a little while later, but I was hearing the same thing from others on campus. At one point I was in the student union and the director of the union, Jack Ostrander, a friend of Grady's, took a moment to tell me that he had heard that I was getting beaten up in the wrestling room and that I wasn't going to make the team.

Later, when I asked Grady about his conversation with Coach Siddens, Grady replied, "Well, at the time, I didn't think you _would_ ever make the team!" So he was simply telling the truth as harsh as that might sound. His position was very plausible, at least to him. I do understand that he was just being frank with my old high school coach as I was performing worse than terrible in the wrestling room. It was just a painful experience for me when I heard about all the stories swirling around about my inability to ever make the wrestling team at Michigan State.

> *To his credit, two years later after I won the national championship, Grady told Bob that he had to "eat his words" about my never making the team at Michigan State. So at least Grady was man enough to admit he was wrong about his prediction.*

In retrospect, I think Grady's comments to people probably helped me a lot toward winning two national championships as they did fire me up. I probably thought that I was not going to let Grady decide my fate, especially when Coach Siddens had such faith in me.

At this juncture, although tangential to the '67 story, I cannot resist a moment of levity, telling a story about the greatest meet and match in the history of Michigan State wrestling. It may be one of the greatest meets in all of college wrestling. I think it is relevant as it is another story about how Grady (inadvertently, I think) motivated another Spartan wrestler to greatness way beyond what I achieved.

On February 17, 1968, my senior year and about a year after we lost to the University of Michigan in the dual meet in 1967, we wrestled Michigan in a meet that a writer from WIN Magazine later wrote up as one of the greatest college wrestling meets of all time. During my three years at Michigan State, we had never beaten Michigan.

Prior to this meet, Grady gave us all a pep talk, where he said all of us should win or at the very least have a good chance to win, except at heavyweight. At heavyweight, we had a transfer from Cerritos Community College, named Jeff Smith, whom Grady had just recruited.

Both Biggie, the MSU AD, and Grady resented the fact that Porter, who lived in Lansing, always used the Michigan State facilities and gave the impression he was going to Michigan State to play football and wrestle. Porter, however, told them as he left for Ann Arbor, that he wanted to be on a team that could win a national championship. Since Michigan State had no chance to do that, Porter enrolled at University of Michigan.

Porter ended up being the greatest football/wrestling combination in the history of the Wolverine athletic program, actually being drafted by the Cleveland Browns in 1968. As a result, he decided not to compete in the 1968 Olympics.

To add insult to injury, the previous two years (1966 and 1967) Michigan State had gone into the heavyweight match ahead of Michigan, but NCAA champion, Dave Porter, pinned our heavyweight to snatch the victory from the jaws of defeat. Grady was hoping that this year the Spartans would be so far ahead it would not matter if our heavyweight got pinned. Just looking at the lineups, it appeared that we would have a big lead by the time we came to the heavyweight match.

Anyway, Grady's comment that we had no chance to win at heavyweight made Jeff mad—really mad!

As it happened, the meet drew what was one of the largest crowds in Michigan college history, certainly the largest in Michigan State wrestling history as the year earlier we had won the NCAAs and the Big Ten tournaments, but Michigan had defeated us in the dual meet and had taken second at the NCAAs. Also, the Wolverines had started this season, the 1967-1968 season, ranked first in the country. So every wrestling fan in Michigan understood the rivalry and the importance of this particular meet.

As the meet progressed, Michigan won a couple matches that they shouldn't have won. I went up a weight and was wrestling an opponent who was much stronger than I was but who had no chance against my intensity. I built a big lead relatively quickly. The problem was that I was beating him 20-5, and our team was only going to get 3 team points. I had to pin him to get 5 team points.

I was sure I was going to pin him, but I soon figured out that he was going to be almost impossible to pin as his coach told him to just sprawl and stall on the bottom. Almost all my falls occurred when my opponents began to stand up as then they were vulnerable to a cradle. I realized that I was going to have to let him stand up and try to either throw him or take him down to his back with a leg drop. The problem with the first idea is that since he was so much stronger than I, I might actually end up on my back trying to throw him. So that was not a good idea.

Every time I would take him down, he would simply sprawl. The ref would not call him for stalling as the ref assumed my opponent just didn't know what to do. Unfortunately, at the end of my match I had slaughtered my Michigan opponent, but our team only got 3 teams. That was definitely a moral victory for Michigan. And a very bad omen for the Spartans.

The worst thing that could occur happened at 160 pounds. The Spartan wrestler, Pat Karslake, picked up the Michigan wrestler and slammed him to the mat. A slam was illegal. When a wrestler picks another wrestler off the ground, the offensive wrestler is responsible for the defensive wrestler's safe return to the mat. The Michigan wrestler allegedly could not continue; so instead of Michigan State winning that match easily (and getting 3 team points), Michigan was given 5 points more. So that was an eight-point swing in the team points, enough to make a difference in which team wins in most meets where the two teams are relatively equal.

Michigan State was in real trouble. Going into the heavyweight match, we were behind, 14-12. So on paper, we now had no chance to win. For the third straight year we were going to lose to Michigan.

I went to talk to Jeff before he went out. I said something stupid to him to try to fire him up, but I could tell that he was in the zone. Thank God, my words of encouragement were not getting through. Almost everybody in the stands got up to leave; but as they began to walk out, they were shocked to see Jeff take Porter down. Jeff wrestled like a lower weight with single leg drops that would make me salivate. I wish mine had been as good.

I'm sure that everyone was thinking this takedown was a bit of an aberration, that national champion Porter would just reverse and pin Jeff in a moment or two as he had done for the past two years to our other heavyweight. Instead Jeff put Porter on his back. Porter got off his back. The referee awarded two predicament points at only 1:49 in the match. 4-0!

What?! Wow! This match is going to be great! Now people were coming back into the gym. The crowd was screaming and getting closer to the mat. It was pandemonium.

Jeff Smith pinning Dave Porter

A little later Jeff put Porter on his back again, and this time the ref slapped mat at 3:31—it was over! David had just pinned Goliath! The greatest match and meet in Michigan State wrestling history—maybe the greatest meet ever!

Grady later commented to the media that this victory was a greater thrill than winning the NCAAs the year before. The athletic director, Biggie Munn, put a huge poster of the fall on a wall in his office. And Grady put the same huge picture on the basement wall in his home.

Kyle Klingman, writer for WIN magazine wrote articles discussing the ten greatest dual meets in college history in no particular order. This was one. Decades later, Porter went to Grady's home to buy a pistol. While in Grady's basement, Dave saw the huge poster depicting the fall and told Grady that he wasn't really pinned. Grady then paused for effect and asked, "Which time?"

The moral of this story is that Jeff our heavyweight had no chance of beating Porter. But he did. How did that happen? Was it Grady's words working on Jeff's pride for an hour or two? I think it was. Grady's words won that meet for us. I'd swear to it on a Bible—and maybe Jeff would too.

Later in the book in discussing what a great coach Grady was, I quote him as saying that he was "half psychologist and half son of a bitch." I don't think he was either, but I do believe that Jeff and I had moments thinking that he might be.

In the context of the Porter-Smith match, when Grady told Siddens that I would never make the team, was it his comments to Coach Siddens and others that proved an important catalyst in my becoming a national champion? I think it certainly was a factor. So…maybe in the long run, he did me a favor!

All I knew was that I was miserable—in every way. I couldn't beat anybody on the wrestling team; I was sick most of the term; I had no money; and I was fearing that I might flunk out as I almost never went to class. All I could think was that I had hit bottom. Could my life possibly get worse? The answer was yes.

Another Shoe to Drop

There was one more shoe to drop. During this period, my high school girlfriend visited me and Michigan State. She was in her senior year in high school at West Waterloo and had applied to Michigan State so we could be together. She wanted to look the campus over in anticipation of her enrolling. I sure needed a morale boost, so I really looked forward to her visit and renewing our relationship when she enrolled.

After coming to see me in East Lansing (and noting my obviously deteriorated physical and mental condition), she said she thought it best we "date around." What she meant, of course, was that she thought it best that she date around. I had no money, no scholarship, and my prospects were even worse.

I didn't blame her at all. It was obvious. Even after three years "going" together, I was too pathetic to continue a relationship with. She decided during her visit not to attend Michigan State. She would stay in Iowa.

I'm embarrassed to say that I assumed that my notion of a "relationship" with her was just another delusion. Again, that's how desperate I was and felt.

I decided my only alternative was to get mentally tough and move on, move forward. I had no other choice. I had gotten myself into this predicament. I was going to have to get myself out—<u>alone</u>.

Things Finally Begin To Improve

Lots of people all over the world were in much worse shape than I, but I was way too egocentric to notice or care. I was concerned only about me. And other people and wrestling were the last things on my mind. After all of my trials and tribulations, I finally got a break from a most unlikely source. I got to spend a lot of time in the MSU hospital. Who would think that a hospital would rescue me and be my saving grace?

No one came to visit me (I'm not sure anyone knew I was there), but the nurses taking care of me were fantastic. Prior to this, I don't think I had ever met a nurse. I had no idea how kind and friendly they are (trained to be). Besides just generally making me feel comfortable and happy, they were fun. I remember distinctly only one specific incident in the hospital. It was raining very hard, coming down in torrents. My hospital window was open and the rain was pounding against the window ledge making a ferocious clatter. A really cute nurse poked her head through the door of my room and yelled, "Dale, use the urinal." That I would remember that corny comment 50 years later should tell you how desperate I was for a "friend" or even a friendly word.

Most importantly, the hospital staff gave me food every day—and it was all <u>free</u>. I rested in bed all day and read my class materials. I never went to class and got almost all A's that term!

As an added bonus, providentially I believe, I met a girl in the hospital who became a friend and was a friend for the next three years. I needed that as suddenly I didn't feel quite so alone any more.

> *And this should inform anybody reading this that if you are ever really down, there is a tomorrow when things will get better if you are mentally tough. And if you are not mentally tough, pray for help to get mentally tough. If I can do it, anybody can.*

Most people I assume can't wait to get out of a hospital. For me, everybody was so nice at the hospital, I decided to make it my home. I wonder if any patient in any hospital has ever said when they were being released, "No, I think I'll stay here." That's what I said.

Every time I was released from the hospital, I figured and finagled a new way to get myself re-admitted. I now realize how easy it is to get hooked on welfare! I certainly was hooked on that (free) hospital care. I'm sure the hospital staff thought I was a hypochondriac or worse. Actually, I was just hungry, for food and friends.

Also, I suddenly found out that spring at Michigan State is incredible. I don't know if there is a top ten in beautiful campuses, but my vote goes for Michigan State. So although my entry to MSU was under terrible weather conditions and miserable overcast days, the end of my first year at Michigan State just four or five months later could best be described by my feelings of spring fever.

Even better and more important, I decided I had the academic part of Michigan State figured out. I tested out of most of my required classes and spent most of my time studying. Learning how to study at Iowa State my first term was really paying off.

At the end of spring term, a great surgeon operated on my knee. Again, I tried to stay in the hospital as long as possible, complaining of pain, etc., but the hospital administration and doctors and nurses were on to me and my freeloading ways and finally kicked me out.

Meanwhile, the Michigan State wrestling team that year improved from last in the Big 10 the year before (1964) to second in 1965. Don Behm at 130 and Jeff Richardson at heavyweight both won Big Ten championships. Michigan more than doubled our score, prevailing in every weight but three and winning its third straight Big Ten championship.

MICHIGAN STATE UNIVERSITY
1965 VARSITY WRESTLING TEAM
SECOND PLACE BIG TEN CHAMPIONSHIPS

The Spartans fared rather poorly at the nationals. Don Behm was our only All-American, losing a close match to Uetake in the semis and then placing third at 130 pounds.

It was a tough year for the team—and worse for me. But both the team and I were finally getting better and feeling better! Next year would be even better for both the team and me!

Most importantly for me, I was growing up. Different people "grow up" in different ways. Some kids have a ritual grow-up event like a "walk about" for Aborigines or a Bar Mitzvah for Jewish boys. I never had anything like that.

I probably prayed, trying to bargain with God and asking for some providential intercession in helping me to get through those trying times. But I knew I had to do this by myself. I know there's no place in the Bible where it says, "God helps those who help themselves." But there should be.

I had to become a man. It was time.

Chapter 10
My Sophomore Year
1965-1966

ଔ

> *"Phoenix rising from the ashes—The Phoenix is a mythical bird with fiery plumage that lives up to 100 years. Near the end of its life, it settles into its nest of twigs which then burns ferociously, reducing the bird and nest to ashes. And from those ashes, a fledgling Phoenix rises—renewed and reborn."*
>
> **Gail Brenner**

The '65-'66 season proclaimed my rebirth as a wrestler. I rose like the Phoenix from the ashes in virtually every way.

Apparently my growth paralleled that of amateur wrestling. Ron Good, long-time editor/writer for *Amateur Wrestling News*, stated in a column in the July 2015 issue that the "golden era of college wrestling" began in 1966. He stated, "Call it myth-dust, nostalgia, whatever…I say the guys from that time span were meaner, leaner, tougher."

I certainly wouldn't debate whether wrestlers were better then or now as I believe wrestlers, just like all other athletes, are getting better all the time.

I was unaware that I was wrestling in the middle of a golden era. When I went back to school in the fall of 1965, I was still in the middle of what I considered to be quicksand. I couldn't move. I was stuck in every way and certainly was not moving forward.

My biggest problem was that I was still broke, hungry, and had no scholarship. The NCAA had a rule that when you transfer, you have to wait an entire academic year before you can go on scholarship at your new school unless your old coach "releases" you. There was no way Nick was going to release me. Even if Nick had released me, Grady would never have given me a scholarship anyway. Grady had offered me a full ride my junior year in high school. Now he was offering me nothing. I was just another walk-on.

Grady had his team already decided with Behm at 130 and Carr at 137—and me on the outside looking in as there was no other weight I could wrestle. My chances of getting any scholarship money seemed slim to none at that moment in time.

Working My Way Through College

So during the 1965 fall term, I had to work several jobs just to survive and stay in school. The best job I had that term was working in the press box at the football games. The food was delicious, and I was welcome to take home everything left over after all the "big shots" had had their fill. Everything was free to them and afterward was free to me. I was in heaven. Often, I lived for several days just on those leftovers. I had no refrigerator, so the perishable stuff I had to eat up the first day or so.

Also, the mood in the press box was very positive and upbeat as the Spartan football team during this period was the best in history. We never lost any of those games. Bud Wilkinson, the great(est) Oklahoma football coach, commented once that Michigan State had the best defense in college football history during this period. Many times that year the noise from the stands was deafening. And who can ever forget hearing 76,000 fans yell, "Kill Bubba kill!"? Besides Bubba Smith, the greatest player on the team was George Webster (linebacker). Both went on to stardom in the pros, but we had several that went to the NFL in the first round, including Clint Jones (running back) and Gene Washington (receiver).

I didn't get a chance to watch much of the football games as I was working; but I was aware that Michigan State did not lose a regular season game during the 1965 season, and Michigan State was ranked number 1 in the country. So, again, the press box was a very happy place to be.

The 1965-1966 Wrestling Season Begins

Prior to January, before I could even try out for the team my sophomore year, the team started the season with a couple of relatively easy opponents, Colorado State and the Air Force Academy. We beat Air Force 36-3, but Colorado State almost beat us. The score was 16-14.

Amateur Wrestling News ranked Michigan State ninth in December 1965. So that was a bit of good news. I'm just not sure what they based that rating on.

The Spartans finished sixth at the Midlands in late December. The Midlands, at the time, was the best, most competitive (Christmas vacation) tournament in the country. Most people thought that it was harder to win the Midlands than the NCAAs as many post grads wrestled in this tournament at LaGrange, Illinois, just outside of Chicago.

I wrestled unattached in the Midlands that year, as I was still under NCAA sanctions for transferring mid-year. I lost decisively in the finals to Behm at 130 pounds. I really didn't wrestle very well and certainly should not have cut to 130 pounds to compete. I have no idea why I made the cut to 130 for the tournament. I'm not taking anything away from Behm as he was definitely better in that match—and he really took advantage of my aggressiveness and used it against me.

He also used a strategy that I would never fall for again right before the match. He came over to me and started a conversation, sort of like we were in the wrestling room, just talking. He was joking around and making light of the moment. I'm not sure he did that on purpose, maybe not; but he totally got me out of my zone. Behm had better wrestling skills than I did. He also didn't ever try to focus that hard, I don't think. He could be laughing about a joke one minute and the next minute go all out and wrestle at a very high level. I had little chance to beat him unless I was in the zone.

Anyway, I was glad when that match was over—and even happier to see the end of 1965. Unfortunately, 1966 started out even worse for me than 1965 ended. It was soon after the New Year that I "broke" a bone spur just above my elbow. I didn't know what it was at the time, and I certainly didn't dream that I fractured a bone spur—and that's not all. The internal problem was worse than just a fracture.

When anyone touched the area, it would create a great deal of pain. Most opponents grab you just above the elbow when they tie up or ride, so there was no relief when wrestling. I didn't go to a doctor as I didn't want him to tell me I couldn't wrestle. I didn't really understand what had happened at the time. All I knew was that it really hurt when someone touched it in any way. Nobody in the wrestling room really cared, so I just shrugged it off.

> *Even in 1965, I guess I could have sought a red shirt in order to let my arm heal. But why? I was a "walk-on"—so I would have had to continue for another year starving without a scholarship and trying to find the money to pay out-of-state tuition. At the time I had no idea what a red shirt was, so the issue was moot anyway. (A red shirt, for those who don't know, is an extra year to compete granted by the NCAA when an athlete gets hurt badly enough that he couldn't compete that year.)*

As a result of my injury, I was unable to wrestle at a quadrangular at Northwestern, even if I could have made the team. Minnesota won the quadrangular with 65 points. The Spartans were second with 55.

During this period, on January 13, 1966, the school newspaper ran an article titled "Hapless Anderson 'Gets the Breaks'." In the article, Ed Brill explained all of the injuries and illnesses I had suffered since transferring from Iowa State. The article attempted to explain and excuse my poor performances in the wrestling room and competition, explaining my inability to stay healthy and free from injury for any period of time. I'm at a loss now to figure out why an article would be written about me in the school newspaper in the first place. Perhaps Grady planted it to make me feel better.

I tried to wrap the elbow/bicep area enough to soften the pain when opponents grabbed my arm. But nothing seemed to help the pain, and the wrap was cumbersome. So I decided to forget the wrap and just deal with the pain, which by now was constant and relatively intense. I was totally unaware at the time that one could take pain medication to help with pain. I just decided to get mentally tough and endure it or better yet, forget about it.

> *Two of our mantras in high school when we suffered an injury were just to "put some mud on it" or "pain is all in your head." Almost everybody has heard those, particularly if you have ever been in the West High wrestling room for more than five minutes with Coach Siddens. We practiced those words there.*
>
> *As I mentioned earlier, just before my junior year in high school football, I fractured and separated my shoulder diving for a pass in a sandlot game. Since the coaches and my parents back then did not believe in seeking medical attention for injuries, I played most of the season with a fractured and separated shoulder. Actually, the term "played" would be using the word loosely. I never played in even one game. And every time I tried to tackle anyone in practice, I winced. I'm sure everyone thought I was a sissy. By the end of the season, the pain was so intense that I <u>had</u> to go to a doctor.*
>
> *I had never gone to a doctor before in my life. The doctor told me and my parents by showing us the x-rays, etc., that my shoulder was in fact fractured and separated. I gave it a rest, but only a short one as wrestling season quickly approached, and I was not going to miss even one day of wrestling season.*
>
> *Anyway, having a broken bone in my elbow area was a little like having a fractured and separated shoulder—put some mud on it and don't complain.*

A few days after the article, Michigan State wrestled a weak Ohio State team and won 15-11. In this meet Carr wrestled at 137. My best friend, Dave Campbell, wrestled at 147 and won. His match really made the difference in winning or losing the meet.

I thought that Campbell's win might mean the end of my wrestling career. If Campbell was at 147, there was clearly no place in the lineup for me to wrestle. Besides being hurt, I was still getting beaten up in the wrestling room.

My First Official College Match

In the next meet we were to wrestle Minnesota, the best team in the Big Ten that year by far. The *Michigan State University News* article, prior to and in anticipation of the meet against Minnesota, stated that Carr would wrestle at 137. A later article discussing the meet said that Carr would be moving up to 147 and that I would wrestle the first match of my college career against Minnesota. No one ever told me anything. It seemed I could learn what was happening only from the newspaper.

I don't remember trying out against anybody. I guess Grady just flipped a coin and then hoped that I would be as good as Coach Siddens said I was. Since Minnesota had already beaten our team rather soundly in the quadrangular earlier in the year, it really didn't seem to matter how we juggled our lineup. We were going down.

The night before our meet with Minnesota, the Gophers wrestled the Wolverines in Ann Arbor and throttled them 18-8, Michigan winning only two out of eight matches. That Minnesota victory broke a 34-straight dual meet winning streak for Michigan—the longest winning streak in Big Ten history at the time!

Michigan was also the perennial Big Ten Conference Champion, having won the Big Ten Tournament for the past three years in a row. The year before (1965), the Wolverines scored 88 points. The Spartans were second with 38. And the year before that (1964), the Spartans scored only one point in the Big Ten Tournament.

So the victory over Michigan was especially sweet for Minnesota. They were no longer the little gophers but were now the new 800-pound gorillas on the (Big Ten) block.

The specter for the following day was ominous for us in East Lansing. I think everyone on the team knew we were in for a serious beat down. I can just imagine how Minnesota felt coming off that big win just about an hour down the road from East Lansing and having beaten Michigan State earlier in a quadrangular. I'm sure they were justifiably confident.

My Minnesota opponent at 137, Terry Barrett, had beaten the returning Big Ten Champion, Billy Johannesen. Johannesen, the Wolverine's team captain, was a returning All-American and would later that year again claim All-American honors at the national tournament at Iowa State. A decade later, he would be head wrestling coach at the University of Michigan. So Barrett's beating Billy Jo was a pretty big upset for the Gophers.

I don't remember anything about the match with Barrett, so there is no sense talking specifics. All I remember is that I went into my "zone" and the next thing I knew, I had beaten him 11-2!

I do remember distinctly what happened right after the match as I came out of my zone and walked off the mat. Grady greeted me with the biggest grin I have ever seen in my life and in his Oklahoma accent drawled, "Son, you can play marbles in my circle any time!" (I'm sure Grady has long forgotten that statement. But I never will.) I didn't know what that meant, but I was hoping that it meant I had "made" the team and had now earned a scholarship (finally)!

I'm sure Grady was as shocked as everybody else in the gym, as I had really been struggling in the wrestling room with my injuries and inability to get in shape. And, after all, this was my first official college match ever and probably the most important match of my life. (Most importantly, if I had wrestled poorly, I might never have wrestled another match for Michigan State—ever.)

Who'd a "thunk" it—maybe a miracle? This was obviously where my miracle comeback began. And I have to give credit to Grady for injecting me into the lineup as there was no particular reason to do so. He definitely was taking a chance.

> *I know it sounds cocky now, but I never doubted that I was going to win. I never wrestled a match where I thought I was going to lose. Never. Ever. But I never really thought about winning—or losing. All I thought about was attack. However, if you were to ask me, I would say that I always thought I was going to win, and I'm sure I would have meant it. If I had had to wrestle King Kong, I would have been sure I was going to win. I'm not sure where my bravado came from. But I was glad I had it as it came in very handy, especially when wrestling opponents who were better than I was.*
>
> *If I were a coach, a parent, or a wrestler, I think a kid should always be encouraged to do his best. Telling kids to win is a bad idea, in my opinion.*

When the dust cleared on my match and the meet, we looked up at the team score board. We had beaten the previously undefeated Gophers

20-8! And we had done it by wrestling aggressively in front of a full house. We wrestled in the men's intramural gym where 1,200 spectators seemed like a very big crowd and seemed to easily fill every seat available. The crowd really helped us to get fired up, and I appreciated how enthusiastic they were during my match.

Ironically, we beat the Gophers as badly as they had beaten the mighty Wolverines the night before. The University of Michigan won only two out of eight matches against the Gophers the night before, and the Gophers won only two out of eight matches against us. It made us all wonder, how good were we really? And, maybe more importantly, how badly were we going to beat Michigan this year? Could we shut them out?

The student newspaper the next day led with the heading "Matmen Crush Gophers." Grady graciously gave me the credit for the victory.

The paper read, "A crowd of 1,200 at the IM sports arena roared as the team swept to victory…The victory was sparked by sophomore Dale Anderson who was wrestling in his first varsity match…'Anderson did a magnificent job' Peninger said after the meet. 'None of us were sure how he would perform under the circumstances in his first bout, but he came through to really spark the team.'"

Continuing to Hurt

My arm continued to hurt constantly and intensely; the sharp broken bone spur in my arm was cutting a blood vessel and was causing me to bleed almost continually internally. Of course, in the meet(s) I never even thought about it. The zone and adrenalin blocked out all pain.

We won a couple of meets after Minnesota, and then we ran into a buzz saw against Oklahoma. All of the matches were close, but Behm at 130 pounds was the only Spartan to win. Ismail Al (Sam)-Karaghouli, my nemesis, and I tied at 137 pounds. Sam had earlier tied the (future) NCAA champion, Gene Davis, so I felt it was at least a moral victory for me. He was extremely hard for me to wrestle as he did nothing on his feet, and he was much stronger than I was. I mention over and over in this book, that particular style was the hardest for me to wrestle.

In the big picture, nobody could doubt that we were humbled by the (hated) Okies. The meet was sobering to the extent of letting us know that we were not ready for prime time—meaning wrestling up to the level of the Oklahoma (and Iowa) schools.

The Oklahoma coach, Tommy Evans, complimented our team after the meet, commenting to the MSU student newspaper that almost all of the matches could have gone either way (which was true), and that our team was "one of the toughest teams Michigan State has ever had."

I was injured again for the next meet. We then wrestled Cornell, one of the best teams in the East, and beat them soundly. We beat Northern Iowa and the University of Iowa in preparation for Michigan.

Wrestling Michigan and Behm Cutting to 123

In a surprise move I did not understand at the time (or even now), Behm said he was moving down to 123 pounds for the Michigan meet. <u>I was moved down</u> to 130. I had no idea why. I just did what I was told to do.

I hated the cut. I had just tied a guy from Oklahoma University at 137 (Karaghouli) who had previously tied a (future) NCAA champion, Gene Davis. And I was undefeated at 137 as a sophomore (and I had a broken bone in my arm). So why should I go down to 130?

That cut was brutal, for both of us. Don was undefeated at 130. His only loss in three years was to Uetake. Don was the best wrestler on the team. The articles in the school newspaper constantly praised Don, and justifiably. I complimented Don in one article stating that he might be the best wrestler in the world at his weight. I sincerely believed that.

Don had an open door to Grady's office. Don and Grady got along great at the time mainly because Don was our star. Both Don and Grady were extremely gregarious, so their personalities meshed well. I was not that outgoing, preferring to keep to myself and just do my job.

Don Behm wrestling at MSU

No one knows now the sequence of events, but I'm thinking that while conversing in Grady's office, the idea of the weight cut arose. Grady and Don both liked the idea, not only because Don was his favorite wrestler on the team but because Grady (and just about every other coach back then) believed that it was always better to cut down to a lower weight. Another reason was because we really had no chance of getting any team points at the national tournament from our 123 pounder. Don might even be favored to win the national championship at 123.

I'm sure, from Don's point of view, no one had ever beaten Uetake—and probably no one was ever going to. I don't think Don was afraid of Uetake, per se. Don just had a tendency to over-think everything. In retrospect, I believe that his over-thinking on this issue was that it was going to be easier to win a national championship at 123 than 130. Who could disagree with that conclusion?

Ultimately, Don's recollection was that the idea to cut to 123 was Grady's. Don said this about the weight cut, "I didn't think about who was easier (Uetake or Caruso). I could beat either one. I'd already almost beat Uetake the year before, so I knew he was beatable. I only went to 123 because of Grady and the team."

At the time, I guess I was just too busy sort of surviving. If I thought anything, I probably speculated that the beat down we took from Oklahoma prompted the coaches to try a different lineup. So I was about to be "thrown to the lion" (Uetake) without ever knowing why.

I wish that Doug Blubaugh would have taught Don how to beat Uetake. After all, Doug pinned the greatest wrestler in the world in one of the greatest upsets in Olympic history. Why couldn't he teach Don how to improve just a couple of points on Uetake? In a parallel universe, maybe that happened and the crowd was treated to one of the greatest matches in NCAA history. But that was never to be.

In my opinion, Don wanted to win a national championship, not place second. And therefore, once the decision to cut to 123 was a fait accompli, he had decided to focus on opponents he thought would be easier to beat—123 pounders, Mike Caruso, eventual three-time national champion at Lehigh, and Bob Fehrs, three-time runner-up to Caruso from the University of Michigan.

The logic of Don's beating Caruso was sound if you subscribe to the reasoning of this syllogism:

- Caruso lost one match in his entire college career. That was to Bob Steenlage, the first four-time Iowa state champion and star wrestler at West Point Academy.
- At the NCAA championships in 1965 the year before, Don beat Steenlage in the quarter-finals 8-7.
- Therefore, Don could beat Caruso. (Since Steenlage beat Caruso and Don beat Steenlage; the logical conclusion was that Don could beat Caruso.)

Where the logic broke down was that Caruso went up from 123 pounds to 130 pounds to wrestle Steenlage. Don was going down to wrestle Caruso—at Caruso's natural weight. In my mind that turned out to be a deciding factor that threw a big monkey wrench into the whole idea.

Also, Caruso was wily, funky, and unorthodox. I would think he would have been very tough to beat the first time an opponent wrestled him, no matter what. Frankly, I think even Uetake would have had a battle on his hands had he cut to 123 and wrestled Caruso. I probably would have bet on Uetake, but I would not have bet the farm.

I would think that a person who worked out with Caruso a lot could figure out his style and get used to it. For example, it seemed that every time Fehrs wrestled Caruso in the finals, Fehrs got closer to figuring out how to wrestle Caruso, but he still lost to him three times in the NCAA finals.

Caruso wrestling Fehrs in the NCAA championship match

I guess whoever thought up the idea of the weight cut, this appeared to be an agreement made in heaven—at least for the coaches and Don—

certainly not for me. But I was still a nobody from my perspective and as far as my opinion was concerned.

I must admit, however, that for me <u>in my admittedly delusional state</u> the idea of wrestling Uetake was one of the most exciting thoughts that I could possibly conjure up. It was like my first match in high school. Instead of preparing to beat a state champion in my very first wrestling match ever, I was now preparing to beat an Olympic, two-time national champion, voted outstanding wrestler in the last NCAA tournament, and possibly the greatest wrestler in NCAA history! And the cherry on top was that our match would be the last of his college career. This was going to be fun—really fun! I couldn't wait.

Obviously, I was delusional (again). In actuality, I think I was a little like the dwarf, Gimli, in *Lord of the Rings* where the good guys are debating whether to fight the enormously overwhelmingly powerful army of evil, and Gimli says something like, "no chance of victory; certainty of death; what are we waiting for!?" That was me, firing myself up to wrestle—and beat—Uetake.

The bigger problem was sucking my body down to 130 pounds again. That was an experience I did not look forward to at all! The last time I did that at the Midlands I got beat by Behm. Then reality set in; this was going to be a very difficult weight cut for both Don and me, making me seriously wonder if there might be an easier way to work my way through college.

I remember Don and me running together after a tough wrestling practice shortly before the Michigan meet. We were almost down to weight and very short on fuel or energy. All of a sudden, Don stopped short and said, "(an expletive) it; I quit." I had no idea what that meant. He just stopped running and headed for the showers. He said he couldn't run any more. He was quitting. I had never seen or heard Don "quit" before, and I must admit, it really bothered me. I thought that it was a bad omen. That's why I still remember it.

> *Any wrestler knows that one of the "easiest" ways to lose weight is to put on rubber suits. I don't think any of us had rubber suits or even knew what they were in high school. Back when I was in high school, we would put on a lot of sweat clothing. After practice, the sweats would be soaked. Some guys would roll up under the wrestling mat to sweat. It was all very primitive. Coach Siddens kept the room hot enough that you could almost break a sweat just walking in the room.*
>
> *Once I started using rubber suits in college, I decided to never use rubber tops. It was just a psychological thing, but I thought they made me weak. I also had a psychological block against using the steam room to lose weight as it seemed like that approach too drained me of my energy. I really tried to stay away from both while cutting to 130 pounds—but eventually I had to use both to make weight for the NCAAs. I think they had a very deleterious psychological impact on me in the tournament.*
>
> *I would never try to tell anyone how to lose weight, but it seems to me that the wisest is to eat right and work the weight off by wrestling and running (easier said than done, I know).*

Little did Don (and Grady) know when they agreed to cut Behm down to 123, it would be the worst mistake Don and the coaches would make that year—and maybe in his entire wrestling career. I still say, without equivocation, that nobody told me the logic of this cut. In fact, nobody told me anything. Dale Carr has recently said that nobody consulted him about the cut from 147 to 137 either. Dale thought that he had absolutely no say in the matter. He was right; he didn't.

Whether or not it was Don's suggestion or Grady's to move us all down a weight, the impact it had on me was the same. I was never going to be a national champion my sophomore year as I had about as much chance of beating Uetake as Larry Owings had of beating Dan Gable.

The Michigan Meet

> *Almost everyone in Michigan bleeds either blue or green. Most people would probably say I bleed green now, but in the mid-'60s I could not make myself appreciate the rivalry with the University of Michigan. I'm not sure I felt a "rivalry" with any team, but I did make an oath that I would never lose to an Okie (or an East High wrestler in high school). So if anything, I saw Okies, not Michigan, as my rivals.*
>
> *Again, don't get me wrong. I didn't hate Okies. I actually admired the fact that they (and particularly OSU) were unquestionably the most dominant program in NCAA history and still are—in any sport!*
>
> *Also, as it related to Iowa State, I had nothing against the Cyclones or Nick. And I didn't blame Nick for my going to Iowa State. It was my decision and my own fault. Anyway, I certainly didn't think of Iowa State as rivals, as I was definitely still an Iowan at heart.*

A few days after Don quit during our run, we wrestled Michigan. He got pinned by Bob Fehrs, a three-time NCAA runner-up at 123.

I was warming up at the time and was shocked (out of my zone). I could not imagine Don getting beat, let alone pinned, even though he had cut more weight than he probably should have. Behm was the guy I had bragged about to the paper who might be the best wrestler in the world at his weight. I think the paper also quoted someone as saying something like, "Behm has about as much chance of losing as the sun not coming up."

Next, I got beat by Dave Dozeman 12-11 at 130 pounds, a match I never should have lost. It was to be my only dual meet loss in a Spartan uniform. It was Don's only dual meet loss in his three years of wrestling for Michigan State, also. I am sure our losses could easily be accounted for as a function of the weight loss. But for me, it was also because I lost focus watching Don get pinned.

We should have beaten Michigan easily; instead, we lost 16-11. Michigan's future two-time national champion heavyweight, Dave

Porter, pinned Richardson, our returning Big Ten champion. This team loss was not Richardson's fault as the meet fell apart when both Don and I lost. Had we been up a weight, we both would have won (almost for sure), and the meet would have been ours, regardless how the heavyweight match turned out. However, at the time, Richardson was a returning Big Ten champion and Porter was still a nobody (like me). Porter's pinning Richardson, a Big Ten champion, made him an immediate "somebody" who had to be reckoned with.

One would think that since the weight cut didn't work at all for the three of us—Don, Dale Carr, or me—in the Michigan meet, we would all go back to our more natural wrestling weights where we could win. But that made too much sense, I guess. Logic was not going to reign here.

Behm asked Grady if he could go back up to 130, but apparently Grady refused. Grady told Don that he would wrestle at 123 at the Big Ten tournament. And that was that. He would not let Don try out with me at 130.

Again, nobody asked me for my opinion. But had Don or Grady asked me, I would have jumped at the idea of going up to 137 in a second. I hated that cut to 130. I think Don, deep down, wanted revenge against Fehrs anyway; so Don cut to 123 again, hoping to avenge his only dual meet loss.

The Big Ten Tournament

At the Big Ten tournament the next week, Bob Fehrs again beat Behm, this time 4-3 in the finals at 123.

Don was simply not himself at 123. I worked out with both Behm and Fehrs. I felt that although Fehrs was good, he wasn't as good as Behm. So I had to assume it was the weight cut or it was psychological damage that was the deciding factor in the match. But then I'm obviously biased toward Don.

Relatively recently, I asked Don why he had so much trouble wrestling at 123 when he took a silver medal at 125 at the Olympics in 1968. He said he thought those last two pounds were tortuous. My opinion is that in 1968 he could devote every minute, every second, every thought to preparation for the Olympics. In 1966 he had school and other things that also took his time and mind, but that's just speculation.

Anyway, I was not going to let Don's getting beat again affect me. In the Big Ten Finals I caught Bob Campbell from Indiana in a cradle and pinned him at 2:50. Campbell had beaten Michigan's Dozeman in the semifinals, so I was unable to avenge my loss to Dozeman a week earlier. But at least I pinned the guy who beat Dozeman. So that would have to do.

I pinned at least a third of the wrestlers I wrestled with a cradle, as it was almost impossible to escape once I got my hands locked. I think the reason I was able to execute this move was that I always hit the cradle just as my opponent was moving his knee to stand up, so I was anticipating his movement. Any time my opponents knee was going to anywhere near his head, I would try for a cradle. I tried to lock my hands as close to his head as possible and then pull my opponent into my chest so that my body then became another point that secured my opponent. I had a pretty strong grip so there was little chance of his breaking my grip or escaping once I locked my hands.

Campbell made the mistake of coming up with his inside leg and keeping his head down, making it easy for me to cradle and pin him. I think Gable was the only one to wiggle out after I had locked my hands and had him in what I believed to be relatively secure in a cradle. He wiggled out of it so easily, I was surprised. Apparently, that's why his teammates named him the "weasel." He could weasel out of even my cradle.

If you want to get good at cradles, you must be able to keep a little weight on your opponent and you must really get good at anticipating when your opponent's knee will be near enough his head to commit to the cradle.

Dale Anderson pinning an Ohio State opponent

Dale Carr won the tournament at 137 pounds also. In order for the Spartans to claim the Big Ten Championship as a team, however, Mike Bradley had to beat his Minnesota opponent, Bob Ramstead, in the finals. Bradley did win 6-4 in one of the most exciting matches I have ever witnessed in college as so much was riding on that match.

So we three sophomores were Big Ten champions! A bright future seemed on the horizon for Michigan State wrestling! Ironically, the two returning Big Ten champions, Behm and Richardson, who were juniors, lost in the finals.

A senior, Dick Cook, took third. Cook would win the NCAA championship a couple weeks later. Another irony, George Radman, a junior, finished third also and would win the national championship as a senior in 1967. As a big picture, when the dust settled, the scoreboard read Michigan State 71, University of Michigan 67.

> *Indeed, the Spartan wrestling program in 1966 was starting a seven-year streak. We won the Big Ten Wrestling Championship from that year, 1966, to 1973. On page 36 of Jairus K Hammond's* The History of Collegiate Wrestling, *Jay writes "The 1966 season marked the beginning of the era of dynasties in the Big Ten. Michigan State won the Big Ten Championship for seven straight seasons." That was, and is, the longest winning streak by any Michigan State team in the history of Michigan State athletics. That is, no Michigan State teams, except our wrestling teams, have ever won seven straight Big Ten Titles. Ever.*

After the Big Ten tournament, *Amateur Wrestling News* boosted our ranking from ninth to sixth—an improvement at least. Since the Oklahoma schools were one and two, we were still not even close to being in the same class as they. But we had slipped past Michigan and Penn State and ranked first in the Big Ten.

The 1966 NCAAs

Ultimately, oblivious to the discussion about "weight" issues occurring, I cut to 130 again for the NCAAs. The nationals were being held that year in my home state on the campus of Iowa State, the college I had left in frustration the year before.

> *Ironically, in 1965 my freshman year, after I transferred the year before, Iowa State won its very first NCAA Championship <u>ever</u>. The tournament went down to the championship match at 177, Tom Peckham, ISU, and Bill Harlow, OSU. Peckham won 5-3 over the number one seed, Bill Harlow. So ISU beat OSU by one team point, 87-86! What an exciting way to win a first national championship! And no wonder Peckham became a legend at Iowa State after that.*
>
> *Gable often cites Peckham as the wrestler he most styled his technique around. I always liked Peckham and looked up to him, especially in high school.*
>
> *Peckham and my college records were very similar: almost the same percentage wins and losses; the same records at the NCAA tournament, one fifth place and two first place finishes. I won more conference championships, but he had more falls.*
>
> *Reflecting on Peckham's win in the finals in 1965 and the Cyclones win over Okie State, Iowa State was in good position in 1966 to repeat on their home mats—and begin their run at a dynasty. But it was not to be.*

Behm hurt his knee in his Big Ten finals match with Fehrs and couldn't wrestle in the NCAAs, so confusion seemed to dominate the coaches' thinking. Our best wrestler was out of commission right when we needed him most. What was the best thing to do?

Now there was <u>no</u> reason for me to cut to 130. But that conclusion made too much sense, I guess. Once again, I decided to think positively about the nationals and talked myself into believing that I could beat, <u>would beat</u>, Uetake. My biggest hurdle before that would be winning my semifinal match, as then I could get a long rest before weighing in for the finals. My only chance of beating Uetake (in my mind at least) was to get lots of rest so that I could wrestle at my best.

Peritore and Leeman

I was to wrestle Joe Peritore from Lehigh in my semi-final match. Peritore was a second seed, and I was seeded third. He was a lot slicker than I was, but I was sure that I was a lot tougher, hungrier, and more intense. As long as I could keep up my strength, I was almost sure I could wear him down and beat him in the third period. The wrestler on our team who was closest in style to Peritore was Keith Lowrance. I actually thought Lowrance was slicker than Peritore, so I had already experienced in the wrestling room what I was in for.

Caruso and Peritore watching a match at the NCAA tournament

As I prepared to wrestle Peritore, I psyched up and was ready to tear into him. I was at the side of the mat and in the zone! I was peaking at the right time—I beat Peritore and then I get to wrestle Uetake.

Seconds before the match as we stood beside the mat waiting to go onto the mat to wrestle, the referee told Grady and me that the Lehigh coach, Gerald Leeman, had leveled an objection to my wrestling at all. He said that I should be disqualified! Leeman insisted that the front of my jersey was too low and was showing off too much of my chest! The wrestling rule book provided that the neckline of the uniform was supposed to be cut only so many inches below my neck or chin or something. The referee measured it, and it was lower than it should have been according to the wrestling rules. So I was going to be disqualified. (I have no idea why any coach or referee would bring a ruler to a wrestling match.)

This whole farce was even more ironic in the context of the fact that a few years before this, wrestlers did not need to wear shirts at all, and many didn't! Thinking about it now, I would have thought that most referees would have said that we should just wrestle and take care of the relatively silly issue of my uniform <u>after</u> the match.

But no! This ref was actually entertaining the objection and was about to disqualify me! I was about to be forfeited in a couple of minutes if I didn't find a "top" that covered more of my chest—at least a quarter inch more. Since all of our wrestling uniforms were the same, it wasn't going to do any good to try on anybody else's uniform on the team.

I was stuck. Then someone came up with the bright idea to just wear a t-shirt under my uniform. I put a t-shirt on seconds before I was to be forfeited and proceeded to the middle of the mat. I was in shock, and I was beat before my match even started—and Leeman and Peritore (and I) knew it.

> *Coach Leeman, a native of Osage, Iowa, had recruited me in high school, even sending Caruso to try to get me to go to Lehigh. Mike actually was a great recruiter. One thing that particularly impressed me was that Mike said that wrestling at Lehigh was the number one sport. He said that on the scoreboard at the football games, they would announce how many weeks until wrestling season. I liked that. Mike also told me that even though Lehigh really didn't offer wrestling scholarships, that Lehigh would take care of me. I didn't understand that part and didn't like it. I didn't know anything about Leeman except that Bill Koll had once said that Leeman was the best wrestler on the Iowa State Teachers College national championship team (which was later to become the State College of Iowa and finally to be named University of Northern Iowa).*

By objecting to my uniform, Leeman had accomplished his purpose. At the moment the referee blew the whistle beginning my match, I was not thinking about wrestling at all. I was definitely out of the "zone." Someone recently compared what Leeman did to a football coach who calls time out right before the opposing team's kicker is about to kick a field goal in order to "ice" him. Of course, I think that analogy is a bit generous.

Be that as it may, I definitely was "iced"—and there was no way I was going to beat Peritore at that point. We were too close in ability. And I needed that edge that only the zone gave me.

> *Thinking back, I wish that someone would have told me what Leeman was doing and "ordered" me to stay focused in the zone. Instead, I became as frantic as the coaches trying to figure out how to avoid forfeiture. My uniform should not have been my problem; it should have been my coaches' problem.*
>
> *I would never have tolerated any coach slapping me, and I think every coach knew that. But I think this would have been one time it might have worked—getting me really mad and maybe back in focus.*
>
> *In this, I am reminded of the movie "Hoosiers" when Gene Hackman, coach of his high school basketball team, tells one of his players to focus after a traumatic event had occurred. I loved that part of the movie.*
>
> *Maybe one day this will help some coach. If you see your athlete forced out of the zone or has lost his focus by something tangential, it is up to you the coach to explain to him that he must focus and get back into the zone.*

Even though I did lose focus in the match and was getting beat, I tried a desperation move toward the end of the match and took Peritore down to his back. Joe bridged from almost the middle of the inner circle to off the mat. The move was ruled to be out of bounds, and the back points that probably should have been scored were not awarded. I have no memory of the move as by then as I was sort of back in the zone, I think. If I had to guess, I would say it was what we called a "pancake" back in the '60s.

The Iowa newspapers, obviously prejudiced for me, wrote this up as a terrible miscarriage of wrestling justice. Little did any newspaper know that the real miscarriage occurred before the match even started. But then it was my own fault for letting the wrestling uniform fiasco affect me so much.

The fact was, I did lose and was inconsolable as I wanted nothing more than a chance to wrestle Uetake. But that was now never to be. After the match with Peritore, I went berserk (and I mean berserk!) in the warm-up wrestling room, acting like the spoiled immature brat that I was. Nothing and nobody could console me.

I think a lot of wrestlers in the wrestling warm-up room thought I was crazy. I probably was. I was in a "different zone" then. I was out of control for a long time after that match.

I absolutely hated the thought of wrestling in the consolations. If I would have had my way, I would have just forfeited my two consolation matches, gone home, and taken my sixth place finish as I no longer cared at all whether I won or lost. I was done for 1966.

However, the next morning, I did wrestle. I went through the motions even though I was sick at heart and was acting like a big baby again. I'm ashamed of myself now for simply throwing in the towel after losing in the semifinals. I ended up taking fifth, getting beat 7-2 by Bob Campbell in the consolations. This was the Indiana wrestler whom I had just pinned in the Big Ten finals the week before.

> *Peritore wrestled Uetake in the finals and ironically, Mr. Siddens, my old high school coach, was the referee in the match. Holding a slight lead, Uetake was apparently "playing" with Peritore. So Mr. Siddens warned him for stalling. Uetake said, "Me no stall." A few seconds later Uetake pinned Peritore. The following may be apocryphal, but the rumor got started that after Mr. Siddens warned Uetake for stalling, Peritore told Mr. Siddens, to "mind your own business" as he had no desire to annoy Uetake with a stall call.*

Three NCAA Champions in 1966. (from left) Bill Harlow (191), Jo Uetake (130), Gene Davis (137)

Oklahoma State Wins the NCAAs (Again)

In 1966, Oklahoma State finished first with 79 points. OSU had three champions: Harlow at 191, Uetake at 130, and Davis at 137. Uetake was voted Outstanding Wrestler. Davis and I would be on a collision course for the 1967 championship. Unfortunately, he would lose in semi's the same as I did in '66.

Dick Cook, a Michigan State senior, overachieved at the 1966 NCAA tournament, winning the championship at 157. That was a pleasant surprise as Cook finished third a week earlier at the Big Ten tournament.

> *For some reason, I have very little memory of Dick during the year as he seemed to be suffering through a relatively mediocre year. I think he had some kind of stomach ailment that affected him during his matches.*
>
> *As mentioned, at the Big Ten tournament Cook took third place. His points were important, but who would think that he would do so well at the NCAAs after that?*
>
> *Dick was a very dangerous leg man, as I will explain in the next chapter. I think at the nationals he was able to put the legs in on his opponents and destroy them from the top position.*

As a team, MSU finished sixth behind Michigan, which finished fifth. It was not great, but it was a lot better than the Spartans did in '65. At least we were improving.

I believe strongly that if we would have had Behm at 130, me at 137, and Carr at 145, we would have done much better and would probably have finished with a team medal (in the top three), particularly because Cook surprised everyone by winning the NCAA title.

The 130-pound weight class, except for Uetake and Peritore, was the weakest weight class in 1966, presumably because everyone wanted to avoid having to wrestle Uetake. Behm would have been a second or third seed and would, in all likelihood, have beaten Peritore in the semis. There is almost no way that Don would have lost before meeting Peritore in the semifinals, so that would have given us a lot of points.

Carr struggled at 137 as that weight class was by far the most loaded weight that year. There were lots of national champions including Bill Stuart (1965 champion) from Lehigh and Mike Sager (1964 champion) from Oklahoma. Sager beat Carr 17-5 in the quarterfinals and Stuart in the semifinals (1-1, 3-1). There were also several place winners from earlier years at that weight. As I mentioned, Gene Davis beat Sager in the finals (1-1, 3-2) in overtime, which just shows how close the two were in ability. Carr would have matched up better at 145 where he was as strong as anyone at that weight and would not have had as many wrestlers whom he did not match up as well against.

I would not have had a high seed at 137. I might not have been seeded at all. But I matched up a lot better than Carr did with almost all of the wrestlers at 137 as the best wrestlers were high-energy, aggressive wrestlers, the kind I loved to wrestle. And Davis, the ultimate champion, did finish third behind me the next year.

On the other hand, all of us at the weight would have been so close in ability that I could have lost in the first round and not achieved All-American status at all. The best part about our weight cut was that Dave Campbell got to wrestle 145 and get experience, which I believe helped to make such a big difference in the Big Ten tournament the next year.

Grady later took all the blame for the debacle related to the weight cut. He basically felt the buck stopped with him and that he was wrong to force the three of us to cut so much weight when we were winning at higher weight classes. I give him a lot of credit for that.

Ultimately, I decided to look back on the year positively. I had finally <u>earned</u> my full ride. I had won almost all of my matches and was an All-American as a sophomore. Our team was going in the right direction. And almost all of us on the team (except Cook) were underclassmen. What more could I want?

Post Season

As for me, after the season was over, I had the fractured bone spur in my arm operated on. As I mentioned earlier, it was only after the surgery that I learned why so much blood filled my arm when anyone bumped or grabbed my arm and why I was in such constant pain. The doctor told me that when he operated he learned that there was a blood vessel "wrapped around" the fractured bone spur (that was the way the doctor explained it to me) and that the bone cut into the vessel every time it was touched. The good news was that pain and frustration was totally taken care of by a relatively simple operation. All I have to remind me of that painful period now is a scar.

<u>I was finally healthy and on full ride!</u> (Even more importantly, I could finally eat!) All was finally well with the team, with me, and my soul.

Next year would be my best season—<u>and the best season</u> in the history of Michigan State wrestling!

Front row: Behm, Anderson, Carr, Hansen, Villareal, Cook, Campbell, Larsen, Tsiminaki.
2nd row: Peninger, Radman, Johnson, Richardson, Weathers, Maidlow, Ott, Young, Bradley, Blubaugh.

MSU		Opponent
16	Colorado State College	14
36	Air Force Academy	33
15	Indiana	9
15	Ohio State	11
20	Minnesota	8
25	Purdue	3
5	Oklahoma	27
27	Cornell	5
25	Illinois	3
21	Iowa	8
24	State College of Iowa	10
11	Michigan	16
	1st Big Ten Meet	

Our 1965-1966 team picture and schedule, with Dale Carr [inset] completing the famous Granby roll he helped to design.

Chapter 11
Our (Dysfunctional) Wrestling Family

ଔ

> *"I think a dysfunctional family is any family with more than one person in it."*
>
> **Mary Karr**

Was our wrestling team one big happy family? It certainly was not for me, at least at first. Let me explain.

I was extremely egocentric in the '60s. I had liberal leanings, which meant that I felt sorry for the poor and downtrodden, but I was not going to do anything to help them. I was way too concerned about <u>me</u>.

I began to relate to my fellow wrestlers from 50 years ago. I think I'm a better person now. I hope so. Thank God for allowing me to live long enough to (try to) change my ways. So let me say without equivocation: I had no idea how other wrestlers on the team viewed the team as family. I did not think of my team as my family, especially during my freshman year.

However, a wise coach once said only half facetiously, "Winning solves everything!" That's a bit of an overstatement, but it sure helped us to build some unity within our wrestling family as we grew as a program. We got better over the four years I was there; and as we got better, we grew closer as a team, as a family, if you will.

Every team is different and every team's esprit de corps is different. These days, when I watch Spartan Football, I love it when they celebrate a victory by taking a knee and praying or singing and dancing together to music in the locker room. There's something about praying together or celebrating together that I think is really special and helps to create a "family" atmosphere among the team members.

We never did that. I don't remember our doing anything together socially except maybe the banquet at the end of the year. I feel bad about that.

Positive Reinforcement and Spectator Support

One thing about our wrestling "family" that I noticed initially when I first transferred was that none of the parents, relatives, or even friends came to any of the meets. In fact, in 1965, almost <u>nobody</u> came to the meets, not even girlfriends!

I went to a meet my freshman year and there couldn't have been more than a handful of spectators. It was really depressing, as I came from a high school where fans packed the gymnasium to watch us wrestle. Dale Carr mentioned that when he went to his first meet at MSU, he wanted to go back to Granby where the fans were hanging from the rafters of the gym for every meet.

The fact that nobody on campus cared at all about wrestling, and even our friends and relatives lacked interest in attending the meets, initially made us even a bit more remote and dysfunctional as a family than normal, I think.

The spectator part picked up fast my sophomore year when students began to realize that we had a really good <u>aggressive and exciting</u> team that—win or lose—was fun to watch. As I mentioned above, in my first meet I ever wrestled as a sophomore, the relatively small gym where we wrestled was packed to capacity with 1,200 spectators and created a great atmosphere in which to wrestle. But soon, somehow, we were packing 2,000 into that very small gym. During the next two years while I was on campus, the crowds grew to around 5,000 by the end of my senior year; so we had to move to a different, bigger venue.

I think what we experienced about creating spectator interest is true of every campus. If the team is aggressive and does well, crowds develop. Like in *Field of Dreams*—build the program, and the fans will come.

> *I remember when our team became good and we visited the University of Iowa. It probably wouldn't be too great an exaggeration to say that you could hear a pin drop when we wrestled. Almost no one was there to watch. The very small section of spectators was a little like a few marbles in a boxcar as we always wrestled Iowa in a huge field house. That made me very glad I didn't decide to go to Iowa at the time.*
>
> *It's hard to believe today that Iowa drew very small crowds in the '60s but it was true. Iowa didn't always have spectator support for wrestling.*
>
> *The success at Iowa really all began with Gary Kurdelmeier, an Iowa NCAA champion who became an assistant to Dave McCuskey and patiently waited his chance to market the sport of wrestling as head coach. When McCuskey retired, Kurdelmeier hired Gable away from Iowa State, and the rest is history.*
>
> *Gable, of course, built a program where it was not unusual to see 10,000+ fans in the stands on a regular basis. J Robinson, legendary Minnesota coach, said that Gable "became the coach of a team that was terrible and two years later, he turned them into a national championship team."*

It seems obvious that where there is a fan base, wrestling is more fun and tends to build cohesion within the team and a fun relationship to the fans and each other. In 1967, we actually had a substantial crowd of fans that even followed us to Kent State for the NCAA championships.

As the crowds grew at our meets and because of the positive reinforcement, we began to feel good about ourselves and bonded together a bit as a team and as a family.

Friends

Our entire team was not one big family of loving friends in the sense of all of us doing things socially together either. We all probably had a friend on the team, but I would be surprised to hear that any three of us ever engaged in a social event together. Our friendship, if that is the right word, came from being foxhole buddies and sincerely cheering hard for and supporting our teammates during meets and tournaments.

I can't speak for anybody else, but here is my take. Like Spartans of old, we stood side by side against all foes. None of us wanted to stand next to a pansy. That meant we were (and had to be) tough and hard-nosed and sometimes harsh. We also knew that every one of us was going to give everything he had; that is, leave it all out on the mat.

From the start and throughout my career at Michigan State, I kept to myself. I ran almost every day, almost always by myself. I did what the coaches told me to do, especially during practice. For the most part, I kept my mouth shut. I think most people and the coaches would agree with that assessment of me and my role on the wrestling team at Michigan State. I did not lead, and I did not follow.

Mike Bradley, our 177 pounder, called me the "phantom" because I was never around except when I had to be. When others would gather in someone's motel room to watch television after weigh-ins, I would go to my own room or for a walk, often to begin to focus on my opponent and my match.

Maybe others on the team thought of me as not one of the "family." I don't know. I never really tried to fit in or not to fit in. At first I was way too concerned about getting squeezed out, so I definitely felt alienated. During the first year, I felt like the ugly stepchild on the team.

Getting Squeezed Out

Had Grady not taken a chance on me, my career might have ended early my sophomore year. This is especially salient as Grady had already told my high school coach that I was never going to make the team at Michigan State.

Anyway, I don't remember ever conversing with either Behm or Carr in or out of practice during my freshman year or the start of my sophomore year. So I never considered the wrestler in the weight right below me or the wrestler in the weight right above me to be friends my freshman year or sophomore year. And I'm pretty sure that they never considered me to be a friend. I don't think they considered me to be an enemy. In reality, I wasn't worthy of being considered at all. I'm pretty sure that for my first year at Michigan State, Behm and Carr (and most other wrestlers) thought of me as someone they could easily beat on. In wrestling terms, I was a "nobody" really.

Since I was such a terrible wrestler in the wrestling room my freshman year, I might well have never gotten a chance to wrestle in a meet. Many times during my career at Michigan State, Grady said to the student newspaper reporters that I got beat up pretty regularly in the wrestling room, "but put Andy in front of a crowd, and he's a totally different person." He was probably half right. I loved the crowd, and I really liked wrestling in the zone, which I just couldn't seem to replicate in the wrestling room. I don't think I wanted to replicate it there.

Everyone on the team was working hard toward a common goal—to win, but mainly as individuals. Again, we all wanted to win, but mainly <u>for ourselves</u>, not the team. So there was no family/team unity there in that sense, at least from my way of thinking.

I think what made me a good college wrestler in the short run—my freshman and start of my sophomore year at Michigan State—was simply my initial threat of Behm and Carr beating me out and squeezing me out of the lineup. That paranoia probably drove me to greater heights. Also, I am a goal-oriented person in the extreme. I always need a goal. The perfect goal for me at Michigan State was to beat out Behm and Carr. I probably didn't think that way specifically, but it was probably subtly always in the back of my mind. I didn't know it at the time, but I should have known that if I could beat Behm and Carr, winning a national championship would be easy. Grady kind of lit the fire that started all this, but Behm and Carr sometimes poured some gas on the flame.

One thing's for sure. You fight a lot harder when you're fighting for your life—in my case, life as a member of the team.

Once my position on the team was secure relatively early in my sophomore year by beating my opponent from Minnesota, I didn't have concerns about being beaten off the team by Behm, Lowrance, Carr, or anybody else any more. The coaches knew then I was a match/meet wrestler, not a practice wrestler. So my interaction with

Keith Lowrance was one of the great recruits at Michigan State during the '60s.

everyone on the team became more relaxed as now I felt I was a part of the team—sort of part of the family.

And our team began to bond a lot closer as we got better and began to respect how each of our fellow teammates was working so hard to make our team the best that it could be. We were about to be like the Spartans at Thermopylae—fighting against the almost impossible odds of beating the Okies!

Leadership

I would doubt that anybody on the team could pick out a leader on the team. I don't remember our ever having a "leader" on the team my freshman, sophomore, junior, or senior years. We all just sort of did what we were supposed to do and went on our separate ways. No one ever called a team meeting. No one ever had a party where the team was invited. No one did anything to even try to pretend that he was the leader.

I have no idea who was the captain my freshman or sophomore years. I think Behm was captain my junior year, and I was captain my senior year. To the best of my recollection, the coaches chose the captains after the season was over; so captainship, at least the word, was kind of meaningless.

I don't have a strong opinion about this, but I'm not sure that wrestlers need a "team" or a "leader" to win. It is an individual sport. And each individual has to prepare himself to win. A wrestler can't depend on any other wrestler to win a match for him. He has to do that himself. Some people on the team have told me that they liked my aggressive winning style and tried to imitate it. No one told me that in the '60s. I guess to that extent, I was a leader—and I am flattered that they would say that, even if it was 50 years later.

As mentioned, I was named captain of my wrestling team both in high school and college. Maybe I led by working out hard, trying to do what was right, and being aggressive. I virtually never talked to members of the team in order to inspire them, fire them up, or cuss them out. I would be amazed if anybody could name one time I gave a speech, a pep talk, or cussed anybody out.

Thinking back, I remember only one time in high school or college that I yelled at a wrestler on our team in anger and that was my senior year in high school. We had just lost our only meet my senior year at Cresco. After that meet, in frustration I criticized our 138 pounder in the locker room for refusing to get in shape, etc. He wrestled 152 against Cresco because he didn't feel like cutting the weight to wrestle 138, where he belonged. I blamed our loss on him, which may or may not have been fair. We almost came to blows. A few weeks later, he won the state championship at 138. Maybe I had something to do with that? All I remember was that I was really frustrated after the loss and felt that our 138 pounder, the best natural athlete on the team, had really let the team down. (Gable would probably remember that altercation as he was there. Unfortunately, almost all of our old high school team have now passed on. That is what makes our 50-year NCAA championship anniversary so special as everyone on that team is still alive!)

Anyway, if I led at all, I led by example. My personality is such that I don't like to tell other people what to do, and I don't like other people telling me what to do. I think if I had to say who was or were the leaders of our team, I would say it was our coaches. They really did lead in ways that molded us into a championship team.

In summary, Coaches Peninger and Blubaugh (and Siddens) didn't lay out a series of rules to follow. I do not remember _any_ rules. They expected us all to be in shape so that we could wrestle our best in all the meets, and they trusted us to do that.

Here is a brief biography of my teammates, our family of wrestlers on our national championship team:

Dave Campbell (152)

My best friend on the team was Dave Campbell, a 152-pound walk-on (like me), an incredibly bright, ambitious, disciplined, and determined guy both in the classroom and on the mat. He had wrestled in high school in New York. I was attracted to Dave as a friend because he took his school work and his wrestling very seriously.

Dave got along with everybody on the team, but I don't recall he did anything with anybody on the team except me. Dave was gregarious and engaging. He became a resident hall assistant and president of the varsity club, so I can be sure he had a lot of friends outside the wrestling room.

When Dave arrived at Michigan State, he had not had much (good) wrestling coaching or experience. He simply decided that he was going to outwork everybody. And he did. Ironically, when he first arrived at Michigan State, he found the practices very hard and exhausting. He soon learned to adapt and later found them almost as easy as I did.

Dave also had some fear when he went out to wrestle. As he developed, he learned to overcome those fears by thinking positively and aggressively. By his junior year he got good, really good, beating out a two-time Michigan state champion to make the team. He won some really big matches against some very tough opponents, placing second in the Big 10's in 1967 and second in the Midlands. He also beat a guy from Minnesota who pinned an Olympic champion.

When we won the Big Ten tournament in '67, Coach Peninger attributed the win to Dave as he upset several very tough opponents to make it to the finals. Had he not beaten those wrestlers seeded ahead of him, we would not have won the Big Ten Championship in 1967. I was happy for him about that.

If he had not gotten hurt his senior year with a career-ending injury, he would surely have been at least an All American and just may have helped us win another national championship in 1968. He was the perfect example of finally finding the "zone"—and losing his fear of losing.

Since he was my best friend, I always felt bad about his suffering an injury before our run even started our senior year. Dave told me later that his older brother, Dick Campbell, also a wrestler on the Michigan State team, had advised Dave to hang out with me and get to know how to wrestle "right." I was flattered by that comment from Dave. Dave went on to a very successful career as a hospital administrator and is now a consultant living in the Detroit area.

Don Behm (130)

Don was about as good they get. I've already talked a lot about Don. He was the star and the start of our team as he arrived a year before the rest of us really, and he almost never lost. In my opinion, he never should have lost. But he did.

I haven't watched wrestling closely over the years; but when I talk to people who have followed the sport, most agree, even Gable, that at least arguably, Don was the best wrestler who never won an NCAA championship. He simply was very sound in every aspect of wrestling, on his feet and on the mat. I can vouch for that.

Here is what Don said about his wrestling career:

> "My freshman year I was not eligible to compete so I went to open tournaments. I went to Canada, Detroit, and New York City (for the National AAU tournament). In Detroit I wrestled Gray Simons and got beat 6-0. I never felt him coming, and his touch was like Keith Lowrance (when Keith got really good). In New York I lost to Dave Auble 8-1. What an experience….
>
> Then I went to a training camp in the summer at Russ Houk's camp in Pennsylvania. I was one of the youngest there….What a great place for a hungry young wrestler to be.
>
> Then I went to the final Olympic trials at New York. This time I was better prepared. I had trained back in Illinois at Northwestern and then finished up at MSU. I hit the trials and did very well. I beat defending NCAA champion Freddy Powell. Then I had a rematch with Auble. This time was different. I learned my lesson the first time. I caught him for two and then I frustrated him. Finally I avoided him. The final score was 2-2. Then I drew Carmen Molino, Auble's training partner. I drew with him too. So I was undefeated at the trials.

However, when it came to the final trials, they did not take me. It was a big letdown. I came away that summer knowing I was on the right track. Being around all the older wrestlers also taught me how to train. I learned from the best—Kristoff and Douglas. I started to see the big picture on wrestling and knew if I worked hard I might be the best in the world.

It was great to win the team NCAA Championship as a team, but for me it was not a very pleasant experience. I was happy, but inside I was upset. I wanted to be the best, an NCAA Champion. I had trained hard, developed my wrestling techniques, skills, and countless hours of training. Morning runs and late night sweating working out—all to take second? I don't think so.

I was in the finals against Oklahoma Sooner, David McGuire, whom I had beaten earlier in the year. Michigan State had won the title before the finals had even started. Coach Grady Peninger had said to me before my match to just go out and have fun. I've lost two matches by not taking it seriously, by not focusing all my energy on doing my best. The first one was against an up-and-coming Dan Gable and now this one—twice in the same year. They did beat me fair and square, so I can't fault them. Never again did I EVER take an opponent lightly.

My life-long goal, to be a world champion, had not changed. I went right back to training to make a world team. I was very fortunate to wrestle for the Mayor Daley Youth Foundation wrestling team. Based in Chicago, they were the freestyle National Champions. They paid my way to all the Open meets and we were the best club in the USA, winning the tournaments all the time. Three weeks after the Nationals, I tried out for the PAN AM team but took second to Rick Sanders, a future Olympic Silver Medalist.

I never missed a day of training. Even with a heartbreak loss, I would be back at it the very next day. Cutting weight to 125.5 pounds was tough. I had learned a lesson dropping to 123 pounds my junior year. It was simple: run my ass off and don't stop till I made weight—just run, run, and more running. It also had the effect of putting me in great shape. Out of season I would be at 145 pounds. I could diet to about 135 pounds, and the rest was just one pound per mile. So to make 125.5 would be 9 or 10 miles. The key to it was to plan for the running at the end, which I did by running every morning and after every practice—at least 5 or 6 miles every day. That also meant not eating for the last 2 days.

I trained the next year at MSU and had great workout partners. I went to the Olympic Trials at Iowa State and took second again. I picked up my training in preparation for final trials in Alamosa, Colorado. I was working very hard, three times a day, and got in great shape for the high-altitude training.

I did make the Olympic team and headed to Mexico to give it all I had. The weight class was 125.5 and was a difficult cut—four days of flat weight. The competition was tough and I had six 9-minute matches. Against Iran I was losing 8-1 going into the third period. I caught up and was down 9-8 with 30 seconds left. I had a chicken wing on one side and half-nelson on the other. It was tight, and he was going over; no way could he stop it. But the referee did. Said it was illegal and made me stop. The head judge said it was ok and told us to keep wrestling. I thought, "Put the SOB back down." They started us on our feet, and he ran the remaining time. I lost 9-8. My next match was against the 5x World Champion USSR's Ali Alieve. I beat him in a very hard match 5-3.

Don Behm, silver medal winner at the 1968 Olympic Games. Don did not get a chance to wrestle Uetake for the gold medal.

My next opponent should have been Yojiro Uetake from Japan, Oklahoma States 3x NCAA champ and defending Olympic Champion. He had beaten me in the NCAAs semi in 1965 5-3. We didn't wrestle due to the fact I needed to pin my opponents. Uetake takes Gold; I take Silver again, in the only no Gold medal match in Olympic history. (Every Olympic tournament had a gold medal match at every weight, except at 125 in Mexico in 1968.) Ironically the Iranian who beat me took Bronze. I was close but no Gold.

I took a job teaching and coaching at East Lansing High School. It was a great job as I could do the things I liked most—wrestling, teaching, and coaching. The school district gave me time off to travel and tryout for the 1969 World Championships which were held in Mar del Plata, Argentina, in March.

Later that year I went up a weight class and won the US Open and won Outstanding Wrestler 136.5 pounds. In 1970 I went to USWF Open at 136 and won outstanding wrestler again. I liked going 136 and did well. Somehow I always went 125 internationally. The 1970 World

Championships were held in Edmonton, Canada. I took fifth and injured my ankle. This was the lowest I ever placed in a world tournament.

1971 was a very memorable year as the USWF sent a team to the prestigious Tbilisi tournament in Russia. I went at 125 and was the only American winner. The Russians came to Evanston for a dual meet and again I went 125 and won.

Later that year the Pan Am trials were held in Oklahoma. I made the team at 125. I won Pan Am Gold without having a point scored on me. I returned to Annapolis to try out for the world team travelling to Bulgaria. Gable and I were the only ones to make both trips. I won Silver again; Gable won the Gold."

Most wrestlers know that the Tbilisi tournament that Don won was more difficult to win than the Olympics. In conclusion, Don was as inscrutable as Gable. He and Gable were totally devoted to wrestling for their entire lives. But during the '60s, it was a true passion. They couldn't get enough of it.

But there was one thing Don did that I think Gable didn't do. For some reason, Don would think and then double think and triple think sometimes, instead of just wrestling and letting his great skills take over. That was his one wrestling flaw.

Dale Carr (145)

About a year or two ago, Dale said he learned more about me in a five-minute YouTube video than he knew about me in the four years we wrestled together. That sort of makes sense as I don't think we ever engaged in a conversation at Michigan State, at least outside the wrestling room.

We have recently re-acquainted and enjoy discussing wrestling and the "good old days." In fact, I've learned much more about him in the last couple years than I ever knew at Michigan State.

After I was not concerned about Dale's beating me out, I sought to learn some wrestling techniques from him. Dale had the best Granby roll in the country; I was eager to learn it from him (and Lowrance). One of my earliest memories in the Michigan State wrestling room was Carr doing a standing Granby on me! I had never seen anything like that. I think when I saw that, I said to myself, "I gotta have me one of those." (Sort of like what Will Smith said when he first had a chance to fly ET's spacecraft in the movie *Independence Day*.) I executed a lot of Granby's when I was at Michigan State. But I must admit that I was never able to execute a standing Granby well enough to try it in a match.

What I liked best about the Granby roll was that since very few wrestlers had ever seen one, it was easy to catch everybody off guard with it. And it was easy to set up as I always moved first on bottom, getting my legs free. After that, it was easy. The Granby roll was made for me and my style of wrestling.

I sincerely believe Carr could have won a national championship too, but I think he tended to wear down more easily than I. For example, in the semis in 1968, he was soundly beating Dale Bahr from Iowa State, the future national champion that year and future coach at the University of Michigan. As I watched the match, I had no doubt Carr would win, as he had a commanding lead. But Bahr came back and beat Carr. In the next round Bahr pinned his opponent to win a national championship.

Also, since Billy Martin taught that Granby wrestlers shouldn't use their strength but should rely on technique, I think Dale often wasted one of his best assets—his power. Even saying all that, Dale was a crucial cog in our winning machine and was an All-American. He also won two Big Ten Championships.

> *I know that Granby guys will deny this and think it blasphemous, but I think that Coach Martin, in his emphasis on technique alone, kind of short-changed the Granby wrestlers at Michigan State. In my opinion, Lowrance and Carr would have been national champions had they reached beyond their high school coach when they wrestled in college.*
>
> *Carr told me once that he was as strong as or stronger than Karaghouli, my nemesis at Oklahoma. And Carr could beat*

Karaghouli. Carr actually said he didn't mind wrestling Karaghouli, whereas Kharagholi drove me crazy. I found Dale's assertion that he was stronger than Karaghouli to be staggeringly unbelievable—inconceivable until he told me that Martin didn't want his wrestlers to use their strength, only their technique. I worked out with Carr a lot, and I don't remember ever experiencing any great strength, certainly nothing like Karaghouli.

I've already mentioned this, but Karaghouli beat Sager off the team at Oklahoma. Sager was an NCAA champion as a sophomore. Sager slaughtered Carr in the NCAA tournament our sophomore year 17-5. The reason was that Carr tried to wrestle with Sager rather than muscle him as Karaghouli did. Sager finally lost a close match to Davis in the NCAA finals. If Carr had wrestled like Karaghouli, he could have beaten Davis in the NCAA finals, in my opinion, as Davis could not beat Karaghouli, at least in 1966.

Since I now believe Carr, I can think of many matches that Carr could have won if he had used his strength, slowed the matches down, and made his technique and power work for him, in other words, wrestling smart. His strength certainly would have permitted him to slow the matches down and not have to push himself so hard the entire match, just to wear out toward the end.

This is a good idea for all young wrestlers—figure out what your style is and make your opponent wrestle your style.

So many wrestlers at West High School also failed to rise above their high school wrestling techniques and thought processes when they got to college. To be fair, maybe Martin and Siddens were just so good that they spoiled their wrestlers. I lost my spirit for wrestling at Iowa State because Siddens had spoiled me.

George Radman at first refused to listen to Doug because George felt that no one had anything to teach him except Martin. But once he did begin to rely on Doug, I think he became 100% better as a wrestler. Doug really helped him to move to that next level higher. In his junior year George was an average wrestler.

> *In his senior year he was the best wrestler in the country, at any weight.*
>
> *I believe that success at the high school level can sometimes be a detriment to success at the college level. All I know is that Doug helped me immensely after I began to listen to him, especially about different techniques to use in college.*

Dale is retired and lives with his wife in California.

George Radman (167)

George Radman told me in anticipation of writing this book that he had no memory of his time at Michigan State, except that he was very "lonely" (his words). George was a loner like me, so I understand.

Coincidentally, George and I transferred in to Michigan State at the same time and lived together in the same residential bedroom a few blocks from campus. George transferred from the University of Pittsburgh. Since we were both lonely and lived in the same bedroom, one would think we would be best friends. I really don't think we were friends at all. We were both way too neurotic to be friends with anyone. I frankly don't ever remember having a conversation of substance with George. I doubt he would remember one with me either.

The owner of the home, Dale Ball, was a former Spartan wrestler who wrestled in the NCAA finals in 1932. Mrs. Ball was an extremely attractive lady, inside and out. Their son, Jim, now a doctor, was on the wrestling team as a reserve.

Barb, their junior high daughter loved wrestling and wrestlers. And we loved her—she was always happy, friendly, and supportive. I was told that when she saw me get taken down and put on my back at the NCAA finals, she started crying. Since I was down by five points relatively late in the match, she figured that I was going to get beat. When I asked her about it she said, "Of course, you were like family to me. You were always like a big brother." She always thought I would win and that I would <u>do</u> something spectacular to win, so she (and her family) began to call me "Doer." They would yell from the stands, "You can do it, Doer!" Barb would yell the loudest and could be heard by everyone in the gym (except me).

The Balls were always loving, supportive, and helpful. And they always attended the NCAAs and most other wrestling events where the Spartans participated, every year. I really appreciated their support.

Suffice it to say for now, the Balls were a wonderful family; but George and I were much too depressed and neurotic to properly appreciate them or their hospitality or their support, especially when we first moved in. And the Balls were bound by NCAA rules, the same as we were. So they would have violated NCAA rules by helping us in a lot of ways, including financially. I wish now I had been much more responsive to their wonderful hospitality. But then there are a lot of things I would do differently if I had it to do over.

I think George's only friend on the team was Carr. Carr was actually the one who talked George into transferring from Pittsburgh as they were both stars at Granby at the same time. Personality-wise they couldn't have been more different.

One day Carr came to the Ball's home where George and I were living. Carr and Radman got into a fight in our bedroom. Radman outweighed Carr by about 20 pounds, but he had a dislocated finger that was in a splint. Carr bent the finger as hard as he could, ran around the room, and then out of the house.

Apparently, the fight created a big crack in the ceiling in the living room below our bedroom. George says about the incident, "I chased him around the room but didn't catch him. I'm glad—bet he is too."

Even by abnormal standards, George could easily be characterized euphemistically as eccentric. One time he gathered a number of big rocks and put them on my bed stating that they were going to stay there—that that was the place for them. That conduct went way beyond bizarre for me. I'm sure George has long since forgotten that incident, but I haven't.

It was rumored that George could often be seen riding his bike around campus using ropes tied to the handlebars as reins, so he could imagine himself riding a horse. He would often whip the bike, like one would whip a horse, to make it go faster. The bike, which he had bought from Dave Campbell for $5, he named "Lightning."

Carr tells an even more interesting story about George which happened before the purchase of Lightning. Dale loaned George his 15-speed bike one day so that George could ride it to class. After class, George forgot all about the bike and walked back. When George and Dale returned to get the bike, it was gone. According to Dale, George felt bad about losing the bike and wanted to give Dale a comic book to make up for it.

In class it was rumored that George would empty out his backpack/book bag on the floor in order to find pen and paper or whatever. The bag would be filled with almost anything imaginable, many things of which are unmentionable.

When Mother's Day rolled around, George went to the school and allegedly picked flowers out of the president's garden to give to Mrs. Ball.

Some of the things George did that related to wrestling were similarly strange, to say the least.

Everybody on the team had great respect for Blubaugh, except George. The reason was that George worshipped Billy Martin, and George felt that no other coach could teach him anything. George got off on the wrong foot with Blubaugh almost immediately. He made the mistake of telling Doug that he left Pittsburgh because the head coach, Rex Perry, was making him cut his hair. Doug's response was, "Go cut your hair."

> *I thought the above story may be apocryphal until I read a book by John Irving. I mentioned Irving earlier as one of our nation's most famous novelists and wrestlers. He wrote about his haircutting experience when he wrestled at University of Pittsburgh in his memoir, <u>The Imaginary Girlfriend</u>. He said that Perry told him to cut his hair. When Irving forgot to get his hair cut, Irving wrote, "Coach Perry put a surgical basin on my head—it was a bowl, but not a round one—he cut my hair with a pair of snub-nosed shears, of the kind used for removing adhesive tape from injured ankles and knees and shoulders and*

> *wrists and fingers…and whatever else could be taped… All things considered, it wasn't a bad haircut…"*
>
> *So I guess George (and Blubaugh) were telling the truth about the haircut.*

George always had trouble making weight. I will discuss later George's nearly being disqualified at the NCAAs for failure to make weight for the 1967 finals. For now, I will tell you a different story about George and his weight.

Coach Blubaugh saw George get off the scales one day after practice and asked him what his weight was. George responded with a smart aleck answer (as George was always way over weight). Doug lifted George up in the air against the wall by his shirt and read him the riot act. After that, George answered Doug's questions with respect.

Another strange thing that George did was to sit and read during meets. He didn't cheer his fellow teammates on and was rarely seen to congratulate them when they won. He just sat there and read. When it was time to wrestle, he put his book down, took off his warm-up uniform, jumped up and down a couple of times and strolled out on the mat. When he was done wrestling, he sat back down and read.

He apparently reveled in being "different" or eccentric in all things, wrestling and life. This technique, of reading during our meets, must have worked for him as he went undefeated in '67. I had one more win than he did that year. So we were and are, 1 and 2 as far as the best records for a single year in the history of Michigan State wrestling.

After some prodding, I forced George himself to remember some of his experiences at Michigan State. George told me that the only thing he remembered doing at Michigan State for pleasure was to ice skate on the river that ran through the campus, a relatively normal pastime.

After rooming with me for the freshman year, Radman and Carr moved in together. They both loved motorcycles, so they would ride them together. According to George, one cold winter night they "went riding on a frozen-over lake in the moonlight, and you wouldn't believe what fun that was. The lake was covered over with about 6 inches of snow that had adhered to the ice and gave incredible traction."

Carr has a story about their rooming together, "The night before a match, I woke up, went to the fridge, and drank one of George's drinks. I was on weight and George was at least 7 pounds over. A little while later, I woke up again, drank the last one, and went back to bed. I woke up with George's hands around my neck strangling me with tears in his eyes pleading, "Did you have to drink both of them?"

As I mentioned, George worshipped Billy Martin, the legendary coach at Granby High School in Norfolk, Virginia. And so, George did not listen to anyone else when it came to wrestling. Unfortunately, Martin was not around to mentor George. However, George said that Martin explained something rhetorically to him after the 1966 NCAA tournament in Ames, where George got beat by guys he never should have lost to and failed to place.

Here's how George explained it, "Billy Martin was at the nationals when I lost and asked why I was letting my opponents move. As I thought about it, I concluded that I had gotten used to allowing my workout partners to wrestle instead of clamping them down. That was the beginning of a change of attitude—next year I was determined to win….My breakdown worked very well and later became known as the Radman ride. Also, my senior year I started with my underarm stuff, which had the effect of getting my opponents out of their defensive crouches into a more upright stance in the later periods. This made it easy to knee-pull into a double leg without getting their weight working against me."

Watching the national finals in 1967, it was very obvious that George was by far the best wrestler in the tournament. He was able to knee pick and heel pick his opponent, Mike Gallegos of Fresno State, a future national champion, at will, beating him 17-8 in the finals. If you didn't know better, you'd think George was giving a takedown clinic.

After Radman arrived at Michigan State, Doug thought the only way to get him to listen was to beat him up in the wrestling room. So he did. In my opinion, this approach was the main reason George lost badly his junior year at the NCAAs in Ames. When coaches beat up their wrestlers over and over, it causes most wrestlers to lose confidence. I think that's what happened to George (although I think George disagrees).

The next year, Doug began letting George win in the room, and it had an incredibly positive impact on George's wrestling. (By the way, don't tell George that. He still thinks he took Doug down, rode him, escaped from him, and reversed him. In other words, to this day he thinks he beat Doug. No way.)

During George's senior year, George said he called Doug late "one night and asked him to go takedowns. He had an extended offer, and so I took him up on it....He turned on the lights in the wrestling room, and we went takedowns." George said he took Doug down that night. (Yeah sure.) I hope that George doesn't read this part because I would hate for him to discover that Doug was letting him win just to build his confidence back up. Doug told me he did that with lots of wrestlers in the room (including me, except I was smart enough to know what was going on).

George presently is an assistant pastor and contractor in Pennsylvania. When George's old Granby teammate, Dale Carr, went out to Pennsylvania to see George, Dale soon found out that George's wife had no idea who Dale was and had only an inkling that George had ever even been a wrestler! How can that be?

When George was interviewed by *Sports Illustrated* right after George destroyed his opponent in the NCAA finals, George said that he didn't care at all about wrestling and that all he wanted was a farm. So I guess George moved on quickly after the NCAAs his senior year to new goals.

One thing's for sure about George and wrestling. George might give a lot of credit for his winning the NCAAs to Billy Martin, but he would never have been an NCAA champion without Blubaugh teaching him to develop into a great college (not high school) wrestler.

Mike Bradley (177)

Mike Bradley grew up in Ypsilanti, Michigan, a stone's throw from Ann Arbor. So Mike grew up wanting to go to the University of Michigan.

Mike played on the football team. I'm not sure whether Mike had a wrestling or football scholarship. Mike won some incredibly important matches for us, the biggest, in my opinion, the Big Ten Championship match in '66. He was definitely the hero in the Big Ten tournament in 1966 as his win captured the team championship for us. He then went on to win three Big Ten championships.

In 1967 he took second at the nationals. Without his rising above his seed that year as he did, we would not have won the NCAA championship as a team. Besides that, he was our soul man, always playing his portable radio tuned in to nearby Motown!

Mike is retired and lives in Michigan.

Jeff Richardson (HWT)

Jeff Richardson, our heavyweight, won the Big Ten championship his sophomore year and was an All-American. He also went through Oklahoma during the dual meet season in 1967 undefeated, helping us immensely to remain undefeated during that period as a team. Jeff had a number of football players who would help him by working out with him. Among those were Neil Peterson and Bill Dawson.

Jeff was on football scholarship and later went on to play professional football for the Superbowl championship team, the New York Jets with Joe Namath. He was just a great guy, someone impossible not to like. I really liked him, and he was my friend.

In discussing playing two sports in college, Jeff said that going to the Rose Bowl caused him to lose part of the season. "It takes time to get going again and time to get back in shape because you have to be in a different kind of shape to wrestle. In football you go 15 to 20 seconds and get a little rest; while in wrestling it's eight minutes of you on the mat, and it's a lot tougher."

Jack Zindel (191)

Jack Zindel also played an important role on the team. He was the 191 pounder and a local recruit from East Lansing. He also played defense on the national champion football teams.

Although 191 was a certified weight class at the NCAAs, it was not an official weight class throughout the year or even at the Big Tens, so Jack did not wrestle in most meets and tournaments. This was a shame because Jack would have won most or maybe all of his dual meet matches and was another wrestler who made the difference between our winning and losing the NCAA championship in 1967 by taking a third.

He did, however, get to wrestle heavyweight on occasion. And one headline in the local school newspaper read, "Jack the Giant Killer" when he beat an opponent from Indiana, Chuck Wertschnig, who outweighed Jack by more than 100 pounds. But even without that win, Jack had beaten six heavyweights in anticipation of Jeff Richardson's return to the team.

After the match, Coach Blubaugh gave Zindel his highest praise, "Jack's a fighter. He's got lots of guts."

Friendships on the team

Even though we were on the same team, we all went our own way with our own friends. As far as being friends with someone on the team, Don Behm (130) and Dale Carr (145) went their way, Mike Bradley (177) and Jeff Richardson (HWT) went their way (probably with friends on the football team), and Dave Campbell (152) and I went our way (usually to study).

We also had a couple other wrestlers on the team who more or less kept to themselves—Gary Bissell at 115 pounds and Mike McGuilliard at 123 pounds. Both were local as both of their parents worked for Michigan State. So I assume both had friends locally outside the wrestling team. Bissell, another walk-on, won the Big Ten championship in 1969.

I have no idea what the other members of the team were doing, probably studying and trying to make it through school in one piece.

(from left to right) Gary Bissell, Mike McGuilliard and Rod Ott

Anyway, Behm, Carr and I are now friends. We have started to do some things together after 50 years, like attending the Big Ten Conference tournament and attending Spartan football games.

Team Specialties that Helped Diversify our Wrestling Family

Some of the moves I used in high school just didn't work in college. Every college wrestler learns relatively quickly that he is going to have to leave some of his favorite moves behind if he is going to improve and compete at the collegiate level.

> *One thing that I learned about wrestling (and life) is that if a skill is required, there will be many levels of "sophistication" reflected in the people involved in the skill. I thought of it in tennis. I was a pretty good tennis player in high school. Yet there were players my age who could beat me 6-0, 6-0. And then there were players who could beat them 6-0, 6-0. (And probably players who could beat them 6-0, 6-0).*
>
> *In wrestling, there is a huge difference between a good junior high wrestler and a good high school wrestler. There is a huge difference between a great high school wrestler and a great college wrestler. And there is a huge difference between a great college wrestler and a great international wrestler.*

> *I think these levels of expertise and talent are true of every sport and profession. I think the sophistication approach is true of every sport and every profession. Where do you fit in that continuum (whatever your sport or profession)—and how can you rise to a higher level of sophistication and performance?*
>
> *I asked myself that in 1967 and realized that the only way I could rise to the highest level in wrestling was to be in better shape than anyone and out-work everyone I was going to wrestle. Gable has said he did the same thing.*

One part of our family as a team was how well we worked together as it related to the development of various skills and moves we used. One of the best characteristics about our coaches at Michigan State was that they did not try to mold us all around a particular move, approach, or skill. They took the skills we had and developed them.

Doug helped all of us with our technique and was constantly working with us to tweak a move so that it would work better in a match. I executed several moves in the NCAA finals that Doug taught me that my opponent had obviously never seen before.

By far, the best thing about our team at Michigan State was the diversity of moves I was exposed to at very high levels. Everybody on the team had different personalities and everybody had different skill sets that I had not encountered in high school. I benefited from this because I would wrestle one person and learn how to defend against his best move. If I could defend against his best move, I could defend against that move in a match.

> *Most of the time in practice, I really didn't care if I was out-maneuvered or beaten. I would often work on a move over and over even though it would cause me to "lose" to my practice opponent.*
>
> *Our team attracted some great ex-wrestlers, one of whom, an Olympian, took delight in pounding on me after I had already wrestled for a couple hours and he was coming in fresh. He was particularly adept at applying arm bars and cranking them in ways that injured your shoulders if you didn't go over. I always*

> *thought he would have been fun to wrestle in a real match when I was fresh. But that never happened.*
>
> *Against him and almost all others, I tried hard not to put myself in positions where I was going to get hurt as it is easy enough to get hurt wrestling. Why should I take a chance and tear a muscle or hyper-extend a knee or elbow just to try a move in practice? That made no sense to me.*
>
> *I know that what I am saying is a bit blasphemous to most coaches and wrestlers. But I simply could not and did not wrestle in practice the way I wrestled in a meet—no way.*

Dick Cook was a perfect example of a guy to work out with even though he was bigger than I. He was easily beaten on his feet, but God help the opponent who let Cook put the legs on him. I say Cook won a national championship in 1966 with one skill set—legs.

Nobody used legs as well as Cook.

> *Cook allegedly learned to use legs from MSU's Assistant AD who was a former national champion in the '40s, Gale Mikles. It is rumored that Mikles put the legs on the legendary Bill Koll once, and Kohl screamed for mercy. Koll won the match, but I was told he paid mightily for his win. Maybe that is just a story among Spartans, but it is plausible. I would love to know if anyone can either confirm this story or refute it.*
>
> *Leg rides began with Gale Mikles in the '40s. Cook later coached Mark Churella, three-time NCAA champion. So if you want to know where Mark got his great "leg wrestling" skills, rumor has that you have to look back to Dick Cook and Gale Mikles.*

So what did I work on with Cook? You guessed it. If I could keep Cook from getting the legs on me, nobody was going to be able to. A couple other wrestlers on the team had excellent skills with legs, and my only goal when I wrestled them was to keep them from putting the legs on. Nothing else mattered. Once they got the legs on, it was almost impossible for me or anyone to get out of them. So the way to beat a leg man is to not let him get the legs in.

Dick Cook

I never wrestled anybody who was as sound all around as Behm, so I could work a lot of areas with him. One facet was particularly important in a few matches. Behm was left handed. Wrestling a left-handed wrestler is totally different than wrestling a right-handed one. I learned to wrestle "left handed" from Behm.

> *When I worked out with the national champion at 145 in 1967, Don Henderson, of the Air Force Academy, I think I did well relatively quickly. He was left handed and most people whom he competed against were not used to that. So he would beat them quite easily. Not me, at least after a short while.*

I never could really cope with Lowrance when we just shot takedowns, but at least he helped me get better at wrestling guys who were really slick, as nobody that I ever wrestled was as slick as he was. That includes Uetake, so not faint praise.

I learned even from my best friend on the team, Dave Campbell. He developed a counter to a takedown where he grabbed your jaw and turned your head around. He learned it from Blubaugh and got very good with it. The first time he did it to me, I felt like that little girl in the *Exorcist* when her head spun around 360 degrees. I never wanted to feel that again.

My point is that because I wrestled every style of wrestling imaginable in the room, I was always prepared in my matches to battle almost any style.

> *I say <u>almost</u> any style, because the only style I did not confront in the room was one where my opponent was very strong and sound on his feet but never tried to shoot. I hated wrestling that kind of opponent. I ran into that when I wrestled Karaghouli at OU and in both national finals matches against Yatabe. I hated wrestling those guys.*

My junior year, we would prove that a wrestling team doesn't have to love each other to win. And we didn't have to all win with the same move(s). I will say that as we began to get better and to win more meets and tournaments, to work hard in the room, it did feel more like a team, a "family" effort, than an individual effort—at least to me. It became even more so in 1967.

Walk-ons

One thing that I loved about our team in retrospect was that it was loaded with "walk-ons" and "average" wrestlers, some of whom became great. I was (at least technically) a walk-on who had to earn his scholarship. George Radman, the only other national champion on the '67 team was also technically a walk-on. Also included in that list was Dave Campbell, Gary Bissell, and Tom Muir, all of whom became great wrestlers at Michigan State.

More than half of the guys on our national championship team were walk-ons who received no money from the school for wrestling when they first arrived at Michigan State. Only two guys on our '67 team were on (full) wrestling scholarship when they first entered the Michigan State wrestling room—Behm and Carr.

Compared to the great wrestling powers like Oklahoma State, Oklahoma, and even Iowa State, we were like a junior high program against the Denver Broncos. All of the best schools were probably two or three deep in full rides at every weight.

All of the walk-ons in the room exuded energy and enthusiasm. Representative was Tom Muir. He was our Rudy. He was a 145 pounder and probably pound-for-pound the naturally strongest guy in the room (besides Blubaugh). The problem was that he had no technique. I found out later that the reason he had no technique was that he never really wrestled in high school because his school had no real wrestling team or coach even in his senior year in high school.

Tom would shoot for my leg—and once he got a hold of it, he had absolutely no idea what to do next, so he would just hold it. Tom told me that for most of the first year at Michigan State, he did not get one takedown on anybody. Blubaugh noticed that Tom was struggling in the room that freshman year, and he told Tom that he wasn't very good and that maybe it would be better to quit. (Blubaugh was always deadly frank and honest.) Tom, like Rudy, said his goal at Michigan State was to wear the green and white just once at a home meet at East Lansing and that he was going to accomplish that goal.

One day Tom was in the locker room crying. The reason was that his father told him he had to quit wrestling. I rarely felt so bad for any wrestler on the team as I did watching him cry because his wrestling career was over in his freshman year. He was so desperate to wrestle. He wanted to wrestle a lot more than I did.

Tom Muir (our "Rudy" at MSU)

The reason his father ordered him to quit was because Tom's dad got a letter from the MSU administration stating that Tom was flunking out of school. The problem was that the Tom Muir who was flunking out was a different Tom Muir than Tom Muir the wrestler. Tom Muir the wrestler was pre-med with great grades. Tom cleared up the problem and came back on the team. He later won a Big Ten championship in 1969 defeating the same wrestler I beat in the state championship my senior year in high school. Tom then went on to capture All-American honors, placing fourth at the NCAAs. Later, he became an alternate on the Olympic team.

The year after I graduated, not only did Tom win the Big Ten championship but another walk-on, Gary Bissell, beat highly recruited (probably full ride) wrestlers to win the Big Ten. Had Dave Campbell been healthy, he would have won one as well.

This was the type of inspiration we all created and thrived on in the Spartan wrestling room. Without wrestlers like these, we never would have been a championship team—and not just because they won championships, but because they were willing to show up every day in the wrestling room to improve and be great workout partners for the first team wrestlers.

Tom ultimately put aside his aspirations for medical school and became a successful high school wrestling coach. He enjoyed telling his young wrestlers that he was the one everybody on the team gravitated toward at the end of practice (when they were very tired) as everybody in the room knew they could beat him no matter how tired they were. That might have been true the first year, but not after that.

Tom and I probably hadn't talked in 50 years; but when we reconnected, I had to tell him how much I admired him as he was our "Spartan" Rudy. He told me that the admiration was mutual. Here is what this walk-on Rudy did in college and beyond besides his great improvement on the mat in college.

- 1971 - (President) John Hannah Award (academics, leadership, and athletics)
- 1971 - Varsity Club President
- 1971 - Outstanding Senior Wrestler
- 1971 - Outstanding Senior Member of the MSU Varsity Club
- 1977 - National Freestyle Champion
- 2000 - Inducted into the Michigan Wrestling Hall of Fame
- 2003 - Michigan Wrestling Association - Coach of the Year
- 2005 - Michigan High School Coaches Association - Coach of the Year
- 2009 - Inducted into the National Wrestling Hall of Fame (for lifetime service)
- 2013 - Inducted into the Bay County Hall of Fame

Finally, when I talked to Tom about his story, he said the one really sad thing presently that he really wanted me to include in the book is that if he went out for wrestling these days, he would be cut from the team within minutes because of Title 9. I agreed. The most devastating effect of Title 9 is that walk-ons in wrestling at most schools are more or less a thing of the past. That is very sad because walk-ons were (and should be) the life blood of almost every wrestling program.

My Epiphany

After writing this, I had an epiphany. I realize now that it wasn't the team that was dysfunctional—it was me. It was very hard for me to dig myself out of the hole I dug for myself my freshman year and the paranoia I felt as a result. But I think after I did dig myself out of the hole I had created, we were a team of friends as much as any team of Spartan wrestlers could possibly be.

Chapter 12
Coaches

ଛ

> *"Great coaches love their kids."*
>
> **Dale Anderson**

What makes a great coach?

It goes without saying that a coach must understand the mechanics of the sport of wrestling, such as basic techniques: stand-ups, reversals, pinning combinations, takedowns, and conditioning. Even average coaches know that.

Jud Heathcoat, who recruited and coached Magic Johnson said that a coach must be a teacher. I suppose that is true too. Frankly, I think Magic could have played for Franklin and Marshall and taken the team to a national championship. Any time he had the ball, you knew something good was going to happen. And as the play-maker, Magic always had the ball. I'm sure his coaches "taught" Magic some things along the way, but let's face facts—that kid Magic was just plain gifted. Maybe it took good coaches to bring that out by letting him play point guard instead of forward, etc. I don't know because I don't know basketball. But even I can see when someone is truly gifted in a sport like basketball.

In my opinion, loving to teach is a characteristic of a good coach, not a great coach. Don't get me wrong, great coaches need to be great teachers too, but I think they need to be more than that.

Read almost any book or article on how to coach, and you will usually see a set of characteristics, most of them as sterile as the three you will see below this paragraph. The article was titled *The Top 15*

Characteristics of Excellent Coaches. It was written by William B Cole, MS, MA, who is listed as "a leading authority on peak performance, mental toughness, and coaching." He starts his 15 characteristics with:

1. Exquisite self-awareness.
2. High emotional intelligence.
3. Broad vision with focus on important details.

I'm sure you get the idea; the other twelve character traits are as meaningless as the first three, so I'm not going to waste the paper to recite them. To me, these look like a lot of intellectual, academic mumbo jumbo, written by athletic nerds who never competed or coached at the highest levels in athletics.

I read an article in *USA Today* (March 19, 2014) that stated that wrestlers trust their coaches more than any other athletes in any other sport trust their coaches. Now that's something I agree with and identify with. The USA Today article reflected the results of a survey conducted among college athletes in all sports. The lowest level of trust for their coaches was experienced by basketball players.

That certainly doesn't appear to be true at Michigan State where Tom Izzo's athletes seem to have bought in totally to Izzo's program and philosophy and seem to trust everything their coach says. And Izzo's players seem to take his philosophy into the pros where Draymond Green is one of the best players in the league. Was Draymond a 3-star athlete coming out of high school? Who cares now? He is a perfect example of a basketball player trusting his coach and profiting from that trust.

Michigan State football coach Mark Dantonio said about his recruits that trust was one of the most important ingredients implicit in the recruiting process—and during all four years of competition.

Anyway, I thought the article reflected an interesting study and result. It wouldn't surprise me if the results about wrestlers at least were accurate. Being in a very hot workout room with your coach every day can begin to resemble a "foxhole" in Vietnam or Afghanistan. Your coach is your foxhole buddy, and you are trusting him with a lot when you go out for wrestling, as wrestlers have to sacrifice a lot just to be wrestlers.

As an illustration, I trusted that when Coach Siddens told me I was going to be a national champion, that I would indeed be a national champion. I didn't laugh at those words; I treasured those words. I trusted that when Doug Blubaugh said that a wrestler in good shape doesn't need much sleep that I didn't need much sleep. He quoted Patton who marched his men for three days and then made them fight the Nazis. It was probably apocryphal, but I needed that advice from him because, as you will read, I didn't get much sleep at the NCAAs in '67. Maybe most importantly, a wrestler has to trust that his coaches are running practices that will bring out the best in them. I truly believed that.

The bond has to be close as you are going through a lot of cutting weight and pain and winning and losing together. I have to assume that it's perhaps like Navy seal training. It's voluntary, it's painful, it is good for you, and you know deep down, your "leader" is doing what he is doing to make you better, to make you a winner.

I participated in lots of other sports, and I simply can't imagine having that close a relationship with coaches in other sports.

I have always thought there is one way a wrestling coach can be sure he was or is "great" whether or not the coach has a great record. Do his former wrestlers call or contact him after they are gone? Do they make a special effort to see him when they are back in town? If you are a retired coach, maybe think about this: Do your wrestlers want to stay in communication with you after they leave town and/or the sport? For coaches who are not yet retired, will your wrestlers keep in contact with you after you're retired? Think about it.

Finally, if you had a great or even a good coach, have you ever contacted him and told him what an important, positive impact he had on your life? Do it. You would be amazed at what it will mean to him and you.

This is just MY criteria for greatness. I really don't measure greatness just in championships but in the way a wrestler "loves" his coach—and the coach loves him and makes him a better person. Without waxing too philosophical, I would like to devote the rest of this chapter to coaches, mostly to those whom I consider to be great wrestling coaches.

Love, Caring, and Respect

I've already used the word "love" at least 30 times in this book. I bet no one reading this far even noticed that. Everybody knows, I think, that there are lots of different kinds of love. Most people probably associate it with romantic attitudes or sex or possibly the love within a family.

Christians have a different idea of what love is. God loves, and Christians are supposed to love God and even their enemies. Think about that for a second. What does love mean in that context? Frankly, I don't know. I have asked lots of people; they didn't know. Even if I knew, how could I do that?

So the word has many connotations, most of which I have no clue. The old Greek language, I heard and read, had six different words for love—and six different kinds of love.

Kids in my day would often say they loved wrestling. What did that mean? Everybody reading this knows. I never heard a kid say he loved his coach—even if he did. I certainly never said that. Coach Siddens was at a banquet once, and one of my female classmates told Siddens that I "adored" him. Mr. Siddens told me that later. Maybe those words are easier for females to say. I certainly would never say that and am mildly embarrassed to even write about that incident.

Every book, article, or lecture I have ever seen or heard that discusses how to be a great wrestling coach does not even begin to mention the word love. Is the word too sissified for a macho sport like wrestling? Back in the '60s I cannot even in my wildest dreams imagine a college coach telling the press or anyone else that he loved his athletes. If anyone reading this book can document that a college coach said this, I would love to see it.

There is a zero chance that my old high school football coach ever said the word love when speaking about his football players (maybe less than a zero chance). Maybe most kids didn't need to hear it from their coaches.

(Frankly, back in the '60s most kids probably never even heard their parents say that word. Maybe it was too "soft" a word even for parents. I can't ever remember my parents saying it. Can you?) If you are old like I am, think back. Did you ever hear a coach in the '60s or '70s say he loved his wrestlers? Do you remember any coach of any sport say he loved his athletes?

Interestingly, now I hear it all the time even from college coaches. I think Coach Kryzewski (Coach K) at Duke started it a few years ago. I saw it on YouTube. It looked like he was embarrassed to say the word, but he did manage to hum and hah and mumble and finally get the word out when he was talking about Christian Laitner. I have no idea why Coach K said he loved him, but I have found no coach who said that four-letter word before Coach K uttered it.

Next, I saw Urban Meyer, the Ohio State football coach, say it over and over with ostensible sincerity that was almost palpable at the press conference right after the Spartans upset the Buckeyes to win the Big Ten championship.

Even most people who know nothing about college basketball and football recognize these names as two of the greatest college coaches in the history of any college sport. Did they just stumble onto the fact that kids who are "loved" play better? Is it that many kids who play high level football or basketball have never heard that word and are more responsive to it?

It may come as a shock that even great coaches in the professional realms are discussing the importance of coaches loving their athletes. No less than Super Bowl winning coach, John Harbaugh, stated recently, "If they are on your team, you're their dad. They deserve your love…Every player should know that you love them and you care about them, even when they act crazy." Is it any wonder his team won the Super Bowl?

Now that it's ok to use the word, you will hear more and more college coaches say the four-letter word. (Maybe female coaches and their athletes will even utter the word "adore" once in a while now, but I doubt it.)

My theory is this. A kid who knows his coach loves him is going to play better and a lot harder than a kid who doesn't know or feel that. That kid is going to give 110 percent in competition—I know I did.

Probably a more appropriate word than love that most readers, wrestlers, and coaches will more easily tolerate or relate to (although not strong enough in my opinion) for the feeling great coaches have for their athletes is the word "caring." The classic line, allegedly created by Theodore Roosevelt is, "People don't care how much you know until they know how much you care." That phrase interpreted for young wrestlers is, "Kids (wrestlers) don't care how much you know until they know how much your care."

I mentioned earlier that presently Michigan State has at least arguably the best athletic program in the country if only the "big two" sports programs (football and basketball) are counted. Michigan State was chosen to be in the play-offs this academic year—one of the top four football teams in the country and at the same time ranked first in basketball. Without question, that is because of the football and basketball coaches, Dantonio and Izzo.

Although I don't know either of them personally, I have incredible respect for both of them and not just for the fact that they coach teams that are so highly rated. More importantly, the way their athletes respond to them reflects love, caring, and trust that appear to go both ways.

That had to start with the coach(es).

Mental Toughness

Besides these coaches loving their athletes, both coaches emphasize "mental toughness," which I think is crucial in football, basketball, and even more in wrestling.

Because Izzo traditionally did not get many, if any, 5-star athletes, he had to make sure his players got more rebounds, which is apparently more a function of mental toughness and coaching than skill. One time, to emphasize the necessity of being tough on the boards, Izzo allegedly made his team wear "pads" and fight like a football team for the ball. That is hard to picture, but I understand it was true.

In one of the biggest football games in Spartan history, playing Iowa for the Big Ten championship in 2015, Dantonio explained right after the game to ESPN why Michigan State won. He simply stated that his players were "mentally tough" during their final drive that ended with a touchdown as the game ended. I don't know how Dantonio builds mental toughness in his athletes, but I'm sure he does it, as his teams simply do not accept defeat easily. Even when they lose to teams loaded with 5-star athletes, they fight to the finish. How do 3-star athletes beat 5-star athletes like those at Ohio State and Michigan? Does it have anything to do with mental toughness? I think it does.

I have heard that many of the members of the Spartan football team were great wrestlers in high school. Maybe that is one answer. I can't imagine a more important characteristic than mental toughness if you are going to be a great athlete, particularly a wrestler.

Robert Siddens

Did my coach, Bob Siddens, love me? Of course he did. Did he say so? Yes. Did he love all his wrestlers? Of course he did (and does), and he has never been afraid to say so. Recently he said in an article, "I had so many great young men who wrestled for me, and they certainly made me look good; I love them all."

Did his wrestlers love, respect, and trust him? Of course they did.

Bob Siddens, West Waterloo High School wrestling coach

Did he care more about his wrestlers as people than he cared about winning? He definitely made us feel like he did. And that was what was probably most important to us. Did he teach us mental toughness? Without a doubt he did.

Many people who know Bob Siddens hold him in such high regard, they would never call him Bob. I thought it very high privilege the day Mr. Siddens told me to call him Bob.

There are too many stories to tell about Bob. I would strongly suggest you read the book *Siddens* by Don Huff and Mike Chapman if you want to know his life story and the impact he had on Iowa wrestling, West High, and on kids like Gable and me. Most importantly for me in that book, at the end there are 25 pages of short letters to Bob upon his retirement, all of them telling Bob what an incredible influence he had on those who wrestled for him. Some of these kids wrestled third string and never had a chance to wrestle in a meet. A lot of us who wrote, including me, didn't even get our letters included in the book because there were so many from which to choose.

One of the characteristics Coach Siddens was famous for were the many stories, homilies, and little witticisms he told us in the wrestling room. Most have been forgotten now but some are as memorable as if they happened yesterday. One thing Bob would do is to say something a little off-color, but particularly innocuous when he was mad—like "darn it!" And then he would add "pardon my French." He did that a lot, and for some of us who had heard words that were much more profane from other coaches (and sometimes our parents and friends) always got a chuckle out of that. Also, Siddens had a habit of saying, "Stop going half 'a'—pardon my French." Everybody knew what "half a" meant. Bob Bowlsby, Big 12 Commissioner, is fond of quoting Coach Siddens on that phrase. But I remember Coach Siddens refusing to say "half ass" a lot in practice too, so apparently the phrase passed through several generations of West High wrestlers.

Many times Siddens would be light-hearted and fun—and he was particularly good at making practice fun. We always had many more kids out for wrestling than could fit in the room. Coach Siddens would not cut kids, so the room got very congested with way too many bodies trying to work out at the same time in the same space. Everyone would bump into the wrestlers next to them during the tussle, sometimes even bang heads. To protect us during these often harsh and painful encounters, Siddens would advise both facetiously and seriously right before we wrestled, "Ok, now watch out for your teeth and testicles," and then he would blow the whistle to start the wrestling. I have heard that warning numerous times since, but I doubt anybody heard it before the early '60s when Bob, I think, made it up.

Bob also liked to tell us not to drive home but to push our cars home and pull up a couple trees on the way.

One of the things Bob talked about in the wrestling room that probably affected me most was his mind-over-matter approach to wrestling and life. "You are not going to give in to pain. You are not tired." "You cannot get sick or hurt during the season. Wait till the season is over."

Siddens would often tell us that we had to develop a higher pain threshold. It was not at all unusual that if we had a sprained or even broken thumb or toe, that we would simply tape it and forget about it till the end of the season.

Most of us believed his words. I certainly did. I never was too sick or hurt to wrestle. Never. There were times, I suppose, when it would have been foolish to wrestle because of injury or illness, but there were many times I did it anyway. And I refused to give in to exhaustion. I'm particularly glad he had that influence on me as I was about to run into some very bad illnesses and injuries in college. And his advice helped me to overcome them with just the mental toughness I learned from Bob in high school.

Virtually everyone who wrestled at West High can recite dozens of quotes and stories from Coach Siddens. Some of them had important impacts that even they don't recognize as they can be very subtle. There are a couple things, outside the wrestling room, he said to me that will always remain with me and had a big influence on my life, particularly in wrestling.

I'm not sure why these two following statements are so burned into my memory. He always had a way of knowing just the right things to say and when to say them.

The first was when I lost early in the district tournament my sophomore year to a wrestler from Cedar Falls, ensuring that I would have no chance to go to state. I was done for the year. I was good enough at that point to win the state championship as a sophomore. I was just not mentally ready. More importantly, I was not nearly hungry enough. In fact, the opposite was the case.

I am embarrassed to say that I was somewhat relieved when I lost as when that happened, I could eat all I wanted! I felt no mental anguish when I lost. If I had qualified for state, I would have had to continue cutting weight for another couple weeks. That was not really on my agenda. Some people might say that was a healthy attitude. Most wrestling coaches and wrestlers would say that I was a wuss and the type of wrestler they wouldn't want on their team.

A few weeks after the tournament, Coach Siddens came up to talk to me when I was reading in study hall in the school library. By this time I was fat and happy. Siddens said that he couldn't sleep thinking about how that Cedar Falls guy rode my ankle so long in the district tournament, knocking me out of the tournament. When he was through talking to me, I was ashamed that he cared about me more than I cared about myself. I was totally ashamed of my attitude. At least that's the way he made me feel. I decided then that no opponent was ever going to ride my ankle again—and that eating was not as important as winning a state championship.

More importantly, it was an epiphany for me. I thought—this guy really loves (cares about) me. The way he talked to me, it wasn't like I let the team down or him down. It was like I let myself down.

The second moment and statement branded in my brain occurred soon after my high school wrestling career was over, my senior year. Bob said to me without equivocation that I was going to be a national champion. He didn't say, "If you work hard, you will be a national champion." And he didn't say I was good enough to be a national champion. He said I would be a national champion as if there was not a shred of doubt about it. And he said it so casually that I was taken aback.

I was shocked to hear him say that as I had no vision about being a national champion. I had never thought about it. But from that moment on, I KNEW I was going to be a national champion. I had a goal, and I was going to achieve it. Apparently Bob told a lot of college coaches that I was going to be a national champion too as a lot of coaches recruited me after that.

In my opinion, Robert Siddens stands head and shoulders above all other coaches, but then I'm biased. Even objectively, however, how many coaches have helped to develop a Dan Gable and all the many other state and national champions that Coach Siddens has? Kids at West High won state championships who wouldn't

Coach Bob Siddens and Dan Gable

even have made the team at other high schools. That's how good he was at motivating kids.

Look at his record—he produced 11 state championship team titles and finished second or third another 10 times, with 14 unbeaten seasons…all in one of the most competitive wrestling states, maybe the most competitive state at the time, in the nation.

> *Presently, Waterloo West is #1 in the country in the creation of NCAA champions. There are around 10,000 active wrestling programs. Although West hasn't had a national champion in about 30 years, we are still #1 in the creation of NCAA champions among active programs.*
>
> *I have been told that a couple of private schools in the country have more high school kids that became national champions than West High. Assuming that is true, since many of their (eventual) NCAA champions were transfers or came to those private schools as "post grads," I don't count them the same as high schools where the wrestlers were all homegrown. I do not lack respect for those coaches and schools; I have heard all good things about them. I just think that comparing West High to Blair Academy is comparing apples to oranges, unless one is counting only the Blair graduates who are homegrown.*

Billy Martin

The only other high school coach who has helped mold as many NCAA champions during our era as Bob Siddens was Billy Martin, the wrestling coach at Granby in Virginia. I was badly outnumbered by Granby kids in the wrestling room at Michigan State. I used to argue all the time with the Granby guys about whose high school coach was better—Siddens or Martin.

The Granby Connection by Dale Carr

"From 1959-1968, eight Granby High School wrestlers left Norfolk, Virginia, to attend Michigan State University, the alma mater of their coach, Billy Martin.

(The eight wrestlers and the year they graduated from Michigan State University: Okla Johnson 1962, George Radman 1967, Dale Carr 1968, Don Cox 1969, Keith Lowrance 1970, Robert Byrum 1970, Mike Ellis 1971, Ricky Radman 1972.)

[from left] Grady Peninger (head coach), Doug Blubaugh (assistant coach), George Radman, Keith Lowrance, Dale Carr, Don Cox

Mr. Martin had attended Michigan State before it entered the Big Ten, won two conference titles, and the nick name 'Wild Willie Martin." After graduation and military service, Billy Martin returned to Norfolk to found Virginia high school wrestling and invent The Granby Roll.

(In possibly one of the most exciting finals matches of all time, Dale Anderson executed three Granby Rolls in his 1967 NCAA championship match with Yatabe.)

His one and only coaching position was at Granby High School where his teams won 22 out of 23 State Team Championships, 114 Individual titles, and a dual meet record of 259-9-4. Six of his wrestlers went on to win 10 NCAA Titles and three-time national champion, Gray Simmons, wrestled on two Olympic Teams.

During the time span 1961-1972 at Michigan State, six of the Granby wrestlers reached the finals of the Big Ten Championship with four winning six titles, and five were NCAA All-Americans. Having eight wrestlers from one high school attending one out-of-state university is unprecedented, but possibly the most impressive tribute to Billy Martin was that all eight graduated with degrees."

One thing about both Siddens and Martin is that all their former wrestlers totally respect/love them and stick up for them. Even though neither has coached for about 40 years (both retired in the '70s), the two would undoubtedly rank at the top of any survey as two of the greatest high school wrestling coaches of all time.

These two great coaches were very similar in many ways. Neither raised their voice in the wrestling room, yet they could always be heard. Either could talk in a normal voice in the wrestling room, and you could hear a pin drop. Both were so popular that their wrestling rooms overflowed with wrestlers wanting to be on their teams. Finally, I have never heard a bad word about Coach Siddens from any former wrestler—always good. And the same goes, I'm sure, for Coach Martin.

However, they were very different in one important respect. In the Siddens wrestling room, the vast majority of the time was spent wrestling. In the Martin room, most of the time was spent drilling. So with Siddens, in my opinion, the most important factor was getting in such great shape that you could wear down anyone and learning moves such that a West High wrestler could execute them in a match.

> *One of my favorite Gable quotes is, "The first period is won by the best technician. The second period is won by the kid in the best shape. The third period is won by the kid with the biggest heart." I think you have to be in great shape to show heart and intensity in the third period. That's what Gable and I prided ourselves on. When my opponent was worn down, it didn't matter that he had better technique than I did, and it didn't matter that he was stronger. I frankly thought that a few of the guys Gable wrestled during his sophomore year in high school might have been slightly better than he in the first two periods—but never the third. I know that lots of my opponents were better than I was in periods one and two—but never in the third.*

Don Huff, West High state champion and longtime assistant for Coach Siddens, had this to say about Siddens and his practice schedule, "A lot of people have asked me through the years what made him such a good coach, and I would tell them he never took a practice plan with him to the wrestling room; he didn't have a warm up. He just told the guys, and they knew that when he came in the room they needed to be warmed up and ready to wrestle."

My summary recollection of Coach Siddens' practices was that the first part of the season was maybe spent more on technique, the last (99 percent) of the season was spent wrestling.

With Martin, it was making sure all of his wrestlers practiced moves so many times that they could execute the moves in their sleep. According to Granby wrestlers, Martin's three favorite words were, "Repetition, repetition, repetition."

They also were willing to even create new moves by experimenting with their technique. I have heard how the wrestlers at Granby, including Dale Carr, invented the Granby roll. In Hammond's "*History of Collegiate Wrestling*" he discusses Billy Martin's influence on wrestling. Almost all of the wrestling world would agree that Martin's greatest single influence on wrestling, technique-wise, was the Granby Roll. But few know that Granby produced more NCAA champions than any other school, except a couple (one of those being West High).

I can't imagine a Granby kid making it through a Siddens' practice. But I also can't imagine a Siddens' kid or even an Iowa kid making it through a Billy Martin practice. According to Hammond, quoting Wayne Martin, Billy Martin's son, about Iowa kids coming out to Martin's farm in Virginia to work out, "Both Brands brothers have been out here. The old Man about killed Tom….By the end of it, they hated drilling," Steve Martin, another son, said, "They kept telling us, 'I don't want to drill anymore.'"

I like to think that the Brands and I had similar mentalities. Let's drill a little—but not too much. Let's wrestle! So it is obvious to any Siddens-Gable-Brands acolyte, that drilling gets boring. It's necessary, but I'd rather wrestle. Virtually every Granby wrestler who ever worked out under Martin believes there is only one way to practice—drill, baby drill.

In the '60s Martin began to offer camps and clinics to high school coaches and wrestlers all over the country in order to share with them the secrets of the famous Granby roll. Coaches from as far away as Oregon would confess that their kids were winning matches, even state championships, with the Granby. And Martin's reputation justifiably spread far and wide.

Even as an Iowan, I had a lot of respect for Martin and would "steal" anything from anybody that would help me—especially Martin's Granby/shoulder roll. I heard that Coach Martin even once gave me a left-handed compliment during a wrestling clinic when he commented that if an Iowan can learn a shoulder (Granby) roll, anybody can.

I worked out a lot with the Granby guys, and I have to admit they were better drillers than I was; their technique was far better than mine. Dale Carr could Granby roll me any time he wanted to, and Keith Lowrance could take me down almost at will—except in the third period. That was when Siddens' workouts began to triumph. I learned a lot from them as they always knew how to do the moves perfectly.

Also, I think I did most of my drilling "live." What I would do is work on moves in practice with my opponent going 100 percent. If I could make the move work then, it would work in a meet. In my way of thinking, if I could only make the move work when my opponent was passive, how would I know if it would work when it mattered? I had to work on it when my opponent was going hard.

I realized how important the Siddens approach was when I heard that most of the guys in the wrestling room thought that Grady's workouts were really tough. I found them relatively easy compared to Siddens' workouts. Anyway, almost everyone who ever wrestled for Siddens loved him and still contacts him often.

During the retirement dinner for Coach Siddens, Gable said that Siddens "ruined" all his wrestlers for ever wrestling in college because he was such a great coach. And that no college coach could ever measure up. That was probably true of me. And I know Granby kids found the transition to college equally difficult for the same reason.

One thing is for sure: Were it not for Siddens and Martin, there is no way Michigan State would have won the national championship in 1967. How fitting then that in 1980, Siddens and Martin were inducted into the National Wrestling Hall of Fame together—the first high school coaches ever to be so honored!

A final irony about Coach Martin and Siddens—Martin wrestled at Michigan State in 1939-1940 and never would have gotten into the hall of fame based on his wrestling ability. Siddens wrestled on some of Iowa Teachers College's (now UNI) greatest teams a decade later, but he never would have been admitted to the Hall of Fame for his wrestling skill in college.

Their honor in being admitted to the National Hall of Fame told the world what we, from West and Granby, already knew. We had the greatest high school coaches—ever.

Grady and Doug

I want to give Grady Peninger and Doug Blubaugh much deserved credit for creating our championship team. Grady and Doug made the best coaching team I ever dreamed of as they compensated perfectly for each other's weaknesses. And what they did well, they did very well.

In retrospect, the thing I appreciated most about them was that they never once threw back in my face the fact that I reneged on the agreement with them when I signed a Big Ten contract to attend Michigan State my senior year in high school. I know that the contract that I signed only applied within the Big Ten, but I went back on my word, and I must admit that I still feel regret about that. I hope I made it up to them. I do believe strongly that had I gone to Michigan State initially, I might never have won a national championship. So maybe all's well that ends well.

Doug and Grady were near perfect for me as college coaches, especially as far as wrestling practices were concerned. After we won the NCAAs in 1967, many coaches around the country wanted to know how Grady ran his practices, so they (other coaches) could copy them. The practices were so unique as to be unable to be copied, especially because of Doug's energy and influence.

We all have good and bad qualities. Nobody is perfect. Grady had some really good qualities and characteristics. He described himself to me one time as follows: "A coach has to be half psychologist and half son of a bitch." I don't think I ever saw Grady as either. I have told many stories in this book where the reader might develop the inference that he was; but when you put the two characteristics together, you can see that a lot of what Grady did was very subtle in getting his wrestlers to meet their potential.

He was a family man, who was smart enough to recruit the best assistant in the country and recruit the best wrestlers in the country. Also, unlike some coaches, he didn't just let his wrestlers roll around on the mat (as was the case at Iowa State), and he didn't micro-manage his wrestlers' lives such that there was a certain time and place that everybody had to run (like Tommy Evans at Oklahoma University), or that all wrestlers had to be able to take 'em down and let 'em up over and over (like Roderick at OSU), or had to eat a certain food, etc., etc.

So Grady wasn't too loose, and he wasn't too tight in managing his athletes. For me at least, he was just right. He treated me like an adult, so I responded like an adult. I think most of the wrestlers on the team felt and did the same.

For me, I really needed to have practices where every minute was regulated. I needed to be working out for at least two hours straight so I could lose weight and stay in shape similar to what I did in high school. I simply did not have the discipline to cut weight without that kind of help.

At Michigan State, Grady had every minute in the wrestling room down to a science. We didn't waste a second of time. I thought he ran a tough practice, not as tough as Coach Siddens, but tough. The part that made the practices as good as West High or maybe even better, was that the competition in the room at Michigan State was obviously so much tougher than high school. I think we all agreed that if we could survive the wrestling room at Michigan State, we had no fear of any opponent we were to face in the meets or tournaments.

Grady thought all great college coaches were, to some extent, half psychologist and half son of a bitch. I think the combination of those two, on occasion, accomplished feats beyond anyone's dreams. To illustrate: First, he told my old high school coach that I would never make the team at Michigan State. That probably was a huge factor in not only making the team, but also winning a national championship. He told Dave Campbell that he was pulling him from the lineup in the meet against Michigan. Dave then upset great opponents and provided the points in the Big Ten tournament in 1967 for us to win. And last but not least, the greatest example of all maybe, Grady told our team in our pre-meet pep talk that the only wrestler on our team who couldn't win was our heavyweight, Jeff Smith. Those words propelled Jeff to the greatest upset win in Michigan State wrestling history in possibly the greatest college meet in our country's history.

So was Grady a great coach in his own right? I think so. Also at Michigan State was Doug Blubaugh.

Doug was incredibly compatible with Grady as he had wrestled for Grady in high school, and they knew each other so well. As Okies, they were very similar in style and personality. Anyone could tell they really liked (can I say loved?) each other.

> *A classic trivia fact about Grady was that he coached two Olympic champions as a high school coach in Ponca City, Oklahoma—Doug Blubaugh and Shelby Wilson were on the same team in high school and college. Both won a gold medal in the 1960 Olympics. Even my Coach Siddens couldn't say that!*

Besides the fact that Doug had a sixth sense about developing moves around the particular wrestler's abilities, he also was always ready to talk, help, or work out. I guess everyone who knew him would say that he was a really nice guy. I considered him a friend.

Doug had a number of fun expressions by which I will always remember him. My favorite one and the one I identified most with went something like this, "No one ever created a workout tough enough for me." I loved that expression, as I felt the same way. Fellow wrestler, Tom Muir, remembered Blubaugh as uttering these corny lines, "If strength was everything, a bull could catch a rabbit," and "That guy was stronger than seven acres of onions."

Grady had his expressions too. My favorite was, "One's scared and the other is glad of it." It so fits so many matches where the two wrestlers dance around on the mat and don't shoot (including, maybe, my match with Gable).

Jack Zindel reminded me of a couple of slightly corny "Gradyisms"—"You have to be fast as a duck on a June bug." And "there are chickens and there are hawks; which are you?" When Grady invited you in for dinner, he'd say something corny to his wife like, "Wanda, put some more water in the soup." It was just his way of making you feel at home, Oklahoma style.

Grady looked forward to his retirement, but was never interested in settling down. He even won a national paddleball tournament after retirement, I think in his 60's or maybe even his 70's. Nobody seems to know. He didn't care for the 'sedentary type' sports and often remarked that he would never play golf until he couldn't do anything else.

A final Gradyism was to be saved for his tombstone. He told me and others that it would read, "I'd rather be here than in Ann Arbor!"

> *Doug was the best wrestler in the world and was declared to be so after pinning Habibi, five-time world's champion, in the 1960 Olympics (see photo below). Mike Chapman, who wrote Blubaugh's biography in his book <u>Legends of the Mat</u> also produced a classic poster depicting Blubaugh pinning Habibi in Rome.*
>
> *But many great wrestlers are not great coaches. The skill of coaching is so different than the skill of wrestling. Doug, like Gable, mastered both the wrestling part and the coaching part.*

Doug was the best coach by far, ever, at working one-on-one with wrestlers. I have seen coaches who take some kind of sadistic pleasure riding a kid for an hour with the poor kid unable to move on the bottom. A (heavyweight) coach did that to me once. He will remain unnamed, but I will say—what a jerk! Why do coaches need to build their egos beating up their young wrestlers?

I told Doug that I didn't need for him to beat me up. I knew he could beat me. I wanted him to help me learn. I asked him to wrestle me this way: If I did the move right while wrestling him, just let me complete it (even though he could easily have stopped or countered it). I said that if I do the move wrong, stop me and teach me how to do the move correctly.

I told him I would never brag about taking Doug Blubaugh down, escaping from Doug Blubaugh, or riding Doug Blubaugh as we (and everybody else) would know that would be a lie. He was more than happy to oblige. He helped me a lot to understand what moves worked best in college—and what moves didn't. Most importantly, he taught me what moves worked best for my style of wrestling. He even taught me some moves I used in the national tournament that were new. I think he might have created them. One of those moves I used in the NCAA finals my junior year. I think it really scared my opponent when I used it on him as it countered his takedown and put him in a cradle.

Everybody in the room knew that Doug could easily beat everybody in the room. So if you beat Doug, he let you beat him. Doug was probably at his best during the mid-'60s. I think he started slowing down in the late '60s, but even then he could beat anybody in the room.

What a great coaching team! To sum it up, Doug helped so much in developing me individually, while Grady ran great practices to assure that we were optimally prepared. Grady was also a great administrator; he always made the trains run on time.

Gable has often talked about the fact that he credits Doug with helping develop his international wrestling skills. I can't imagine anyone better working one-to-one with a wrestler, any wrestler, no matter how good, than Doug Blubaugh.

Those people on the team who gave Doug the credit for winning the championship in '67 have to remember that it was Grady who "stole" Doug away from the University of Michigan.

> *Doug was an assistant coach for Cliff Keen at Michigan. But Grady, drawing on the relationship he had as Doug's old high school coach, asked Doug to come to Michigan State. The big persuader was that MSU President Hannah had a farm, and Doug was going to work it while he coached. With that combination, Doug was in heaven.*
>
> *The coach at Michigan, Cliff Keen, thought that Grady "stole" Doug away, and there began the feud between Grady and Cliff. Ironically, I think Coach Keen should have been thinking—which school was better for Doug?*
>
> *Doug was very happy at Michigan State as he had everything he could want—the ability to work on the farm every day and the ability to work with his old high school coach on the mat every day.*
>
> *On Doug's part, he told me often after he left Michigan State in 1973 that going to Michigan State was the best move of his life and leaving Michigan State was the biggest mistake he ever made. I agree. Up to the time of Doug's departure, Michigan State had won seven straight Big Ten championships. After that, they never won another Big Ten championship. Iowa won almost all of them after that.*

To repeat and in the final analysis, Grady was an excellent administrator/head coach, and Doug was excellent in making sure we were prepared technique-wise in every way to wrestle. As I mentioned, Doug had a sixth sense about what moves we could do best and how to execute them just right. What more could any college wrestler want?

> *Let me speculate about present college coaches. I would say that Tom Brands, University of Iowa coach, is a Gable-style coach—always attack and wear your opponent down type. I would guess that John Smith, OSU coach, is closer to a Billy Martin type, with emphasis more on technique.*
>
> *I see Cael Sanderson, Penn State coach, as sort of a combination of the two. He was quoted as saying, "Unless you continually*

> *work, evolve, and innovate, you'll learn a quick and painful lesson from someone who has."*

I think the greatest compliment in wrestling I was ever given was this. A friend of mine asked Doug Blubaugh, "What was Anderson's best wrestling quality?" Blubaugh immediately responded, "He was smart." I think Blubaugh helped to make me "wrestling" smart, but I loved the fact that Doug would say that about me. I never thought of myself as smart, more as obsessed and berserk.

> *Again, if you are young wrestler, you have to figure out what style fits you best, but it's impossible in this day and age to be a great wrestler without great physical shape and great technique. But given that, what's next?*
>
> *When you graduate from wrestling and into the "real" world, you must try your best to figure out how to be great in whatever job you choose. In order to be great at what you do, you must love it, which means that you must try to revolve your "work" around something you love.*
>
> *Whatever you have chosen as your sport, do you love it? Whatever you have chosen as your job or profession, do you love it? Are you great? Are you good? How do you know?*
>
> *I am hoping that people of every vocation and avocation read my book. In this chapter I tried to explain from my perspective that the most important and greatest job in the world is coaching kids to become men and women.*

I don't think I would have won a national championship without Coaches Siddens, Peninger, and Blubaugh all working together to make me the best wrestler I could be—truly a trifecta of great wrestling coaches.

Chapter 13
Our Magical Championship Year
1966-1967

ଔ

> *"Win with humility. Lose with dignity (but don't lose)."*
>
> **Bob Siddens**

I awoke in January 1967 to another dreary, cold, and cloud-filled day in East Lansing. January would get worse as Mother Nature was about to unleash arguably the greatest blizzard in the history of the world with drifts of six, seven, even eight feet or more. And February would see temperatures rise to 60 degrees only to drop to 23 degrees below zero (that's -23° and probably a wind chill of -40!) only a few days later. Brrrrr! It was another nasty winter in the Midwest. And East Lansing was one of the worst places to be weather-wise.

But for now, all was well. We, the Spartans, had just won the Midlands tournament. And we had out-pointed Iowa State, the number two ranked team in the land!

> *Prior to the 1966-1967 season, I spent the first half of the summer in Estes Park, Colorado, with my girlfriend recovering from my injuries, relaxing, and preparing mentally for the battles that were about to take place. I worked at a resort there and made 14 cents an hour, but I did get free room and board! And I loved just looking at and climbing the beautiful Rocky Mountains.*
>
> *I spent the last half of the summer trimming trees, building houses, and taking a class at Michigan State. I didn't realize it*

> *before I took the job, but trimming trees was a great way to build my forearms and grip.*
>
> *Almost all of my fellow wrestlers spent the summer wrestling in tournaments and camps—but not me. I really needed to get away from wrestling for a while, recover, re-energize, and rebuild my mind and body.*
>
> *When we all got back to campus, nobody really talked about the upcoming season or how well we were going to do. I certainly didn't.*

It felt wonderful to finally be healthy and able to work out hard at every practice. All wrestlers know that they are going to get hurt during the season, so you deal with minor injuries like sprained fingers and toes and back pains, etc., and you try your best to ignore them. But at least I didn't have torn cartilage in my knee, like my freshman year, or a broken bone spur in my arm, like my sophomore year, or a torn up shoulder, like (I would have) my senior year.

During the 1966-1967 season I said, "Bring on those hard workouts—the harder the better. I feel great!" I now took on as my own Blubaugh's greatest quote, "No one ever created a workout too tough for me."

And finally I could wrestle at 137 pounds the entire year. Even though I started the season at around 155 pounds, I belonged at 137. Even during the year, my weight would bounce up to 145 or 150. But with hard workouts it was relatively easy to make 137 every week.

We always started the practices outdoors in the fall. We did a lot of exercises with partners. For example, we would carry a partner around the track or the football field as fast as we could run. We would do wheel barrel races where one person holds a partner's legs up, so the partner has to run with his hands and arms rather than his legs. Since everyone could walk on their hands alone great distances, we would have races and see who could go the furthest and fastest on their hands. My memory tells me that everyone also had to run a six-minute mile before they could go into the wrestling room. So those outdoor practices were very rigorous but fun in getting us ready for the wrestling room.

The regular season started in early December with three easy warmup meets at home, which we won with ease. We beat Air Force 40-0, Northern Iowa 25-5, and Indiana 25-5.

Going Back to Waterloo for Christmas Break

Prior to the heart of the '67 season in late 1966, we all went home for Christmas break. Grady warned and reminded everyone (several times) to be sure to return to campus a couple days before the Midlands Tournament at the end of December in LaGrange, Illinois, located in the West Chicago area.

I asked Grady about the logic of going to Waterloo, Iowa, for the Christmas break, then the day after Christmas, returning four hours to Chicago, passing Chicago by, and driving another four hours to East Lansing, only to turn around two days later and drive the four hours back to Chicago. That made no sense to me at all and seemed to me to be a colossal waste of time and energy. Plus, it forced me to leave family and friends two or three days earlier than necessary. My final argument was that the extra four to five hours driving in a snowstorm might end up getting me killed.

I suggested to him that it made sense for everyone else on the team (who lived east of Lansing) to return early, as Michigan State was more or less on their way to Chicago. Grady told me that the most important reason why I must return early was so that I "could get at least a couple of good workouts before the Midlands." He said it loud and slow so that I could understand him better, the implication being that I was not going to get any "good" workouts in Waterloo at West High.

I responded slowly (but not loudly), "Grady, I've got news for you. The workouts here aren't nearly as tough as my workouts back in the West High wrestling room." And since the room at West would be filled with tough college wrestlers like Gable, et al, I knew it would be easy to find great workout partners just as tough as at MSU. The biggest challenge at West during the Christmas break was finding space on the mats to work out, as mat space, especially during the holidays, was at a premium.

Normally, when Grady ordered me to do something, I did it without question. And since I was now on a full ride, he had some right to order me back early (whereas he didn't my sophomore year). I held my ground on driving all the way back to Michigan State and then driving all the way back to Chicago after a couple of workouts in East Lansing. I don't remember who got in the last word, but I knew I was not coming back to East Lansing again in 1966 before the Midlands—not going to happen.

I think that Grady sensed that I had dug my heels in for one of the few times when he had ordered me to do something I didn't want to do—and was not going to do. I'm sure he thought it would cost me a Midland championship if I didn't get back for an extra workout or two. I do know one other thing for sure: Had I been overweight or out of shape—or lost—at the Midlands, Grady would have been angry and would have read me the riot act. And I would have deserved it.

But I do appreciate that Grady did not do what some coaches would do and threaten my scholarship if I refused to obey him. In fact, he didn't threaten me at all. I think one reason was that I seldom asked for anything from him; another reason was that I was a returning Big Ten champion and All American. So Grady realized that not returning to East Lansing before 1967 was very important to me, and I was not going to let him down at the Midlands.

One thing I really appreciated about Grady was that he never hung my scholarship over my head like the sword of Damocles. A lot of coaches during my time constantly threatened their wrestlers with loss of scholarship in conjunction with every order or request. I think I heard Roderick threatening one of his wrestlers even during a match!

Just before I left for Waterloo, I assured Doug that I was going to be a national champion. Doug, always deadly frank, told me that I didn't "know" such a thing…that winning the NCAAs was also luck and lots of other stuff that no one can control. (Even Doug only won the NCAAs once.) Doug was always the realist, deadly frank and honest—sometimes too honest and candid, at least for me. I liked Siddens' style better when it came to the power of positive thinking.

I kept near and dear to my heart what Coach Siddens said to me in high school, promising me that I would indeed win a national championship, and left for Waterloo. Whatever Doug said about that issue, I simply repressed.

During my time in Waterloo, I think Doug worried about my getting out of shape, eating too much pie and ice cream, and not working out. He wrote informing me that I got great grades for the fall term (as the coaches got our grades before we did), and then as a reminder explaining to me that Gene Davis, returning national champion at 137, would be working out hard through the Christmas break—and that I must be working out hard also if I expected to beat him in January (dual meet) and March (the NCAAs).

A great competitor and a great person, Gene Davis, after winning the NCAA championship in 1966. We never got a chance to wrestle each other. It would have been a great match.

I did work out very hard, and I was right about the difficulty of the workouts. Coach Siddens cracked the whip and created some great two-a-day workouts—much harder than any I experienced at Michigan State.

> *I have only one small regret about those workouts. I wish that Dan and I would have gone one match in the wrestling room with Coach Siddens refereeing, just so that every West High wrestler could have seen, live, what would have happened in the finals of the national championships in 1968 (or '67 had Dan been eligible). We could have given every wrestler in that room a match they never would have forgotten.*
>
> *I'm not saying I would have won. I am saying, without equivocation, it would have been a great match—and fun—as both of us really liked to mix it up, and we loved an opponent who loved to wrestle. The next year, we could have done the same thing. I never even gave it a thought in '66 or '67, and probably Dan didn't either. I frankly don't think we even worked out together at all during the Christmas breaks, but Dan remembers better. I'll trust his memory (and his journal) on that.*

The Midlands

I went into the Midlands tournament feeling fantastic. No injuries, no pain—perfect. All the pains of the last two years, both mental and physical, were gone.

I stormed through my bracket easily and met Norm Parker, former Iowa wrestler, two-time Big Ten Champion and Outstanding Wrestler in the Big Ten tournament in 1964, in the Midlands finals. I beat him 9-0.

As an aside, I must admit that I was surprised at the time to see Gable beat my teammate, Don Behm, in the semis. I think that was the first time I realized that Gable had some kind of mental power to "will" himself to greater heights and victory. At that time Dan was just not as "skilled" as Don, in my opinion. But Dan had a stronger will. In the match, Don took Dan down easily in the first period with a fireman's carry. The rest of the match, more or less, belonged to Dan. Dan won 10-5.

Despite Don's loss, the Spartans won the Midlands Tournament with 92 points. Iowa State got only 79, and the University of Michigan achieved only half our score, 46.

> *If Gable's points would have counted, the score would have been closer. But Dan was just a freshman then, and freshmen were ineligible to contribute team points.*

Going To—and Through—Oklahoma

It was obvious at that moment, still in 1966, that we were a team to be reckoned with that academic year. But were we ready for prime time—the Oklahoma teams? That reckoning came soon as we travelled to, and through, Oklahoma in January.

The first ranking that came out in December figured that Oklahoma State was the number one team in the country with Iowa State number two and Oklahoma number three. Michigan State was ranked sixth.

After mauling the competition at the Midlands, including Iowa State, we were not going to take the Oklahoma schools by surprise. We were no longer under the radar. Prior to our visit to Oklahoma, the University of

Oklahoma won the first "Bedlam" dual meet relatively easily, 18-11 over OSU. OU won six of the first seven matches in the meet.

Wrestling Oklahoma State

The Stillwater newspaper headed its article about our meet with OSU as "*Cowpokes Await Powerful Spartan Challenge.*" After discussing the matchups, the article disclosed that Oklahoma State had <u>NEVER</u> been beaten by a Big Ten team. Never? Wow!

It also said that Myron Roderick, the OSU coach, had never lost a meet to any school except Oklahoma! Wow again! And, of course, the hype was added to by the fact that Grady himself had been a star at Oklahoma State during his college days, finishing second in the NCAA tournament at 121 pounds in 1949.

Another editorial by Otis Wile, a sportswriter, stated that the 1967 team may be Michigan State's best since 1942, a quarter century earlier when the Spartans, with three national champions, finished a close second to Oklahoma State at the NCAAs.

Tryouts for the meet against us were intense. According to another newspaper article, J Robinson, the present coach at University of Minnesota was beaten out for the meet by Jerry Stone. An article commented that Robinson may have been hindered by an ankle injury.

With this great introduction, the wrestling crowd in Stillwater came out of the woodwork to see the meet on January 20, 1967. There were about 6000 fans in the stands, a full house at that time, and virtually all of them rooting against us.

I loved it—great for my adrenalin. I had always been awestruck by Okies, but I was not a bit afraid. That may seem like a contradiction, but I can't imagine any college wrestler in the '50s and '60s not being awestruck by Oklahoma State.

Putting all of that aside, I remembered my old high school coach who said, "Never take a back seat to anyone." I couldn't wait to get on the mat in front of that hostile crowd and against the best wrestlers in the best program in the country. As Rudy said, "I was born for this moment." But I was not remotely ready for what was going to happen to me when my match rolled around.

Our 123 pounder, Gary Bissell, lost to Tommy Green. Behm then beat Herb Jimmerson 14-4. The outcomes of both of those matches were expected. So the meet was tied 3-3 when I went out on the mat to wrestle.

Gene Davis went up two weights, so I did not get a chance to wrestle him. My opponent was Ray Murphy. Ray Murphy was kind of tall for the weight and a bit unorthodox. I didn't know anything about him, and I really didn't care. I wrestled all my matches the same—straight ahead. I threw myself into the match by shooting immediately on the whistle. Maybe it was my nerves, and I was off balance or something. Murphy hit me with a counter that landed me on my back. I have no idea what the move was, and I still don't know what happened.

Probably everybody in the crowd was just as shocked as I since I was a pretty heavy favorite. There was a moment of stunned silence after the takedown; then the entire crowd of spectators went berserk. I must admit that it was momentarily traumatizing for me to hear 6,000 people screaming at the top of their lungs in a relatively small gymnasium. The roar was deafening. I'll never forget the feeling I got from hearing that much noise. I had never experienced anything remotely like that before or after.

I managed to get off my back, get control of the match, and somehow ride Murphy for over five minutes to pull out a 5-4 win for us. I don't remember the match at all—just the explosion from the crowd when Murphy put me on my back to start the match, which I will never forget. As an aside, I think that was the only time in college that I was on my back except in the NCAA finals.

Things went back and forth in the meet so that at the time of the heavyweight match, the meet was tied. Unfortunately, the heavyweights, Richardson and Wilhelm, tied 1-1 too as both escaped and neither could take the other down. So the meet ended anticlimactically tied 14-14. We had so-to-speak "kissed our sister," and OSU remained undefeated by any Big Ten team. But we also remained undefeated by any Oklahoma team, at least in 1967.

> *Woulda, Coulda, Shoulda, and Who's got Soul?*
>
> *As an aside, under the present rules, we would have won as Behm won his match by 10 points, which would have given us an extra team point. But in '67 every point was meaningless after you won by one. Winning 20-1 was the same in team points as winning 2-1. I think it was a good move that the rules committee changed that rule.*
>
> *After Don and I won, Don held his hand out facing up waiting for me to slap it. I grabbed it to shake it as I had never seen anyone slap a hand before. He looked at me solemnly and said, "You ain't got no soul!" Then he laughed. I guess he was right—no soul, at least not the kind he was talking about. Why I would remember that 50 years later, I have no idea.*

Wrestling OU

The next day we were headed to Norman to wrestle OU the night after the OSU meet. We knew OU was a lot better than OSU, so we were pessimistic about our chances in Norman. No school had ever gone through Oklahoma, wrestling both OSU and OU, without a defeat. Never. We were about to try to do it. And we were halfway there. But the second half was going to be a lot harder than the first half.

One good thing though was obvious and very motivating: Oklahoma had already beaten Oklahoma State 18-11. So the winner of our meet with OU was going to be number one in the country in the next ranking. Again, around 6,000 spectators attended the meet.

> *A word about OU wrestling...Apparently Coach Tommy Evans believed in tryouts like no other coach I've ever heard of. I heard that if you were a national champion on the OU team but got beat in a tryout, you sat the match out, even if that might cost OU the meet. The problem with Oklahoma (for us) was that they were loaded with talent, especially at 137 (my weight). We were loaded with walk-ons.*
>
> *I heard further that the amount of your scholarship depended on whether you were on the first, second, or third team. The first team, of course, got a full ride.*

> *Sager, at 137, was a national champion as a sophomore in 1964. He had many tryouts later with (Sam) Al-Karaghouli. Apparently, Sager simply couldn't score against Karaghouli, but then who could? The rumor is that during one tryout Sager got down in referee's position and began to howl like a wolf. This apparently unnerved Karaghouli, and Sager finally won that tryout; but Karaghouli won some too, not only against Sager but also against other talented wrestlers at 137 at OU at the time.*
>
> *I tried to find out what happened at the tryouts at OU in 1967, but no one at OU seemed to know or would tell me. I'm not sure why. It was like some secret to be hidden in the practice room at OU, like the moose club handshake or something. What I know is that those tryouts were probably the difference between our winning or losing the national championship as a team. I'll explain why later.*

I had wrestled Karaghouli my sophomore year, and, as I mentioned earlier, we had tied as I just couldn't get him to wrestle at all. He just stood there in the middle of the mat and "muscled" me, so we tied. Our team was beaten badly as Behm was the only winner. It was hard to conceal my disappointment when I learned I would have to wrestle him again in the dual meet. I would have much preferred Sager or Haxel, as, win or lose, they would have been a lot of fun to wrestle.

Karaghouli was no fun to wrestle. Sam was exactly the type of wrestler I hated to wrestle, one who is very strong and who simply under-hooks or ties up refusing to shoot and refusing to let me shoot; so there was probably almost no action during the first period of the match. There really wasn't much I could do against someone like that, especially if he was very sound on his feet, kept really good position, and was a lot stronger than I.

Somehow I managed to beat Karaghouli this time, as I rode him the entire period gaining riding time points and wearing him down.

Like the night before, going into the heavyweight match, we were tied 12-12. The OU heavyweight, Tony Bennett, decided to try to win his match and the meet by shooting a single leg takedown in the third period with the score tied. Richardson countered and went behind for a 3-1 lead.

Bennett escaped but could not take Richardson down in the final seconds. So Richardson was the hero of this meet, winning 3-2.

We beat Oklahoma 15-12. I guess we just matched up better against Oklahoma than we did against Oklahoma State. But then, had the heavyweight from OSU shot on Richardson, we in all likelihood would have won that meet too, as Jeff was very athletic and hard to take down.

Oklahoma beat OSU in both dual meets and won the Big 8 title in 1967, so our hold on first place was sealed as long as we stayed undefeated.

Grady commented in the *Lansing State Journal*, January 23, 1967, that "We looked so much better Saturday night than Friday. Our reaction time was better and our fight was better. People who say you can't get up for two nights in a row are making excuses for losers."

As to Grady's former point, I think our win was much more the result of match-ups. The latter point is absolutely true. I would never blame a loss on the fact I had to wrestle two nights in a row—or even two hours in a row—or two minutes in a row. Excuses are for losers. I made excuses for my losses, but I am not proud of them.

After beating Oklahoma, the number one team in the country, we were ranked first in the nation on February 8, 1967—the first time Michigan State had ever been ranked number one in wrestling—ever! We had come a long way in less than three short years—from last in the Big Ten to number one in the country!

Wrestling Michigan

But we could not hold onto that ranking for long.

After the Oklahoma trip, we beat Minnesota (17-12), Iowa (24-8), and Illinois (32-3). About a month after the Oklahoma meets, February 25 to be exact, we wrestled Michigan.

Prior to the meet, Grady decided to unilaterally insert George Sinadinos into the lineup even though Dave Campbell beat him in tryouts. George was a two-time Michigan state champion who came to Michigan State on a full ride. His older brother, Jim, was a national champion for the Spartans back in the '70s. Grady thought that because of the matchups, George might be better able to win at 152.

U of M was also undefeated at the time. So the crowd was enormous and spirited for the meet in Ann Arbor—over 6,000 spectators!

I beat my opponent up pretty badly, but could not pin him. Carr won. Unfortunately, the gamble on Sinadinos did not pay off as he and his opponent tied. If George had won the match, we would have won the meet. Besides that, all went as expected up to the 177-pound match, where Mike Bradley, our retuning Big Ten champion, was upset by the U of M wrestler.

We still went into the heavyweight match ahead. If our heavyweight just got beat, but not pinned, Michigan State and Michigan would tie. At the time that was the best we could hope for. Unfortunately, like the year before, Porter pinned Richardson, so we lost 16-14.

Michigan went undefeated that year and Michigan State lost only that one meet.

> *The University of Michigan was never ranked #1 during the 1966-1967 season. Michigan would have been ranked #1 after they beat us, except that no rankings came out until after the Big Ten tournament.*
>
> *Michigan did begin the next season, 1968, ranked #1. That year we got our revenge in the dual and at the Big Ten tournament.*
>
> *Ironically, in the 1968 season, the Spartans were arguably stronger than in 1967, and we never were ranked first in the country. At the NCAAs, instead of everything going right like it did in 1967, everything went wrong. So maybe Doug was right—there's a lot more to winning a national championship than skill.*

The Big Ten Tournament

For the second year in a row, we won the Big Ten tournament at Columbus, Ohio, in early March. In the *Lansing Journal*, Grady later was quoted as saying, "It was not only an outstanding performance, but it was super outstanding. Everyone did a great job."

Grady gave credit to Dave Campbell, our 152 pounder, for our Big Ten win stating, "Dave Campbell was the key to our success. Here was a boy with a losing season, and he came through to take second place in the conference, upsetting two opponents and beating Bob Schneider of Northwestern to make it to the finals. He gave the whole team a winning lift." During the tournament, Campbell scored a fall and two decisions, including a big upset victory to get to the finals.

The University of Michigan still had a chance to win until Dale Car at 145 beat Burt Merical, the U of M wrestler, 13-4 in the finals. I beat an undefeated wrestler from Wisconsin named Mike Gluck in the finals, 3-0 at 137.

> *Gluck later played a huge role in the Spartans winning the NCAA championship, as he went up a weight and beat the #1 seed from Oklahoma State at 145, Jimmy Rogers, in the first round and Merical in the quarterfinals of the NCAA tournament. More on that later as some bizarre things happened between the 137-pound class and the 145-pound class that meant the difference between our winning or losing the team championship in 1967.*

So in summary, the Spartans won five of the nine weight divisions at the Big Ten. Behm (130), Anderson (137), Carr (145), Radman (167), and Bradley (177) all won individual titles. Dave Campbell (152) and Jeff Richardson (Heavyweight) placed second. And Gary Bissell placed third at 123. The only weight in which Michigan State did not place in the top three was the 160-pound class.

Michigan won all the other (four) weight classes. We ended up with 92 points and Michigan with 78. Minnesota placed third with 32 points.

The Big Eight Tournament

For some reason, the Big Eight had eleven weight classes, instead of nine like the Big Ten. The Big Eight added the weight classes of 115 and 191. This was probably a good idea as these weights were also important at the NCAA tournament. Having them at the conference tournament gave those wrestlers a little more experience and a few more matches in preparation.

Oklahoma took first with 79 points and three champions. Iowa State was second with 68 points and one champion. Oklahoma State was third with

66 points and four champions, and Colorado was fourth with three champions.

Probably the most interesting match for me in the championship round was that Gene Davis, Oklahoma State returning national champion, pinned Dickie Haxel at 137 pounds. I heard that the match was very close before the fall. Prior to the Big Eight, Davis wrestled 145 and 152. In fact, prior to the Big Eight tournament, he was ranked first in the country at 145 pounds.

OSU's Jimmy Rogers beat ISU's Willie Hoosman 12-5 in the 145-pound championship match. Willie from East Waterloo was a state champion my senior year and *Des Moines Register* Prep of the Week for that feat. Ironically, OU's David McGuire, future national champion in 1967, took third at 130.

The Eastern Tournament

While the Big Eight had eleven weight classes and the Big Ten had nine, the Eastern Wrestling Tournament decided to include ten weight classes, leaving out the 115-pound class but including the 191-pound class.

Lehigh won the tournament with 85 points; Navy was second with 79; Penn State was third with 71; and Syracuse was fourth with 43.

Caruso at 123 and Peritore at 130 were the champions for Lehigh and would be expected to be the number one seeds at their weights at the NCAAs.

Final Rankings in '67

The final rankings of the year put the Oklahoma Sooners back in first place as OU beat OSU a second time 19-13. Michigan would have been first, but by the time the rankings came out, the Spartans had outlasted the Wolverines in the Big Ten Championships 92-78, and in the process, set a new Big Ten record for points scored. Our win in the Big Ten championships, however, was not enough to give us back the number one ranking.

We did not get respect from the Oklahoma-based *Amateur Wrestling News* as we were mainly just a bunch of walk-ons who would never be able to stand up to the mighty Okies twice, i.e. at the NCAAs. The first time was luck.

So on March 22, 1967, just before the national tournament, Michigan State was ranked number two. Oklahoma, which won the Big Eight Conference championship, was number one. Oklahoma State was number three, Iowa State, which finished second in the Big Eight tournament, was number four. Lehigh was number five, and Michigan was number six.

Any of those six teams could have won the 1967 national championship at Kent State University. All had an equal chance. Obviously, the Oklahoma teams were favored (again) just because they were <u>Oklahoma teams</u>. But it was possible for Iowa State or Michigan to sneak in for the championship. Iowa State had done it two years earlier, and Lehigh, which had earlier in the season beaten Iowa State, had a good shot, as it (Lehigh) was going into the NCAA tournament with more points returning from their 1966 team than any other team.

Chapter 14
The 1967 NCAA Wrestling Tournament

> *"Wrestle like the champion you are."*
>
> **Bob Siddens**

Every time I went out on the mat my senior year in high school, Coach Siddens would shake my hand and say those words. I'll never forget those words, "Wrestle like the champion you are." Did that break my focus, pull me out of my zone? Maybe, but it was worth it. He was telling me subtly that because I was a champion, I was expected to wrestle like one—every time.

I don't know if he said those words to anyone else. I do know he thought of all of his wrestlers as "champions" and has mentioned that often.

Our 1966-1967 team picture.
Front row: Behm, Bissell, Anderson, Lowrance, Campbell, Larson, Hoddy
Second row: Zindel, Ott, Guidiness, Carr, Sinadinos, Alsup, McGuillard
Third row: Coach Peninger, Manager Charles Beatty, Radman, Cox, Johnson, Peterson, Richardson, Schneider, Bradley, Coach Blubaugh

As we prepared for the national tournament, I don't believe any of us on the Michigan State team was thinking about winning the NCAA tournament as a team. In other words, was I thinking—Michigan State can be the first Big Ten team to win an NCAA championship? Absolutely not. Was anybody thinking that? I doubt it.

Sports Illustrated quoted Behm, "We didn't come down here with the idea of winning (the team championship), but we knew we had a chance." And further the article deduces, "Their lack of great expectations may have been the thing that kept the Spartans loose. What pressure the team felt was placed mostly on the shoulders of Behm, who had won his second Big Ten title; Dale Anderson, a two-time champion who was undefeated in 1966; and a 167-pounder named George Radman…"

The article was right about me. But I was too busy worrying about every match I would have to wrestle in order to win a championship myself to worry about the team winning. For some reason, long before the tournament began, I began to "over-focus." It was as if I was constantly going into the zone, exhausting myself as I began to ruminate and obsess about my opponents.

> *Relatively recently, Coach Dantonio, Spartan football coach, talked about an expression he used to keep his team cool and calm until game time, "Keep the lion in the cage." By that, I believe he meant don't let your lion-like spirit get out of the cage too early and burn yourself out. But then as soon as the game starts, let the lion out of the cage, play ferociously (and have fun).*
>
> *For some reason, it was impossible for me to think that way in '67. In '68, by contrast, I was perfectly calm until just before my matches. I definitely had the lion in the cage until I was about to wrestle. What a difference that made—both for my sanity and my endurance. Actually my NCAA experience in 1968 was fun. I learned a lot from my (exhausting) experiences in 1967 and would never make that mistake again. I slept great and ate great—and wrestled great.*

Previously, I could control my focus. I only began to really focus on my next wrestling opponent—and go into a zone—about an hour before my match. But the NCAAs in 1967 were different.

Preview: Who Was Going to Win? Who knows? Lots of Guesses and Prognostications

The tournament itself was shaping up as the biggest by far in history. Many coaches were saying that in the future there would have to be a way to reduce the numbers by requiring wrestlers to qualify.

The local Kent State newspaper had an article titled "Kent's NCAA Mat to Be Best Ever." There were 411 entries from 93 colleges and universities. The home team coach, Joe Begala, the winningest wrestling coach in the country at the time, predicted for the article that although Oklahoma was top ranked, either Michigan State or Michigan would win the tournament that year. That was prescient.

There were five returning NCAA champs, all from different schools. Rick Sanders (115) from Portland State; Mike Caruso (123) from Lehigh; Gene Davis (137) from Oklahoma State; Dave Reinboldt (167) from Ohio State; and Dave Porter (HWT) from Michigan. Only two would repeat in '67.

Myron Roderick, coach at Oklahoma State, predicted that he would have two national champions for sure, Gene Davis (137) and Fred Fozzard (177). He was right about one of them.

Tommy Evans, coach of the Sooners, said that conditioning and aggressive wrestling would win the championship. I totally agreed with that. He also said he ran his wrestlers at 6:45 every morning. They all ran three miles of wind sprints. I totally disagreed with that. Thank God I didn't go to OU. I would not have appreciated getting up at 5:30 to run three miles of wind sprints at 6:45 a.m. In fact, I would have hated that. I probably would have ended up hating wrestling—and maybe Evans. (Evans was a very hard guy to hate, but I might have).

When Grady was interviewed in anticipation of the tournament, he said it would be the "luck of the draw" that decides the champion. I think he was right on that too. We got a great draw, and all the other potential champions got bad draws, at least as it turned out. More on that later.

My Obsession and Exhaustion

I don't know the minds and spirits of my teammates, but going into the tournament, I couldn't sleep. I couldn't eat. I began to feel totally exhausted.

I had never wrestled in a tournament of this magnitude with so much on the line. **I had to win for us to win.** I just didn't know how to handle it. And no one, it seemed, was prepared to help me deal with it. I was especially nervous because I felt I had blown my chance to be a national champion as a sophomore. Now I was concerned about blowing my chance as a junior.

The others on the team during break time or after weigh-ins would watch television, relax, and would get away from wrestling—or more importantly, stop thinking about wrestling. They were smart, and I was dumb.

I was way too obsessed and obsessive to do that. Nobody told me that my approach was going to get me beaten for sure and may end up getting me admitted to the local insane asylum.

The previous year (1966), I think I had been too caught up in making weight to focus on my opponents that much before my matches. So I wasn't nearly as anxious in 1966 as I was in 1967. Besides nobody expected me to beat Uetake as a sophomore, so I really experienced no pressure.

During this period in 1967, I kept one thing in mind that Doug Blubaugh told me. You don't need to sleep if you're in good shape. You'll wrestle just as well with or without sleep. I'm sure he was lying, but thank God, I believed him, as psychologically I really needed to believe that in 1967.

> *Ironically, a little known fact about Doug was that he was narcoleptic. He could actually fall fast asleep during practice, even just leaning against the wall. Narcolepsy is a disorder which causes an irresistible desire to sleep. I suspect that his disorder also caused him to have many bad accidents while driving—and may have been the cause of the motorcycle accident that killed him.*

Obviously, I was getting some sleep but not what I'd consider "good" REM sleep. And not much sleep, I was just too anxious. And I wasn't eating right, so I wasn't getting much fuel either.

I was in great shape. No one in the world (in my opinion) was in better shape; but I was a mess in my head, and now my body was starting to break down from all the stress I was feeling.

The First Day

Usually on the first day there are only a few upsets. And the few that occur are usually mild. In 1967 there was a monstrous upset that virtually closed the door on Oklahoma State's chance to win the national championship. Mike Gluck, whom I wrestled in the 137-pound Big Ten championship, went up to 145 pounds and beat Oklahoma State University's #1 seed, Jim Rogers 7-5.

> *There have been a few other #1 seeds who lost in the first round, but none so important to his team as Rogers to his team in 1967.*
>
> *I find it astounding that there can be several #1 seeds who have lost in the first round of the NCAA when the brackets consist of 64 wrestlers. Theoretically, the #1 seed is wrestling the 64th seed.*
>
> *In basketball there has never been a first seed who has lost in the first round, and in basketball the first seed is playing a sixteenth seed. Given the parity of teams, one would think a first seed would have gotten beat some time.*
>
> *But in wrestling, one would think it could never happen.*

In the second round, Lehigh was dealt a devastating blow to their championship aspirations when OU's unseeded 130 pounder, David McGuire, beat Lehigh's #1 seed, Joe Peritore. This was great for Oklahoma but disastrous for Lehigh.

The Second Day

The quarterfinals then proved to be a debacle for Michigan when Dave Porter, Michigan's returning national champion heavyweight was defeated by Nick Corollo from Adams State 5-4. This was probably the biggest upset of the tournament (or any national tournament) as Corollo couldn't beat Porter once in a thousand times they wrestled. Michigan had one very pleasant upset surprise at 167 when seventh seed Pete Cornell pinned returning national champion Dave Reinbolt from Ohio State. So that should have offset the upset of Porter.

Michigan State went into the semifinals with 26 points and five wrestlers still alive in the undefeated bracket. Oklahoma had four alive and Michigan had three. Michigan, however, was still in the running with 25 points, just one point behind the Spartans. Michigan would have been well ahead in the point count if Porter would have won.

In the semifinals, Oklahoma State lost their #1 seed at 137 pounds when Masaru Yatabe beat Gene Davis in overtime, referee's decision. So OSU was down to only one finalist, Fred Fozzard at 177.

OU got three wrestlers in the finals when McGuire (130), Wayne Wells (152), and Cleo McGlory (160) won their semifinals matches. Oklahoma, however, failed to score even one point in the consolations bracket and thereby lost any chance for a title at that time.

The only finalist for Lehigh was Mike Caruso. Most of the rest of the Lehigh team had been eliminated with only Peritore wrestling back in the consolations to score points.

Michigan State advanced four wrestlers to the finals: Don Behm at 130; Dale Anderson at 137; George Radman at 167, and Mike Bradley at 177. Behm and Radman were heavy favorites to win it all. Bradley and I were (sort of) designated second-placers with little chance to win.

Day Three

In the morning consolation session, Jack Zindel (191) wrestled back for a third place. Richardson at heavyweight lost to Michigan's Porter and ended up fourth. Dale Carr took a sixth and, along with Zindel and Richardson, became an All-American again.

Besides Porter, Michigan had two others who claimed All-American status in the consolation bracket. By the end of the consolation round, OU, OSU, and Lehigh were all decimated.

Gary Ronberg, who was following the Spartan coaches around at the time, began his *Sports Illustrated* article about the "miracle" of the moment as follows:

> "Coaches Grady Peninger and Doug Blubaugh, seeking to convince themselves of the inconceivable, stood beneath the white scoreboard at Kent State University and counted up the points on their fingers, one hoping the other would not suddenly come up with a combination of small disasters that would deprive their Michigan State team of its first National Collegiate wrestling championship....But because it was Saturday—even these two pessimists could find no way to lose."

In his two-page *Sports Illustrated* article, Ronberg discussed the Spartan's rags-to-riches miracle finish focusing mainly on the fact that all of the potential winning teams were somehow reduced to "skeleton" forces even going into the semifinals. Those great wrestlers from the top teams that made it to the semifinals lost in the semis. The only team left standing with four wrestlers (Behm, Anderson, Radman, and Bradley) in the finals was Michigan State.

Oklahoma had two in the finals, Oklahoma State one, Michigan two, Lehigh one, and Iowa State two. We led second place Michigan 68-60, so going into the final round the team championship was a fait accompli. We had won it all before the finals round even started. Now it was up to us to walk away with four individual championships.

Behm

Don was our most likely champion. Behm wrestled Dave McGuire in the finals. McGuire was unseeded as he had taken third in the Big Eight tournament and had an unremarkable season. When they wrestled in the dual meet, Behm beat McGuire with such relative ease that almost no one expected that McGuire would get past the second round of the NCAA tournament, let alone the finals against Behm—let alone beat Behm!

Don said later that McGuire had sort of sticky hands, meaning that McGuire sort of controlled Don's movements both on his feet and on top.

In my opinion, Don simply "over-thought" the match instead of just going out and wrestling to his ability. Don had a tendency to think, then to double and triple think matches, instead of just letting his wrestling instincts take over. In reality, McGuire was nowhere near Don's talent. Don had to more or less beat himself for McGuire to win. And that's what Don did. He beat himself by thinking too much.

> *Let me give you a classic illustration of Don's over-thinking: (Maybe this will help you to not do this.)*
>
> *In 1972, Don wrestled Rick Sanders for a berth on the 1972 Olympic team. Don was a 1968 silver medalist in the Olympics. Don won tournaments around the world (Like Tbilisi) that were even tougher to win than the Olympic tournament.*
>
> *Sanders was a 1969 World Champion and also a silver medalist in the 1968 Olympics (at a lower weight than Behm) and a 1967 NCAA champion (and voted outstanding wrestler in the 1967 NCAA tournament).*
>
> *Don later told me that toward the very end of the regulation match, he and Sanders were tied. Don **thought** that he would just sit back, wait, and win in overtime. With only seconds remaining in regulation, Sanders shot and took Don down to win the match. Don's thinking was what kept Don from winning gold in Munich. Sanders later won a silver medal there.*
>
> *Gable has said many times that the Behm/Sanders match was one of the most exciting matches he ever saw. It was a classic. It just would have been better had Don won. And he would have— <u>if he just wouldn't have been thinking so much</u>!*
>
> *Anyway, for Don it was his last chance to win an Olympic Gold or to win a championship of any magnitude.*
>
> *So my advice—if you are going to think, think <u>attack</u>.*

Don swears that when Grady told him to just go out and have fun, that Grady's words caused him to lose focus. I suppose that is true too. Who knows?

Anderson—(Yatabe and) Me

My match with Yatabe was surreal. As previously mentioned, I had had almost no sleep in three days and very little to eat. I was a mess as I had let anxiety and super-focus get the best of me.

Just before I went out to wrestle, I thought I was going to faint from lack of energy and sleep. I was not nervous or afraid (I don't think), except about fainting or passing out from lack of fuel and sleep. I once again refreshed my memory about what Doug told me—that sleep wasn't that important if you were in shape. I kept telling myself to let my adrenalin take over, get into my zone.

Right before my match, I watched in disbelief as Behm lost to McGuire. That was disappointing and a big downer for me. It brought back memories of the Behm-Fehrs matches the year before. But I was not going to let his loss affect me or get me out of my zone. Frankly, Behm's match against Fehrs taught me never to allow myself to get out the zone just because somebody on our team loses, especially Behm.

My opponent, Masaru Yatabe, from Japan and Portland State, was seeded fourth. I had been seeded second behind Davis. I really knew nothing about Yatabe except that I had been told he was a staller who would wait till the last second of the match to shoot. That's how he beat Davis.

When the match started, I realized that Yatabe was almost impossible to shoot on. No matter what kind of motion I tried to create, he stood solid, unmoving. This was a worse nightmare than wrestling Karaghouli! When I would shoot, he would under-hook me and do nothing. So there was nothing I could do.

I always had a pretty good fireman's carry, so maybe I should have tried that. But it just didn't feel right against Yatabe. I knew, also, if I tried to muscle him or try to take him down while he was under-hooking me, he could easily take me down. I kept trying to find an opening, any weakness. I could find none. He simply would not wrestle. He was a total counter wrestler simply waiting for me to make a mistake or become overly aggressive. The first period ended 0-0.

Yatabe took the down referee's position in the second period. I had always prided myself in my ability to ride anybody. As soon as the whistle blew, Yatabe went into a ball with his head on the mat grabbing my wrist. I liked that as I then put all my weight on him knowing that there was no way he could stand up or do anything when he had 140+ pounds on his back. I have no idea how he did it, but he stood right up on me! He lifted my entire weight beginning with his head on the ground. I had never seen that before. I was shocked (and impressed).

My brain and my instincts were not working as I tried to pull him back as he stood up, and he landed on top of me. I had never in my wrestling career ever pulled an opponent backward when they stood up. It was like I was back in junior high. Even a junior high wrestler would not do something that stupid. I'm embarrassed every time I see it.

We then went out of bounds with Yatabe on top in the flurry. (Score 2-0)

Yatabe rode from the right side, meaning his left hand was around my back and waist, which was a little unusual. But I had had numerous opponents in the practice room ride me from that side before so I felt perfectly comfortable with it.

I sat out, leaned against Yatabe with my butt off the ground, and hit a Granby roll. The first time I hit the move, I did it wrong and didn't get enough impetus, enough thrust. So Yatabe stayed on his knees and kept his position riding me. The second time I hit the Granby with a lot more thrust. Yatabe tried to roll with it, which was a big mistake on his part. All of a sudden I had him on his back.

I would bet that up until this moment, Yatabe had never seen a Granby roll, let alone experienced one by an opponent. Remember, this was the mid-'60s, and the Granby roll was a move almost unknown outside of the east coast, mainly Virginia. Yatabe wrestled for Portland State, a

West Coast team. The reason I believe Yatabe had not seen the move is that Yatabe did the same thing a junior high wrestler would now do when countering the move, which was to try to follow me. The result? He ended up on his back.

So now I had Yatabe on his back, but I think the ref was as surprised as Yatabe. He wasn't really sure what had happened. So he sort of stood there wondering what to do next. He just stood there watching for a moment. Then, as he saw Yatabe struggling helplessly on his back, the ref gave me two points. Finally, he knelt down to see if there were back points. By that time Yatabe had wriggled out and was back on top. Two more points for Yatabe. (Score 4-2)

I hit another Granby. Yatabe wisely decided to just let me go, instead of ending up on his back again. (Score 4-3)

I immediately shot hoping to catch him off guard, but he just sprawled. I kept shooting on him, hoping to tire him and also hoping that the referee would notice that I was not going off the mat a lot, in case it ever came down to my needing a stall call. Also, I always crossed the mat first. Masaru always just stood there on the other side of the circle, waiting for me to come across the circle after him.

Finally, at just about the end of the period, he shot a single leg drop. As a counter, I executed a move Blubaugh taught me. This was a very fun move that college wrestlers had not seen before at the time. I've never seen any other wrestler use it, but they probably have. Yatabe was already in very deep on the single leg, so there was no use to sprawl and whizzer as that would be a sure two points for him. I decided to put all my weight on the foot he had tackled, throw Yatabe's head to the outside, pivot, and put Yatabe into a cradle. It worked to perfection. The only problem was that as I started to put him into the cradle, we went out of bounds.

I think Yatabe had to be a bit concerned as I had already hit him with two moves that I very much doubt he had ever seen before. Already I had shown him that if he tried to ride me, I would put him on his back; and if he tried to take me down, he would end up in a cradle. So that made it even more natural and imperative for him to do nothing on his feet and to just let me go in the third period when I chose the down position.

The second period ended 4-3 in favor of Yatabe.

I was now down in referee's position to start the third period. I immediately hit a Granby, and Yatabe just let me go, learning after the first two times that it was foolish to try to follow or counter when he didn't know what he was doing. It was now 4-4.

I kept shooting on him, wanting him to back up and be sure he was the one who stepped off the mat in case it came down to a stall call. I kept shooting and shooting. One time he actually sprawled so hard that I was almost able to snap him down and spin around him.

On one of my shots toward the end of the period, I got sloppy and did not penetrate at all. That was a big mistake. Yatabe under-hooked me, took a big step into me, and picked my knee—his right hand to my right knee. Off balance, I fell to my butt—two points. There was no place to go but back into referee's position.

Yatabe let me go but then led 6-5. I started to chase him desperately as there were only maybe 30 seconds left in the third and final period. He started to back pedal. I would shoot, he would under-hook me. There was simply no way I was going to be able to take him down.

Finally, I tried to do a Japanese whizzer, which I had never practiced or executed before. It was the only move left given what he was doing with his under-hooks. So I tried to execute Japanese whizzers several times, but each time Yatabe would just push me away and back up. I shot and shot and shot. Every shot was reckless—and had Yatabe decided to take me down instead of backing up, he could have taken me down easily and won the match.

When I shot with about 10 seconds left, he backed off the mat and got a warning for stalling. I then began to half shoot, but he tied up and backed off the mat. The referee gave me a stalling point with about one second left in the match. That tied the match 6-6.

Yatabe's entire body shook in anger and frustration as he knew the momentum was now on my side. I think he knew deep down at that moment that he was going to lose. Little did he know that I was so exhausted and that I could hardly breathe or even move either. But I definitely wasn't going to show Yatabe that.

As we stared at each other from across the circle, I knew I had him for one reason. He bent over looking at the floor with his hands on his knees. I thought he might tip over forward. As I walked past him and to my corner, he stayed in the middle briefly, not moving.

At the end of regulation, I knew I was going to beat Yatabe the moment he leaned over and put his hands on his knees. Notice where my hands are. I knew he had broken. I had pushed him to exhaustion. The last straw on his back was the stalling call with only one or two seconds left in the match.

> *I always knew I was going to win (because my opponent was broken):*
>
> - *when my opponent delayed getting back to the middle of the mat after going out of bounds; or*
> - *when he clasped his hands over his head; or*
> - *when he leaned over and put his hands on his knees for support.*
>
> *When any opponent did any of those things, the match was as good as over for them as that made a tiger out of me. When an opponent did all three I was in heaven. I became even more aggressive.*
>
> *I made sure in this match (and all matches) that I hustled back to the middle of the mat when going off. I made sure I always bounced when I got back to the middle, like I couldn't wait to tie up and wrestle. I was sure that always had a demoralizing impact on my opponents, who were already really tired.*

I was more than sure I was more tired and more exhausted than Yatabe. But I was not going to let him see that. So I refused to sit down after the regulation and before the overtime (as I didn't want to pass out) when I went to my corner. Behm attempted to cool me off by waving a towel over me, and the coaches attempted to counsel me.

I didn't hear a word they were saying. I was focused on one thing—making sure that Yatabe knew he was in for a hellacious overtime period. I jumped around letting Yatabe know I couldn't wait to get back out to the center of the mat to start the overtime.

I was staring at Yatabe and wanted Yatabe to know I had plenty of energy left for the overtime. So I continued to bounce and stare and focus. We had gone eight hard minutes. And I was going on no fuel and no sleep—just adrenalin. And I had almost drained my supply of that too.

Now there were only three minutes left (the overtime matches then were 1-1-1). I was going to leave it all out there on the mat (Remember? "Come back with your shield—or on it!").

I thought back to my practices in high school and how Coach Siddens would tell us that nobody practiced as hard as we did and that we could and would outlast anybody we wrestled. Coach Siddens was right. He was always right. I knew I would win.

Before the referee called us back out on the mat and before Yatabe got there, I rushed out toward the center, bouncing up and down, letting Yatabe know that I was fresh, renewed, and ready for the tie breaker. Yatabe was still in his corner trying to recover. He returned to center of the mat very slowly and deliberately, conserving every ounce of energy he had. He looked very unsteady. If nothing else, he was psyched out. I could tell.

After we crossed the mat and shook hands, I bounced up and down. Yatabe again bent over putting his hands on his knees. I loved it—just exactly what I wanted to see him do. His putting his hands on his knees again increased my energy and adrenalin.

I circled him in the middle of the mat. I'm sure his coach (and probably Rick Sanders, who had just won his second NCAA title for Portland State at 115 pounds) told him during the break not to back up any more or it might cost him a referee's decision. So he stayed in the middle of the mat. When I shot, he under-hooked me, and we went out of bounds.

When we went back to the middle of the mat, Yatabe again put his hands on his knees. Yatabe tried kind of a half shot, almost no penetration. I snapped him down and went behind. I almost got the takedown, but Yatabe quickly stood up before I could get control and hustled out of bounds with me right behind, holding on to him—no points scored. But if it came down to a referee's decision, that one move might be the deciding factor. Again, he returned to the middle slowly and put his hands on his knees.

I then made my second huge mistake of the mat—actually my biggest mistake of the match. I tried a half-"a" (Coach Siddens' word) double leg drop, and we both went to our knees. He kept my head down and with his right hand he tripped the outside of my right leg, sort of a cross arm tilt. I went to my side and then to my butt again. It was virtually the same move he took me down with in regulation, except this time we were on our knees. He was given the takedown for a 2-0 lead. He then held me there at the edge of the mat waiting for the period to end. Finally the referee called us off the mat as we were right on the edge and there was no activity at all. We started again at referee's position with only a few seconds left in the first overtime period.

Since there were only a few seconds left in the period, I knew I had to hurry to score. So I started to try a Granby without his wrist, just sort of a shoulder roll. He just followed me. I then was able to escape as I had then, by virtue of my motion, created a little space between us. Because he tried to stay with me instead of letting me go we were now facing each other on our knees and very close to each other. I snapped him down and went behind him. He stood up and I threw him down just as the period ended.

The referee gave me one for the escape and two for the takedown. (Score 3-2) For some reason, right after that, the escape was taken away, and I was given just two points for a reversal. So it was 2-2 after the first overtime period. (I'm not sure how it could be that I did not get a one point escape, as we were facing each other and he had no control over me at all before I took him down. It seems to me that the ref should have either given me 1 point for just the escape or 3 for the escape and the takedown—not 2, as no way this was a reversal. I think the ref(s) just decided on a compromise.)

In the second overtime period, I could tell he was really tired. He took the down position and tried to do what he did before by carrying my weight and then standing up, but he was just too tired to do it. I locked his leg in between mine, so there was no way he was getting away.

For the rest of the period he hardly moved, so I figured he was saving himself for the third period. Or maybe it was that he was too exhausted now to move. All I did was to slightly advance my position without giving him any chance to escape as I wanted to show the referee and the judges that I was not stalling on top. But I think everyone could tell I was just riding.

As the period ended, I jumped up and bounced like I couldn't wait for the third period to start. Going into the third period then, we were still tied 2-2.

In the third period, I couldn't figure out if I escaped or Yatabe just let me go. If I had to guess, I'd say he let me go, hoping that he would have the entire minute to take me down and win the match. As soon as I escaped, I immediately shot on him, and we went out of bounds. I was now ahead 3-2.

We were both totally exhausted; but when we went back to the middle, I bounced, and he put his hands on his knees. I shot a couple more times. I then started in toward him. Then it hit me that if no more points were scored, I was a national champion!! I was <u>thinking</u>. Thinking had just caused Behm to lose. And now it was going to be my downfall. I tried to remind myself never to think during a match. But the thought of winning a national championship was too powerful.

The most important reason Yatabe could not take advantage of my sudden defenselessness was that Yatabe was a counter wrestler, and in all likelihood he was not going to be able to take me down unless I shot. Suddenly I was too scared to shoot. I was now wrestling not to lose, a terrible feeling.

Instead of being aggressive, I started to celebrate and got scared realizing he could still take me down in the last seconds. A million thoughts were racing through my mind. What should I do? It was the first time in six years that I was <u>thinking</u> during a match—<u>and it scared me to death</u>. What a time to start <u>thinking</u>!

So for the first time in my wrestling life, I went defensive. I didn't shoot again. And with a few seconds left, as tired as he was, he tried to shoot on me. But I was not going to give him a chance. I back-pedaled. I admit it—he was not going to catch me. I knew that even if I got a stall warning, I was going to win.

What really saved me was that he was so tired that when he shot in on a double leg drop as I began to stall, I easily snapped him down and went behind. We went off the mat, but at least I was ultimately the aggressor on his shot, even though on a counter. (Now he was finding out how it felt to have to shoot and be easily countered.)

He shot again and again. I just snapped him down. I saw that there was only a couple of seconds left on the clock, so as we went back to the center, I threw my hands up in triumph.

I would never have remembered the details of the match were it not for the fact that Wide World of Sports captured it all for their show and then sent me a copy. And Rick Smith, a friend from Waterloo, put it on YouTube. The match was not pretty. Actually, it was the opposite of about every match I had ever wrestled, and I am not proud of it. But it was a win. And a win is a win! A national championship is a national championship!

Coach Doug Blubaugh gives me a congratulatory hug after my win.

Right after I won, I was told that I was to be interviewed for Wide World of Sports.

> *Rick Sanders, who won the Outstanding Wrestler award in 1967 with his win at 115 pounds and who was Yatabe's teammate, accosted me as I was walking toward Frank Gifford, the former NFL star who was doing commentary and interviews. Sanders started his rant by explaining to me that I wasn't good enough to even be carrying Yatabe's jock or tying his shoes. He called me a bunch of names that I never heard in (or out of) church and continued to rattle my cage all the way over to Gifford and the interview.*

> *The next year (1968), Sanders got beat by Duane Keller in the finals. So by the time I wrestled Yatabe in my finals match that year, Sanders was probably already dressed and in one of the local bars, as I never saw him after that match. Sanders and I were never going to be best friends.*

George Radman

The next Spartan to wrestle was George Radman at 167 pounds.

During the '67 tournament, Radman was grossly overweight every day. On one occasion, he was within minutes, maybe seconds, of the referees forfeiting him. Apparently there has never been a wrestler who didn't make weight for the NCAA finals. George probably came the closest.

Once George made weight, he was really scary good in 1967.

In the semi-finals, George pinned his opponent Jeff Smith from Oregon State. In the quarterfinals, he beat Don Miller from Wyoming, 10-4; and in the round of 16, he clobbered Rick Martin from Ohio 13-2. Not one of his matches was even close.

When Radman weighed in the morning of the finals, he was way overweight. Nobody knows exactly how much he was overweight, but some have claimed that it was about 10 pounds. He didn't seem to care whether he wrestled in the finals or not.

Sports Illustrated Gary Ronberg wrote it this way, "George Radman [is] acknowledged by Peninger as the 'cleverest wrestler I've ever coached.' The most nerve-wracking too. 'There wasn't one week that George didn't practically drive me out of my mind worrying about his weight,' moaned Peninger.'"

The article continued, "On Thursday, the day the NCAAs began, there was Radman again, a pound over the limit with 35 minutes to go. Peninger, frantic, rushed him into his sweat clothes and then into the steam room, where Radman ran in place and did push-ups...."

What the article left out was that, while in the steam room, Grady reminded George that he, Grady, could still take George's scholarship for the rest of his senior year. Grady must have been desperate as I don't think Grady could cut a scholarship during an athlete's final term. But apparently that was all that Grady could hold over George's head to get him to lose the weight. George didn't seem to care. George was not one who responded well to threats.

> *Knowing that George was always overweight, our coaches should have brought in Billy Martin to talk to George. If Martin would have told George to make weight, George would have immediately obeyed.*

Every day of the tournament George struggled to make weight. On Saturday, the last day to make weight, George made weight at the last minute—not even by an ounce.

George wrestled a Fresno State wrestler named Mike Gallego, a future national champion in 1968. Radman destroyed him 17-8. George just kept taking Mike down over and over with an under-hook and heel pick. It was like Gallego had never seen the move before. One important aspect of Radman's heel pick was that he was so strong that when he under-hooked an opponent, he could literally drag the opponent's shoulder down toward his feet. Since George had long arms, he had no trouble reaching the opponent's heel or knee.

So George sailed to an easy national championship. It was like falling off a log for George. What a difference from the year before when George was dominated by wrestlers in his weight division. I think George owes that championship to Doug, who stopped beating him up his senior year and taught him how to win.

Mike Bradley

Mike ran into a buzz saw in the finals when he wrestled Fred Fozzard. Fozzard beat him 8-3. Our team was ecstatic that Bradley made it to the finals as he bettered his seed and ensured that we would win the team championship before we even wrestled the final round.

How the Other Finals Matches Played Out

Here is how the other finals matches played out:

- Rick Sanders, Portland State (115), beat Jim Anderson, Minnesota, 19-2
- Mike Caruso, Lehigh (123), beat Bob Fehrs, Michigan, 7-6
- Don Henderson, Air Force (145), beat Mike Gluck, Wisconsin, 8-1
- Jim Kammen, Michigan (152), upset #1 seed and future Olympic Champion Wayne Wells, Oklahoma, 6-5
- Vic Marcucci, Iowa State (160), beat Cleo McGlory, Oklahoma, 2-1
- Tom Schlendorf, Syracuse (191), defeated Don Buzzard, Iowa State, 5-0
- Curley Culp, Arizona State (heavyweight), pinned Nick Corollo, Adams State

Every match except 115, 145, and heavyweight had at least one competitor from the six teams that had a shot at winning it all.

What Was the Big Picture At the End of the Night?

When the dust had settled on Saturday night, March 25, 1967, our point total was in the 70's; Michigan's was in the 60's; Iowa State was in the 50's and the Oklahoma schools were both in the 40's.

Michigan State finished with 74 points, Michigan 63, and Iowa State 51. Oklahoma was at 48 and OSU had 40. Both had only one national champion. These were the teams that were ranked first all year except for the short period when the Spartans took over the number one spot.

And now we had almost doubled their scores. We had finally broken the stranglehold of the Oklahoma schools on the national championship. In fact, in 1967 neither Oklahoma School was even close to winning the championship. This might well have been the biggest beat down of the Oklahoma schools in NCAA history at the time.

Ironically, Michigan's finishing second completed the coincidence of the alignment of the stars. There had previously never been a national wrestling tournament where neither an Oklahoma team nor an Iowa team finished either first or second. In other words, every year since the inception of the NCAA wrestling tournament, an Oklahoma or an Iowa team had finished first or second every year. They had usually finished first <u>and</u> second. But not this year! So 1967 was a watershed year in that regard too!

There are many ways to explain the miracle finish of 1967, but there aren't many that leave out the word miracle. *Sports Illustrated* explained that by the "third and final day the three Big Eight powers had been reduced to skeleton teams" and Lehigh "had lost 10 of its 11 men;" "Michigan had grown used to losing close ones." "The Spartans entered the finals with a 68-60 lead over Michigan. It held up…"

Here is my more explicit and specific explanation, discussing briefly why each of the five teams did not win and why we, Michigan State, did win.

Why Oklahoma University Didn't Win It

Going into the tournament, Oklahoma beat Oklahoma State both times they wrestled in '67 and won the Big Eight tournament. They were undefeated except for their loss to us. After we lost to Michigan in the dual meet and then beat Michigan in the Big Ten tournament, Oklahoma was again back in the driver's seat as the number one team in the country. The logic of how Oklahoma could be number one when we beat them in the dual meet was probably our tying OSU in the dual meet and losing to Michigan.

The biggest reason why Oklahoma should have won it all, besides the fact that they were rated the best team in the country, was the surprise victories of David McGuire at 130. Oklahoma got an enormous lift from McGuire, who was unseeded when he knocked off the first seed, Joe Peritore (Lehigh), and then second seed, Don Behm (Michigan State), in the finals. That should have been enough to put OU over the top in the tournament and given them the team championship.

But the NCAAs turned out to be a disaster for Oklahoma for several reasons:

First, Bryan Rice at 123 was seeded third. He lost to #6 seed, Gary Burger from Navy, in the quarter finals. This was a disaster point-wise for Oklahoma as Burger was beaten by Fehrs in the semis. Since Burger did not make it to the finals, Rice was ineligible for the consolation points, and his team points were therefore negligible.

Probably the biggest disaster for Oklahoma, however, was Dickie Haxel, who was seeded third at my weight, 137. Haxel would have undoubtedly done better at 145 where he wrestled all year. In the quarter finals he ran into Rick Stuyvesant, who was even more aggressive and smarter than Haxel. I beat Stuyvesant in the semis, which knocked Haxel out of the tournament and unable to garner any consolation team points for Oklahoma. (Stuyvesant was, by far, the <u>most fun</u> match I ever wrestled—as he really wanted to wrestle—no holding back or stalling. He was a worthy opponent, and the match featured lots of action. The match ended 11-7.)

The next biggest loss for Oklahoma was (Sam) Al Kharaghouli. In the first round, Kharaghouli was beaten by the Michigan State's Dale Carr. Kharaghouli's going at 145 and Haxel's going at 137 turned out to be the biggest blunder of the tournament for Oklahoma—and definitely cost them the championship. Had Kharaghouli stayed at 137 and Haxel stayed at 145, Oklahoma might well have won the team title. I suspect that Haxel went down to 137 to avoid Gene Davis from OSU, who pinned him in the Big Eight finals. Ironically, Davis went down to 137 also, so that part of his plan backfired also.

So the biggest reason Oklahoma did not win the NCAA championship in 1967 was probably Dale Carr and Stuyvesant.

Wayne Wells was seeded first at 152. He got beat in the finals by one point. This certainly didn't cost Oklahoma the championship, but did cost them a few team points. Another big disappointment for Oklahoma was Tony Bennett at 197. Bennett, seeded fourth, was beaten in the second round and only garnered first round team points for the Sooners. And at heavyweight, Granville Liggins, placed sixth after being seeded third.

Finally, Oklahoma failed to score any points in the consolations as the Sooners only had one wrestler in the consolation bracket, and he lost. In summary, almost all Oklahoma wrestlers failed to live up to their seeds. (Maybe they were worn out from running sprints at 6:45 in the morning. I know I would have been.)

Why Oklahoma State Didn't Win It

First, since we tied OSU in the dual meet and OSU usually wins the NCAAs, we thought the Cowboys might be our biggest nemesis. They weren't.

The most important reason Oklahoma State didn't win the nationals in 1967 was because #1 seed Jimmy Rogers (145) got beat in the first round by Mike Gluck. It had to be depressing for a team that needed everyone on the team to match, or better, their seeds.

Another reason for their failure to challenge us: OSU had a number of wrestlers who could have wrestled at 152, J Robinson or even Ray Murphy, etc. But no one wrestled at 152 for OSU that year. So OSU did not (could not) score even one point at that weight. The same with heavyweight—why did OSU have no one wrestling heavyweight?

At 160, Jerry Stone, seeded third, finished at sixth. Finally, most of the Okies who were unseeded lost in the first round. 1967 was a disastrous year for the Cowboys.

Why Michigan Didn't Win It

Michigan came closest to winning the team title.

The Wolverines had one unexpected national champion, Jim Kamman, who beat a future NCAA and Olympic champion (Wayne Wells) in the finals. Also, they had a second place finisher at 123 in Bob Fehrs. They had third place finishers in Pete Cornell (167) and Dave Porter (heavyweight). Michigan had a fourth place finisher in Fred Stehman (160).

Fehrs lost the championship to Caruso 7-6, in a match that could have gone either way. Had Fehrs won and had a few other things gone Michigan's way, they might have won it all.

Gluck, who knocked #1 Jimmy Rogers out in the first round, also beat Michigan's Bert Merical in the quarterfinals in overtime 4-4 (2-0). Merical had beaten Gluck several months earlier in the Midlands tournament in Chicago. Had Merical beaten Gluck again and wrestled in the finals, Michigan could have won the national championship. To add insult to injury for Michigan and Merical, when Merical lost to Gluck, he ran into an angry, fired-up Jimmy Rogers in the consolation bracket and lost again 10-4.

Finally, had Michigan won the nationals at heavyweight, where Porter was a huge favorite, and Merical beaten Gluck, the Wolverines would have won the team title.

Grady felt that Porter's losing, and that loss a big factor costing Michigan the national championship, was poetic justice since Porter "deserted" Michigan State so that he could wrestle on a national championship team in Ann Arbor. The irony of it all.

Why Iowa State Didn't Win It

Iowa State ended up third behind MSU and Michigan. Several Cyclones either failed to rise to their seeds and/or didn't get out of the starting gates at all.

Five Cyclones placed. They had a first in Vic Marcucci; a second in Don Buzzard (seeded 1st); a third in Dale Bahr (seeded 2nd); and a fourth in Gary Wallman (seeded 8th). John Hanson placed sixth at 130 pounds. This was enough for third place in the team race, 12 points behind second place Michigan.

Why Lehigh Didn't Win It

Lehigh had beaten Iowa State earlier in the year. Also, Lehigh had the most points returning from the 1966 NCAA tournament. So Lehigh fans felt, justifiably, that Lehigh had as good a chance as any team to win its first championship. Their chances were certainly as good as Michigan State's chances.

The match that appeared to kill Lehigh's chances for a team title was when Joe Peritore at 130 lost to unseeded Dave McGuire from Oklahoma in the second round. Most of us thought that since Peritore was out of the tournament, Lehigh's chance for a national championship was over. But McGuire won the NCAAs at 130, so Peritore was allowed to wrestle back and took third; certainly not as good as first, but also not as disastrous as losing to an unseeded wrestler who gets knocked out the next round.

The worst thing about Peritore's loss (from Michigan State's perspective) was that McGuire's win meant that an OU wrestler had clear sailing to the finals when he "should" have been eliminated in the very early rounds.

Most of the other Lehigh wrestlers were knocked out in the first or second rounds and so none of them placed. The only bright spot for Lehigh was Mike Caruso, who cruised to the finals and then beat Bob Fehrs in a barnburner for the third time in a row.

Why Most Spartan Wrestlers Shouldn't Even Have Been Wrestling for Michigan State in 1967

Virtually all of us who scored points at the NCAAs that year shouldn't even have been wrestling for Michigan State—at all. Most of us who scored points did not start out at Michigan State or were going somewhere else to school when our direction was changed to East Lansing, or, as in Behm's case, Michigan State was not even a second choice school.

Another anomaly—why did we go to Michigan State in 1964 when the Spartans had just finished last in the Big Ten tournament with only one team point in 1964? This is what Dale Carr describes as "the perfect storm." Others say the stars aligned. You can decide.

Don Behm (130) was recruited by and going to Oklahoma State. But somehow the school administrators at OSU lost his records. Behm could not get a hold of Coach Roderick to straighten out the mess, as Roderick was in Europe. Behm contacted Grady, and the rest is history. What a break for Michigan State!

His points for OSU (had he gone to OSU) might have made the difference in their having a perfect season and a national championship! I bet Roderick was kicking himself for letting Don get away.

Dale Anderson (137) enrolled originally at Iowa State and transferred in my freshman year. Had my scholarship been registered by Coach Nichols my winter term in '64, I probably would have stayed at Iowa State and might have been able to help them win the NCAA championship in both '66 and '67. Although I have lived in almost every state in the country, I consider myself an Iowan—and I'll always be an

Iowan. Even given the "mistake" by Nichols, perhaps had I been more mature, I would have just stayed at Iowa State and lived in Iowa the rest of my life.

I think another reason I transferred to Michigan State was because I did sign an agreement with Michigan State (a Big Ten agreement), and I regretted that I had let Grady down by reneging on my agreement and enrolling at ISU.

Dale Carr (145) signed a Big Ten letter of intent to Michigan State, but then decided to attend Lock Haven, where his wrestling hero, Gray Simons, was coaching. Dale changed his mind to go back to Michigan State after his mother shamed him, saying that when you commit, you don't back out. (I wish my mother had done that! She always thought it was better if I made my own mistakes—and got to learn from them.)

Dale's points scored were the difference between winning and losing the national championship; plus his victory over Karaghouli was crucial in keeping OU from winning.

George Radman (167) enrolled originally at Pittsburgh because a wrestler named Harrison, from Granby, had just won the national championship at George's weight class. He transferred in to Michigan State as a sophomore because the head coach at Pittsburgh told George to cut his hair—and George did not like being told what to do.

Without George's points, Michigan State, obviously, would not have won the national championship.

Mike Bradley (177) had always wanted to go to the University of Michigan as he lived within a stone's throw of Ann Arbor. Ironically, had Michigan given him a scholarship, Michigan (not Michigan State) would have been national champions as Michigan had no wrestler at 177 in 1967. That was a big mistake for Cliff Keen as he would never have a national championship team—and to this day Michigan has never won the NCAAs.

Jeff Richardson (heavyweight) was going to play football only at Michigan State and not wrestle. Grady apparently didn't even know that Richardson was going to wrestle for us. And he never got a penny for it. Richardson, a New York state champion, just decided to wrestle after football season was over. When he graduated, he was drafted by the New York Jets and played with Joe Namath when the Jets won the Super Bowl.

Had Jeff decided to just play football, we would not have won the NCAA championship.

If <u>any</u> of the six wrestlers above would have stuck with their original plans, Michigan State would not have won the national championship in 1967. Was all this just a coincidence? I don't believe in coincidences; so what was it, a miracle? Who knows?

Why Did We Score So Many Team Points in 1967?

Besides the fact that none of us should have been at Michigan State, how did the stars align for us to win the team championship? Half of our team, remember, were walk-ons. Walk-ons do not beat 5-star athletes—ever. By the last day, all of the walk-ons (except George and me) were eliminated. But all of us, except one, wrestled at our seed or above. That is remarkable in itself!

Let's start with **George Radman**. He was seeded first and won the championship. George was probably about 10 pounds overweight the day of the finals. He came within a hair's breadth of being disqualified for not making weight. In the finals, George destroyed a future national champion, Mike Gallego 17-8. So the closest George came to losing was at the scales. That would have cost us critical points and maybe the championship.

I, **Dale Anderson** was seeded second. I was fortunate that I did not have to meet Yatabe until the finals. Davis, the 1966 NCAA champion, had to wrestle him and Yatabe beat Davis. I was fortunate, also, that Davis might well have been a tougher match than Yatabe for me—but it definitely would have been a lot more fun as we were both the type that liked to wrestle—not stall. Finally, in both my final matches in 1967 (and 1968), Yatabe had pretty good leads. (In 1968 Yatabe was 5 points ahead relatively late in the match.) So there was no reason in either match that I would win as they were both very close matches. Finally, there was no reason that the referee gave a stall point with about a second left in the match, sending the match into overtime—pure serendipity. Had I lost, it would have cost us team points. Finally, I did not have to meet

Kharaghouli at all. A great relief, as he went up a weight, and Carr took care of him in the first round.

Don Behm was seeded second and he finished second.

Dale Carr: It was incredibly fortunate that Haxel was at my weight and Karaghouli was at Carr's. Although Carr was the only wrestler on our team who did not rise to his seed (3rd), he did take out an Okie in the first round and did wrestle back to claim All-American status. Haxel had outlasted Carr in the dual meet—and probably would have done the same in the tournament as Carr had trouble with Haxel's style. Another luck-of-the-draw scenario.

Mike Bradley at 177 was one of the biggest surprises. Seeded third, he beat the #2 seed and made it to the finals. So according to the seeding committee, Bradley should have been in consolations after the semifinals. His win was another big reason we had won the championship before the finals began. Had he not risen to or above his seed, the Spartans probably would not have not finished first.

Jack Zindel at 191 was seeded seventh. He finished third. His points alone counting above his seed could have made the difference between winning and losing the team championship.

Jeff Richardson, our heavyweight, was seeded seventh. He took a fourth and in the process, pinned the heavyweight from Oklahoma, Granville Liggins, adding extra points to the Spartan ledger and making sure the Okies did not add to their point count.

Even our 115-pound entrant, **Gary Bissell**, although unseeded, made a contribution by winning in the first round. Every point mattered and every point counted. Had we not risen to or above our seeds, we would not have won the national championship.

So was it a miracle that we won? Was it providential? Was it natural? Was it serendipity? Your call. One thing is for sure. Our win was a watershed moment in college wrestling history as we were the first Big Ten team to win the NCAA championship.

I am proud that I was a part of that victory. We all fought the good fight. We finished the course. We kept the faith to the end.

Epilogue:
Life's Lessons Learned from Wrestling

ଔ

> *"There are only two ways to live your life. One is as though nothing is a miracle. The other is as though everything is….Don't wait for miracles. Your whole life is a miracle."*
>
> **Albert Einstein**

Characterizing our national championship in 1967 as a "miracle" may be a bit of a stretch, but only a bit. In my opinion, miracles come from God. I personally do not believe that God becomes involved in sporting events. I never once prayed before any athletic event I was ever involved in. I don't criticize anyone who does pray before, during, or after an event. That is just not me.

I would never argue with anyone who believes that God is involved in everything we do, so it is good and right to pray for God's assistance in everything. Again, that's just not me.

One line I love from *Rudy* was when Rudy was ready to beg to get into Notre Dame University so he could play football. He had almost given up hope. He asked a priest if the priest could let him know what God was thinking about all this and how to get God's help. The priest said something like, "In all my years in priesthood, I have learned only two things: there is a God, and I'm not him." I do think that as we get older, we draw closer to God as we consider all his miracles.

I probably didn't pay much attention to God during most of my lifetime. Ironically, although I will never attribute my wins to God's grace, I have witnessed a couple of miracles. The miracles I witnessed put our NCAA championship "miracle" to shame.

I will say this as part of my "miracle" moment in wrestling history. A lot of kids wrestle. Few win a state championship, let alone a national championship. Fewer still win a national championship on a national championship team. And only two of us were national champions on the <u>first</u> Big Ten team to win a national championship. And only one is writing this book as his wrestling autobiography. I am very blessed to be that one. Is that coincidence or a miracle?

So my "Spartan Journey" began inauspiciously among depression and misery January 1965. My Spartan Journey ended March 1967 amid celebration, joy, and the success of winning an individual NCAA championship and standing on the podium as our team accepted the national championship plaque too.

What did I learn from my wrestling journey in general and that championship moment in particular that I can impart—and hopefully not be written off as too preachy, hypocritical, or didactic? Maybe there is something to be learned by my successes (and failures) that I can explain. I'll try.

Here are my 10 lessons, sort of as an epiphany for me as I write this book 50 years after that joyous moment in time. If they can help even just one young wrestler, parent, or coach, this project consisting of nearly 100,000 words will all be well worth the time and effort.

In each of the following, I will explain the wrestling lesson and then the life's lesson.

1. **Love and Trust**
   It all starts with the coach. If you are a coach, you must realize that the relationship is too important to fail. If you fail, kids fail. In my opinion, it fails if you don't let <u>all</u> your wrestlers know you care about them like family. If you can't tell them that, show them.

   Knowing technique and teaching it is not enough. Caring about your wrestlers is far more important than teaching takedowns or winning. But I am convinced in the final analysis that you are going to win if you build love and trust in your team. Make sure your kids know that they are more important to you than winning. Think about it. How do you do that?

Nothing in life is more important than love and trust. I didn't quite get that when I was younger, and I made a lot of mistakes. I think I understand it now. But I'm always working on it. The sooner you know it, the better wrestler you'll be, the better coach you'll be, and the better person you'll be.

2. **Parents and Kids**

Parents must support the coach and their kids. Any time parents criticize a coach (or even a teacher or referee) in front of their kids, they are hurting their children. If you are a parent, realize that your kids have to respect their coach and the referee(s) to wrestle at their best and be their best.

Never let the referee or coach be an excuse for a loss. Make sure your kids realize that they can't blame anyone but themselves when they lose. If they lose, they need to work harder to win the next time. Gable and I both believed strongly that if we let the match be close enough that a referee can decide which of us wins, then it is our fault—not the referee.

(I do not even remotely want to leave the reader with the inference that I blame the referees for my losses in college to Gable and Peritore. If you don't want to leave a match in the hands of the referee, then you must beat your opponents decisively enough that the referee cannot make a difference in whether you win or lose.)

In life, encourage your kids if you are a parent; don't always criticize them. Stay positive. However, on the other hand, way too many parents mollycoddle their kids who wrestle. If your kids are going to be mentally tough, then you have to be mentally tough. You can't expect a child to grow up to be mentally tough if they are not taught when they are young to be mentally tough. Playing video games does not help a kid to be mentally tough. Watching television does not help a kid to be mentally tough. You know what I mean. Control what your kids watch and do when they are young, and they will be more likely later to engage in constructive activities. I know this is a radical idea, but I sometimes wonder if kids wouldn't be better and healthier if they had no television, video games, or iPhones at all.

Also, parents, go to the meets and support your kid(s)—win or lose. Maybe even watch them in practice. Gable once said that his greatest influence was his parents who always came to his meets. And his father even frequented Dan's practice sessions in the wrestling room. Now that was a father who wanted his son to succeed.

I believe strongly that a kid who is taught to just <u>wrestle his best</u>, will do better than one taught that the important thing is to win. One thing I really appreciated about my parents as I get older was that they never criticized me for school or athletics. They simply asked me if I did the best I could. That's all they ever asked of me. That's all you can ask of your kids.

If you are a wrestler, get rid of "friends" who bring you down or encourage you to think bad ways or do bad things. If your parents do not encourage you, try to find a mentor who will help you to look at life in a positive way. Remember that in life there will always be times when you lose or you are down. Those times are not fun. But you can get through those times a lot easier if you have support and keep a positive attitude. There is an old expression, "What doesn't kill you will make you stronger." Remember that. Whatever the problem, this too shall pass. Don't let circumstances control your attitude. Think positive.

3. **The Zone and Focus**

   I have made much (maybe too much) of "the zone" as it related to wrestling for me. "My zone" was perhaps more extreme than anyone else in the history of wrestling, as mine put me into another world. But I believe strongly that I would not have won as many matches without that intense focus. I certainly would never have been a state or national champion. The zone for me was very intense focus.

   Many, maybe most, of the opponents I wrestled were better than I in technique, strength, and/or quickness. My ability to focus and become overly aggressive and intense, always in attack mode, was the difference, and that was a direct function of being in the zone. Since my only strategy was to attack, I never needed to think.

The real problem is thinking. You should have your moves down to where you don't need to think in order to execute them. An even worse problem is over-thinking. Don Behm was probably a better wrestler than I, but he over-thought everything. He even stated that when he wrestled in the finals his senior year, he lost his focus when Grady told him to just go out and have fun. I almost never thought when I was on the mat, except attack. That was my one mantra.

If you want to develop creating your own zone, focus during the week on your next opponent. And maybe at first just when you run, begin to learn how to eliminate fears or outside distractions by thinking about wrestling your opponent and how you are going to attack him. Think only about attacking your opponent during your entire run. If you have fears, put them out of your head and think only how aggressive you are going to be when you wrestle.

Most importantly, don't worry about winning or losing—stay focused on attacking your opponent. Winning will take care of itself and will come in time. When you are on the side of the mat preparing yourself for the match, think only about attacking your opponent. If you have sight of him, look at him and think how you are going to attack, attack, attack. Don't worry about any moves you are going to do, let your instincts and muscle memory do that for you.

Whether you go into a zone or not, it is crucial that you focus during your match so that nothing interferes with your ability to score. In my opinion, "thinking" is a distraction that interferes with your achieving your goal. The more you stand around on the mat and don't shoot, the more you are going to start thinking.

Maybe your style does not allow or permit you to attack constantly. Some wrestlers wrestle better when they are totally relaxed and just use their better techniques and mat smarts to win. This still requires focus. Try to figure out what approach creates the best focus for you.

Many times for important tasks in life, you must be focused. I have written over 20 law books and manuals. I could never even have started them (or this book of nearly 100,000 words) without the focus and concentration I learned in wrestling.

You, too, will find how important focus is later in life. Learn it while you are young. Wrestling will help you create and develop that skill. (Drinking and drug use will kill your focus. Avoid them like the plague!)

4. **Aggressiveness v Defensiveness**

    I have spent some time in this book emphasizing aggressive wrestling. A defensive counter wrestler can never control a wrestling match against someone really good. In my opinion, if two wrestlers are equal in ability, the aggressive wrestler almost always wins. You must try to "control" the matches to win.

    As I discussed earlier in this book, my high school coach, Bob Siddens, always said, "Never take a back seat to anyone." To me that meant, win or lose, you should be attacking your opponent.

    I believe that is true in life too. In life, you will find yourself in many situations that are challenging or problematic. The more you ignore them, the worse they get. Always learn to address and attack your problems. Otherwise they will wear you down and out. Wrestling is a perfect place to learn to not sit back and wait for your opponent to make the first move. "Attack firstest with the mostest." (another Gradyism)

5. **Preparation**

    I heard a quote by Paul "Bear" Bryant that I liked, "It's not the will to win that matters—everyone has that. It's the will to prepare to win that matters." Everybody wants to win, but few want to prepare (enough) to win.

    There is no way to win in wrestling—or in life—without preparation. I always had great coaches who worked us so hard we were sure to be prepared when we went on the mat during a meet. Some people say you wrestle in the meet the way you wrestle in practice. I'm sure that's true for most people.

For me, I wanted to try new things in practice. If you are going to try new things in practice, you are probably going to lose or get beaten up at times in practice. So what? It never bothered me to get beat in practice. It did bother me to get beat in meets and tournaments. I will say, though, I never went into an athletic event thinking about winning or losing, except for those few seconds at the end of my national championship match. I thought only about giving my best by being aggressive—every second. You can only give your best if you are properly prepared.

If you are willing to prepare in wrestling, you will also be willing to prepare in life. When I would run to improve my endurance, I would always say that if I don't finish now, I will not finish in other things I have to do in life. That was a great motivator for me. Another approach that I used that was successful in preparing was to <u>always do more</u> than the coach asked of me to do. For example, if the coach wanted us to do 50 push-ups, I always did at least 51. You should try to do that too. It will give you confidence that you are out-working your opponents, an important thought process in preparing for your next opponent.

Later in life, you will find that almost all positions or jobs you hold require that you be prepared. Learn that character trait in wrestling first, and it will carry over.

6. **Mental Toughness**
All wrestlers need to be mentally tough. Most are. The longer you wrestle and the more obstacles you overcome, the tougher you will become mentally. Later in life, you will find out it's easy to overcome many difficulties that others find impossible because you learned mental toughness in wrestling. Also, some wrestlers will find that the more they give in to difficulties—like quitting—the more likely they are to give into difficulties later in life.

Parents and coaches can teach their wrestlers mental toughness by not babying them. Life can be tough, very tough. Many athletes believe that when they graduate, everything will be easier. It's not. It's harder.

If you learn mental toughness during wrestling in school, you will be amazed at how that toughness will carry you through hard times later in life. Probably most important, always remember that if you are going through tough times and you are mentally tough, the times will get better, and you can push through the bad times.

7. **Weaknesses and Strengths**
We all have weaknesses and strengths. Many of us never figure them out or refuse to recognize them. In wrestling I was never going to be as strong as Carr at the weight above me. Why then try to wrestle him strength against strength? I had to use other techniques to win. I was never going to be as slick as Lowrance at my weight. Why then wrestle him at his strength?

My strengths were probably my stamina, desire, and intensity, so I absolutely had to wear people down to overcome their strengths. How would I have ever figured that out if I had been a defensive wrestler?

Certain moves in wrestling work better for some people, but not well at all for others. For example, I don't believe I ever finished a double leg drop. Some (stronger) wrestlers use it as their only takedown. It is absolutely the same in life. Everyone has to figure out what his strengths are and seek out professions/jobs/avocations that allow those qualities and strengths to be used.

For example, some of the greatest wrestlers were terrible coaches, and some of the weaker wrestlers, who never won a high school state tournament or national tournament, turned out to be fantastic coaches. You have to find out in life what you are strong in and what you love and then use it.

Finally, because we all have weaknesses, we are all going to make mistakes in life, some of them doozies! I may have made more mistakes than everybody reading this combined. Try to <u>recognize</u> your mistakes, forgive yourself, (and, if possible, ask those whom you have offended to forgive you)—and then move on. Virtually no weakness or mistake is so bad that you can't overcome it with mental toughness and perseverance.

8. **Have Goals—And Get Better Every Day**
   I believe strongly that everyone needs goals they can accomplish and goals beyond their grasp.

One goal I have that I will accomplish is writing this book. Vocationally, my goal now is to professionalize all peace officers in Illinois and Arizona such that they understand the Constitution and can carry out their responsibilities within the constrictions of the Constitution. As everyone knows, officers' constitutional mistakes are extremely expensive for taxpayers.

Back in my junior year in high school, I began writing in my journal every night what I did that day to win a state championship in wrestling. So I had one goal. I wrote it down, and I accomplished it.

What are your goals? Do you have goals that you can accomplish and goals that will always be slightly beyond your reach?

You should always be thinking how you can get better today than you were yesterday. In wrestling, the way I did that was to try new moves in the practice room that I had never executed before. For conditioning and preparation, I tried to do more chin-ups, push-ups, etc. Always better, every day, every week, and every month.

Don't ever go backwards—<u>never take drugs—never</u>. Never drink at all during the season. Better yet, don't drink at all. There is no reason to. Drugs and drinking will take you backwards. Always go forward.

Think of all the great athletes and potentially great athletes who have ruined their lives as alcoholics and junkies. Almost every day I read about another great athlete who threw away a great career because he got hooked on drugs and/or drink. Right now there is a Heisman award winner, Johnny Manziel, who appears to be ruining his life because of alcohol. Right now, no professional team wants him, and his career may be over. So many great athletes throw away their careers that way. It's always best to learn by other's mistakes.

Write down your goals and keep a journal to track your progress. You will be amazed at how much it will help you get better and better as you accomplish your goals. Start slow and low—think of some goal you know you can accomplish for sure; then accomplish it and put that in your journal. Then move on to greater things.

Long after wrestling is over, have goals, work hard to get better, and be better every day in life.

9. **Think Like a Winner**
There are a lot of books on how to succeed. Maybe you should read them. I think that the first step in becoming a winner is to think like a winner. In order to think like a winner, you might start with small successes. Every time you succeed, imbed in your brain that you are a winner. Grow with those successes.

I have always felt like I was a winner (even when I wasn't). I think the reason I thought like a winner, and still think like a winner, is that <u>I never was afraid to lose and I was never afraid to fail.</u> Too many wrestlers are afraid to lose. Never fear to lose; never fear to fail. Everyone loses and everyone fails. You will lose, and you will fail. So what? Our greatest leaders in American history lost and failed at one time or another—some, many times. They learned from their losses and failures and became successful. When you lose and fail, get back up off the mat and try again.

The best lessons, and perhaps the most important lessons, are the direct result of failure. When you fail and then overcome your failure, you will be amazed at what that does for your attitude—and your future. You will begin to win. For example, in everything I attempted to do that was important, I failed at first. But then I always ended up winning. As Tim Tebow says, "End well."

10. The Greatest Miracle—Decision-Making and Wisdom

This one is the most important factor in life, by far, in my opinion.

I have made lots of mistakes. I do not blame anyone else for my bad decisions or mistakes. I blame me. And I have reaped what I have sown. Whenever things have gone wrong in my life, it was my fault and my fault alone based upon my bad decision-making. Everyone makes bad decisions. Put them behind you and don't make the same mistakes twice. Learn from your bad decisions.

How did I make good decisions? And how did I make bad decisions in wrestling and in life?

I was fortunate in wrestling (and life) to have a role model like Bob Siddens when I was young. Had I always listened to him or thought about him when I made a decision, I probably would have made better decisions. Bob Bowlsby, Big Twelve Commissioner, often says that before he makes big decisions he often thinks, "What would Bob Siddens do?"

My strong suggestion for you if you are young—find a role model or many role models who have character and will lead you down the straight and narrow. This may not be easy, but it may be the most important decision of your life. If the people you choose know that they are your role model, you will be amazed at how responsive they will be in fulfilling that role and helping you to have good judgment and make the right decisions in life.

What about important decisions? It really didn't even occur to me to drink or smoke when I wrestled in high school. Sometimes in important decisions you must consult someone whose opinion you respect. Maybe it's a teacher, a parent, or a pastor. Some people might pray over the decision. I believe strongly in the power of prayer to give me wisdom about an important decision.

What are important decisions? Maybe…Where will you go to school? What type of job is best for you? Who should you choose as friends or a spouse? I'm sure you can think of many more.

In my opinion, the worst decision anyone can ever make is to take drugs. I have mentioned this several times, but if I can prevent **one** wrestler from taking drugs, that will be at the top of my list of personal accomplishments in my life. If you never take drugs, you never have to worry about being an addict and ruining your life.

I never even tried any "hard" drugs, and I'm glad I didn't. That may well have been the wisest decision I ever made. If you are presently taking drugs, stop it—right now, today. If you can't stop today, get help to stop. That will be the best decision of your life.

I like the idea of ending well. It doesn't matter that I lost every match when I started my wrestling career. It matters that I ended it ("the journey") by winning a national championship. I ended my wrestling career in 1967 by standing at the top. I hope to end my life the same way.

Thank you for reading this book. It was a labor of love for the team, the program, the sport, my teammates, and all the great people I have come to know through wrestling.

May God bless all wrestlers, coaches, parents, fans—and even referees!

Best –

DA